S0-AXW-291

MUSLIM
COMMUNITIES
IN THE
NEW EUROPE

D
1056.2
.M87
M855
1996

MUSLIM COMMUNITIES
IN THE
NEW EUROPE

Edited by

GERD NONNEMAN

•

TIM NIBLOCK

•

BOGDAN SZAJKOWSKI

GOSHEN COLLEGE LIBRARY
GOSHEN, INDIANA

MUSLIM COMMUNITIES IN THE NEW EUROPE

Ithaca Press is an imprint of Garnet Publishing Limited

Published by
Garnet Publishing Limited
8 Southern Court
South Street
Reading
Berkshire RG1 4QS
UK

Copyright © 1996 Gerd Nonneman, Tim Niblock, Bogdan Szajkowski

All rights reserved
No part of this book may be reproduced in any form or by
any electronic or mechanical means, including information
storage and retrieval systems, without permission in writing
from the publisher, except by a reviewer who may quote
brief passages in a review

First paperback edition, 1997

ISBN 0 86372 223 7

British Library Cataloguing-in-Publication Data
A catalogue record for this book is available from the British Library

Jacket and book design by David Rose
Typeset by Samantha Abley

Printed in Lebanon

Contents

LIST OF TABLES

PREFACE

This book is the final outcome of a three-year project, undertaken with support of the Council of Europe, the British Council, the Saints Kiril and Methodius University in Skopje, and the Universities of Exeter, Durham and Lancaster. On the basis of two international conferences addressing the theme of Muslim communities in post-bipolar Europe, and further work with researchers throughout Europe, the intention was to produce a coherent comparative overview of the issues relating to the role and position of these communities. In the changing context of both West and East, such themes have acquired increased importance, yet for long remained relatively under-researched. This volume cannot claim to be comprehensive, but by presenting focused analyses and information both at the thematic and country-specific level, it is hoped that it may contribute to a better understanding of the trends and dynamics involved, and provide the basis for further work.

GERD NONNEMAN

Part I
Themes and Questions

1

MUSLIM COMMUNITIES IN THE NEW EUROPE: THEMES AND PUZZLES

Gerd Nonneman[1]

1. The New Europe

The role and position of Muslim communities, in both Eastern and
Western Europe, has attracted increasing social and political concern
over recent years. In Eastern Europe, the end of the Cold War
has brought the release – and, at times, fanning – of ethno-religious
feelings of belonging partly in reaction to domestic as well as international developments, and in turn feeding back into the domestic
and international scenes. One such focus of identity has been Eastern
European Islam – an indigenous presence for centuries. The emergence and cultural as well as political assertion of this identity
has interacted with the emergence of other, at times conflicting,
reasserted identities of a similar nature, and brought into question
models of modernisation, as well as the nature of some of Europe's
new states and systems. In Western Europe, where Islam is mainly
associated with communities of immigrant origin, there has been a
continued increase in the number of Muslims (however defined), and
also a spreading of this phenomenon to 'new' immigration countries
in northern and southern Europe. This has occurred at a time of
domestic economic recession and in an international environment
where political upheaval and Western–'Oriental' friction has at times
become acute. All of this appears to have led, on the one hand, to more
explicitly political positions being taken by elements of the Muslim
communities in Western Europe, and, on the other, to increasingly
hostile reactions to the Muslim presence and activities on the part

of the 'host' societies and governments (both of these developments also being related to one another).

The position and role of Muslim communities in Europe has been a neglected field of academic study. While this has recently begun to change with regard to Western Europe (as exemplified by Nielsen's excellent *Muslims in Western Europe*), the case of Eastern Europe, newly liberated from communist authoritarianism, has been given less attention. Whether separately or in comparison, therefore, the study of the evolving fate of these communities in the new Europe is both fascinating and important.

A series of questions present themselves: How does the situation of Muslims in Western and Eastern Europe compare? How 'Muslim' are the Muslims in Western and Eastern Europe? How important are religious elements (rather than ethnic/linguistic elements) in these Muslims' relations with other Europeans? What role is or has been played by the variation in historical experience? What does the case of the 'new' immigration countries such as Scandinavia and Spain and Italy, tell us? What is the effect of governmental policies and citizenship rules? How important are economic factors? What international linkages come into play? How is public opinion affected by these and other factors? In a project sponsored by the Council of Europe, supported also by the British Council, and organised from bases in the Universities of Durham, Skopje, Exeter and Lancaster, a group of researchers from around Europe set out to address these questions. The present volume is the outcome of this project. It cannot claim to be comprehensive, but by presenting analyses of the situation of Muslim communities in both parts of the new Europe, both through country-chapters and thematic contributions, it is hoped that the reader will be offered useful new information and pointers towards possible answers, in a comparative context.

2. Muslims in Western Europe

2.1. *A brief overview*

For Western Europe, as Nielsen has pointed out, Islam remained, until the 1960s, very much alien, 'out there', notwithstanding the establishment of a few mosques in some cities.[2] It was only in the late

1950s and the 1960s that the situation began to change with the expansion of labour migration, but even so, this whole phenomenon was still essentially regarded as foreign and temporary. These immigrant communities, including those of a Muslim background, were still defined by the host society by their economic function (guest workers), their colour, or their nationality, and only to a much lesser extent by their culture or religion. This reflected the migrants' own perception of their place in their European surroundings, and their relative lack of concern with opportunities for socio-religious expression within the context of the host society.

From the 1970s, however, the religio-cultural dimension did become an important social issue in the relations between Muslim communities and host societies. This, Nielsen observes, 'was the unforeseen consequence of the drastic change in European immigration policy at the time of the 1972–4 recession'.[3] Governments halted further labour immigration, but allowed family unification. With the arrival of wives and children, the Muslim presence in Western Europe was no longer simply one of migrant workers, but of social communities in the full sense. In the present volume, the chapters on Britain, Belgium, the Netherlands, France and Germany are particularly illuminating in this respect. As a result, 'the contact surface between the immigrants and the host society saw a major expansion', Nielsen points out, especially in the sectors of health, social services and education. These sectors, he goes on to argue,

> were the very areas which impinged immediately on those aspects of culture which lie at the very centre of family life and identity, areas which often are reinforced by religious norms and taboos, namely childbirth and rearing. It is therefore no coincidence that expressions of religious community life . . . proceeded apace in the decade following.[4]

In the wake of this, and in part linked to such expressions, Muslims in Western Europe became increasingly politically active. Political activism, moreover, was reinforced by the emergence of the 'second generation': Muslims who had been born in Europe and were familiar from the start with Western assumptions about political participation. Especially in Britain and France, where it was relatively easy to acquire citizenship, the effect of the concomitant expectations on the part of this Muslim element of society became apparent in their increased willingness to agitate for what they perceived to be their rights.

It was in Britain and France, also, that a backlash could first be observed. Chronologically, this development coincided with the intrusion, from the early 1980s, of international events and concerns into the domestic scenes of Western European countries. The situation was characterised by a vicious circle. Perceived discrimination and insensitivity to cultural differences led some Muslims in Western Europe to identify with some of the causes of their fellow Muslims in the Middle East, for instance the Iranian revolution. Large sections of public opinion in the host societies then reacted to these attitudes and to the perceived excesses of radicalised Islam abroad, by stereotyping the Muslim communities in their midst as a threat. This was exacerbated by growing unemployment in Europe. The potential for misunderstanding and ever-increasing friction, therefore, was considerable. It is true, of course, that, additionally, cultural differences between immigrant/Muslim communities on the one hand, and the host societies on the other (increasingly accentuated precisely in the context sketched above), have proved problematic in certain circumstances.

2.2. A Muslim challenge to Western secularism?

Conflict situations between Muslims and host societies, as seen in the Rushdie affair in Britain and the Headscarves affair in France, centred around the questioning by Muslims of the secular principle in Western European socio-political life. Even if the West European past features enough instances of the role Christian religion and institutions have played in the organisation and running of the state and politics, it remains true that, by and large, the area witnessed, over the past two centuries, a 'privatization of religion and public secularization of the state'.[5] As Clark has noted, the secular assumptions underlying political and civil organisation in Western Europe today are the result of a particular combination of events and developments. Crucial elements of this were: the Enlightenment and the emergence of thinkers such as Voltaire; the historical event of the French Revolution and its impact outside France; the determined secularism of Napoleon; and, from outside Europe, the influence of the American revolution (where legal/constitutional sanction was given to religious pluralism).[6]

It is legitimate to speak of a certain 'identity' of Western European society, underlying the way this society has come to function. Whatever the earlier history, and whatever the earlier cultural mixes, the last three hundred years have, via the above factors and the 'invention' of the nation-state in a context of industrialisation, resulted in a broad similarity in the underlying principles of socio-political organisation and the symbols which are used and understood among the indigenous populations, including among those who became 'indigenised' during this process (such as the Jews, who adapted their socio-religious institutions at least in practice to the prevailing model). This commonality was, and is, based on and reinforced by common myths, common or related languages, education, to some extent a shared religious background and/or folklore, and the idea and practice of the secular state along with private religion. The latter principle, indeed, along with the more or less implicit assumption of a Christian 'background', had become part of the 'national project' in Western Europe's emerging countries, just as the non-secular principle and Islam have increasingly become part of the national projects in many an Islamic country.

The questions of citizenship, citizens' duties, the social contract, and the relationship between religion and state, therefore, had for the most part been solved and considered settled in the West (in contrast with Eastern Europe, where this is much less clear).

In the 1970s it became clear that the cultural and religious integration of Muslim communities would not necessarily happen along the established Western European lines of secularisation. With the emerging friction, conflict and disagreement between host societies and elements in the Muslim communities especially since the 1980s (exemplified and fed into by the Rushdie crisis and the war over Kuwait), Nielsen writes,

> Muslim demands, and reactions to their demands, were threatening to place the issues back on to the table . . . In the West the new presence of Muslim communities has reopened the agenda, while in the east the disappearance of communist authoritarian rule has exposed the unfinished agenda.[7]

Is there, then, an incompatibility between Islamic values and the secular organising principles of the Western European state? The debate on whether Islam must of necessity be 'political' and whether,

for Muslims, there can be an essentially secular state, cannot be settled in these pages. The usual assumption is that, in Islam, politics
and religion cannot be separated. At the very least, however, the
blanket nature of this assumption can be strongly challenged. Khaldi,[8]
Ayubi[9] and Piscatori,[10] among others, have convincingly argued that
both in theory and in practice, Islam has in many respects had a
history of pragmatism, separation between the essence of the 'religious' principles and institutions on the one hand and those of
the temporal ruler and the state on the other, and compatibility
between its precepts and the imperatives of 'a world of nation-states'
(Piscatori). In the words of Khaldi: 'Islamic history contains innumer-
able instances of thought and action in which *din* and *dawlah* have
been sharply distinguished'. Indeed, he adds, '[o]ne of the most
interesting aspects of the Iranian revolution is its complete historical
novelty'.[11]

There would appear to be no insurmountable obstacle of principle, then, to a fair degree of compatibility between 'Islamic' practice and 'Western' practice as regards citizenship and the nature
of socio-political organisation. Indeed, European Muslims' reactions
(themselves varying strongly) may often be less a matter of 'Islamic
practice' than of a cultural minority's sense of discrimination leading
to a search for rallying points. Yet this very intertwining of the
religious and cultural aspects with socio-political ones, together with
the state and likely development of the debate in the foreseeable
future, means that the realisation of optimistic sentiments about
compatibility of the 'practices' must probably be relegated to a
rather distant future. In the shorter term, indeed, the question of a
society's 'cultural absorbancy' remains highly salient.

2.3. *The general question of societies' 'cultural absorbancy'*

The concern with Muslim communities' 'cultural coherence' and 'security' which is expressed by many of their members and a good
number of writers on the subject, does not, it should be stressed,
apply only to the Muslim community itself. It also applies to the host
societies. That much should be clear from the observations made
earlier about the 'identity' and functioning of Western European
society, as it has developed over the last three centuries. This is a point
which appears to have been relatively neglected in the academic

literature on the subject outside the xenophobic camp. The concern for the cultural accommodation of the Muslim community is occasionally expressed and pursued in ways which lack both balance and the potential to convince the essential target audience. Thus, accusing the European host society of 'Eurocentrism'[12] is rather like accusing the population of the Arab world of Arabism or of an Islam-centred world view.

The most sophisticated and careful treatment of the issue is probably to be found in Nielsen's work.[13] He points out that, although early European history contained multiple cultural cross-fertilisations, the coming of the nation-state altered the nature of developments, by elevating the notion of a common national culture to unprecedented importance:

> The very success of the concept of nation involved creating an ideological identity which, whatever its variety of cultural sources, presented a common culture as an essential distinguishing characteristic of the nation.[14]

Nielsen therefore dismisses the 'liberal myth of a multi-cultural Europe': in these countries, a 'national culture' clearly *can* be identified – with differences but also (European) similarities between them. At the same time, however, he still seems to imply that this national culture is itself largely a 'myth', and holds little real substance. There is, he argues, a *social* 'multiculturality', in the sense of the differentiation between the elite – the carriers of what is ostensibly 'national culture' – and the other groups in society. While this premiss is correct, the implied conclusion is unfounded. First, the myth *itself* (as myth) is a reality, as it has become inculcated to varying degrees in the population at large. Secondly, the general and widespread evidence of resistance among this population to the 'foreign' or 'alien' element, and to the idea of adapting its own ways and assumptions, demonstrates that there is, at some level, the same commonality as can be found (and is indeed claimed) by Muslims (and others). Thirdly, the general assumption and acceptance of the secular state and privatised religion is, again, an instance of the common national or European culture that has evolved, whatever the multicultural, and very gradual, processes which preceded it.

Language, acquired myths, legends, history, symbols used and understood, and assumptions about how society and state can and should function, are all elements of this 'culture'. A relatively sudden and large influx of a culture which is different in the above terms, which in modern West European history is typical only of the post-1945 labour migration era, is almost certain to lead to friction, incomprehension and conflict, especially in economic crises: the evidence, sadly, confirms this. The chapters on Italy, Spain and Scandinavia in this volume also provide a further illustration that such friction remains far less significant as long as numbers are small and the central elements of what is perceived as 'national culture' are not yet put in question.

Specific evidence of this is the very incomprehension which Nielsen cites in the case of the Rushdie affair (e.g. the unawareness among the minority of British Muslims involved in the book-burning, of 'the significance of book-burning in European history, with its associations of Inquisition and . . . Nazi . . . Germany'). The reverse incomprehension among non-Muslim Europeans (demonstrating 'to what extent European society . . . had become distanced from religious priorities'[15]), again illustrates the reality of common European cultural elements, rather than their *mere* mythological nature.

The above discussion holds both for the West European level and that of the individual states. One instance where the national culture of a country has had a major impact on the interaction with elements perceived as being outside this culture, is the case of France (regardless of how 'mythical' the origins of that culture may be, or how inaccurate a reflection of some of the social dynamics at work). Of particular relevance here would seem to be the sense of being *the* country of the Enlightenment, and the related conviction that *the* common ground for the French is *rationality* – with religion being at most an addition. Very visible signs of religious identity are, in this context, almost inevitably regarded as disturbing: they may be perceived as 'eating away at the very element that is our common ground.'

Truly 'plural society', Nielsen acknowledges, has hardly any precedents; moreover,

> the threat of social disintegration as a consequence [of efforts to amalgamate such differences] cannot be ignored. Differences and plurality, especially of a religious kind, have historically been more destructive than constructive. Differences have to find a place within an overall political, social and legal consensus. In

10

Europe, we have tended to find this consensus in overarching institutional frameworks and in a basic core of common cultural and national identity.[16]

This solution, of course, has not been limited to Europe but seems to have been (and still to be) the rule. Nielsen's suggestion that it 'is equally possible to imagine a socially cohesive consensus founded on modes of intercultural and interreligious relations', directly contradicts his earlier observations, and therefore seems little more than wishful thinking. It can hardly be surprising that a host society defends its 'inherited solutions and models of action'. To say that 'concepts such as nation, constitution, laicism, secularism . . . are the products of history . . . [and can] continue to evolve into the future',[17] is, of course, historically correct. To use this observation as the basis for policy prescription *today*, however, rather than as a description of broad, slow processes which happened over vast stretches of time, is ahistorical and, in its effects, may vary between the irrelevant and the counter-productive.

A difficulty for those concerned with the fate of Muslim communities in Western Europe, and with their harmonious interaction with the 'host society', has been that the above problematic has not been seriously tackled; this has left the field free for the xenophobic right, and has undermined the credibility with the general public of the pronouncements and writings of those not associated with that tendency. A recognition of the difficulties, and of the substance of the phenomenon of cultural resistance among the host populations (rather than dismissing it as merely misguided), is necessary both to come to a genuine understanding of the problems faced by Muslim communities, and to begin finding a hearing for non-xenophobic arguments among the population at large.

The concern among Western European populations for their 'national identity' has probably become more acute in line with the spread of industrialisation and, particularly, urbanisation. In this context people are likely to try to recover the old and lost sense of community, by, among other things, returning to their part-real, part-mythical 'roots'. A consequence of this in turn will tend to be a blaming of problems on 'outsiders', who do not form part of this new, initially imaginary but increasingly real, community. The case of Germany in the late 19th century would seem to bear this out. The nationalist project meshed and meshes well with this.

If such a trend, as in the 1970s–1990s, is combined (a) with a more sudden and larger influx of such 'outsiders'; (b) with an economic malaise; and (c) with a context where, because of the instant network of global communications, the international situation acquires an impact on the mutual perceptions of both communities, then the extent of problematic interaction (more problematic, that is, than in earlier instances of cultural cross-fertilisation), is less than surprising.

In the specific case of mainly Christian (if secularised) Europe, and Islam, the historical 'baggage', or 'collective memory' of the 'other' has remained an important factor. This has stayed alive through various elements of folklore, among other factors, becoming increasingly mythologised and stereotyped in the process. Since these elements are part of the same folklore which is re-employed (and developed) in the course of the search for 'roots' referred to above, an even more skewed and potentially negative view of the 'other' is likely.

3. Muslims in Eastern Europe

3.1. *Historical background*

The Ottoman conquest of the Balkans in the 15th century (the victories in the late 14th century, including the Battle of Kosovo in 1389, were temporarily undone by Mongol conquests) brought not only an influx of Muslim settlers but also, eventually, an 'indigenised' presence of Islam. Both the religious and ethnic make-up of the region therefore underwent a process of change. Islam did not remain simply the religion of the conquerors. Many of the indigenous populations also converted, arguably largely for pragmatic reasons, including social, political and economic benefit. This was the case for a majority of the Albanians, and for the ancestors of today's 'Pomaks' and Bosnians. Many sections of the population, indeed, welcomed the Ottoman system of rule, which replaced a relatively more oppressive feudal system. Non-converts were incorporated into the Ottoman Empire as *dhimmis*, or protected communities. This was in accordance with Islam's traditional view of Christians and Jews as 'people of the book', or those who have a faith which shares some of Islam's precepts, based on a book of revelation, even if that book was only an imperfect reflection of God's word. The empire was administered along religious, rather than ethnic or linguistic lines: the different religious communities were allowed to run their own socio-cultural affairs, in what became known as the *millet* system. Until the 19th century, when modernising administrative reforms known as the *Tanzimat* were introduced, this meant that the different religious communities (*millets*) were not directly interfered in by the Ottoman state apparatus: the relationship was mediated through the communities' own leaderships. As Poulton has observed, this non-assimilative system meant that the members of these various communities to some degree could retain separate identities.[18]

With the weakening and gradual contraction of the Ottoman Empire in the 19th century – culminating in its dissolution after the First World War – Orthodox Christianity increasingly became a focus for political and nationalist assertion. The states bearing down on the borders of, and arising from, the disintegrating empire were largely Orthodox (except for Albania). Orthodoxy, in other words, became linked to a large extent with the struggle for independence and with the new project of state building. Greece and Serbia are perhaps the most striking examples of this. The Orthodox past, prior to the Muslim conquest, acquired mythical status. All of these new post-Ottoman states were left with Muslim minorities (in significant numbers in Bulgaria, Greece and Yugoslavia), and a Muslim majority in the case of Albania. Even if, in areas of mixed populations, peaceful coexistence was often the rule, the struggle between Orthodoxy and Islam became part of the collective memory that Orthodox leaders and others could henceforth call on or, in part, develop.

The imposition of Communist rule in Eastern Europe and the Balkans (except in Greece) to a large extent suppressed ethnoreligious differences. Where, as in Tito's Yugoslavia, such different identities were recognised, it was in a 'sanitised' form, which did not allow for any form of separatist expression. Religion was to varying degrees emasculated as a major force in society, to the extent that in Albania, possibly a majority of the population became agnostic (even while remaining part of one or other confessional 'tradition').[19] In Poland, of course, the Catholic church did remain a powerful autonomous actor.

3.2. The post-Communist 'release' and its effect on the role of religion

With the end of Communist rule in the region, many latent dynamics were suddenly released and new ones emerged. It is perhaps no exaggeration to use the label 'chaos' in describing socio-economic developments since this 'release'. Not only did the situation on the ground become fluid and chaotic, the ability of academic or other observers to establish the nature of developments was severely constrained. Data were either not available, or unreliable, or continually shifting. At the very least the interpretation of any such data was problematic. Even five years on, this must of necessity introduce a *caveat* in any discussion of the current position of Islam in Eastern Europe, but at the same time it only heightens the need for attempts at such an inquiry.

Existing political, economic, and to some extent also socio-cultural structures were destroyed, leaving only the Church (Orthodox in the east, Catholic in the west) as a more or less functioning autonomous (or newly autonomous) body. The non-hierarchical organisation of the Muslim communities meant that there was nothing quite comparable to these Church structures for them. Nevertheless, the socio-cultural and (to varying degrees) religious identification with Islam and the mosque had persisted at the personal, family and indeed communal level. In the post-Communist vacuum, or chaos, this identification was therefore one constant that remained and hence acquired potentially increased relevance.

The potential relevance of religious identification which resulted from this 'release' and from the destruction of the previous frameworks of society and polity, was increasingly turned into reality as a result of the psychological impact of the political and economic strains pervading the region in the first half of the 1990s. A sense of threat to people's individual, communal or national well-being and security (political or economic) has, as elsewhere, led them to seek increased recourse to ethno-religious identification. This in turn has heightened the potential for, and indeed the occurrence of, ostensibly 'religious' conflict.

A further factor has been the phenomenon of religion as a 'fashion'. With the advent of political liberalisation and the rejection of the old system which had kept religion suppressed or under a tight reign, it became fashionable to identify with, and join in the rituals of, one's nominal religion, even if this implied no religious belief. It became an expression of the new, free 'ambience', a folkloric-cum-political social experience. Whether Catholic, Orthodox or Muslim, thousands joined in the religious festivals who otherwise would have had little inclination to do so.

The fluidity of polities and political principles in the chaos that became post-Communist Eastern Europe, was a further important factor. The still ongoing process of defining what the state, state structures and constitutional principles are or should be has had a two-fold effect with respect to the role of religion. First, it led to a concern for national consolidation, and hence a fear of, and resistance to, group rights for ethnic or religious minorities. Secondly, the enthusiasm among many of the post-Communist elite for the constitutional principle and the *Rechtsstaat*, as a reaction against the previous system, also has resulted in a distinct lack of sympathy with, or outright opposition to, calls for group rights, as these are seen as incompatible with the kind of civic society which is being aspired to (with equality of all individuals before the law, which guarantees their rights *vis-à-vis* each other and the state). The resultant sense of aggrievement on the part of the affected minorities (in terms of language or otherwise) clearly has a potentially destabilising impact, whether it is expressed in strictly ethnic or also in religious terms.

4. Overall comparative points

The evidence and analysis presented in this book would appear to point to a number of tentative comparative conclusions; these are listed below in an attempt at formulating answers to some of the questions listed at the outset of this chapter.

- There is no evidence that the political economy of the state (e.g. the size and strength of the public sector within the national economy) has affected the character or form of political activity of Muslim communities in Europe, whether positively or negatively.

- Economic difficulties always cause or exacerbate problems of integration, understanding and conflict between non-Muslim and Muslim communities. In a climate of economic hardship, competition for resources becomes inevitable, and often becomes tied in with the search for scapegoats. For both processes, 'otherness' based on religion and culture becomes a visible tool, all the more so when this 'otherness' is combined with 'foreignness' in the case of immigration-based communities.

- Socio-economic status has a major impact in affecting the attitudes which individual members of Muslim communities have towards the dominant societies, and which individual members of the latter have towards the Muslim communities. The majority of the members of the Muslim communities – except in Bosnia-Hercegovina and Albania – can be classified as among the lower socio-economic strata. This in part explains their lower level of awareness of non-Muslim European conventions and values, as was shown during the Rushdie case. In the middle class and professional segments of the Muslim communities, greater awareness is generally combined with greater pragmatism and a moderate position.

   This would seem to be similar on the 'other side': among non-Muslim Europeans of lower economic status, the awareness of Islam and Muslims' values and sensitivities is lowest. A difference on this side of the fence, though, is that there is generally less familiarity with the 'other' (i.e. Islam and the Muslims) among the non-Muslim population at large – including middle class and professionals – than there is among the equivalent strata among Muslims. (These observations probably apply in particular to Western Europe. In Eastern (ex-Communist) Europe, the different class structure under Communism and the different post-1989 stratification, suggest different dynamics.)[20] One of the problems in Western Europe is the 'bias', referred to in section 2.3 above, in much of the literature on the subject of Muslim communities. This has detracted from the power of persuasion which these writings have had among the non-Muslim middle class in this part of Europe. Moreover, it is these strata who are the main 'carriers' of the West European national culture which seems to 'clash' with the other (usually stereotyped) culture.

- There appears to be little consistent difference between Catholic and Protestant dominant societies in their attitudes to Muslim communities within their states. The state has played a more active role in society in European countries which have a Protestant majority, and has therefore been more active also with regard to Muslim communities. Yet in Catholic countries the Church itself has often played a positive role in engaging with the Muslim community, as for instance in the case of Italy. There appears to be no correlation between the Catholic/ Protestant divide and variations in popular and societal attitudes to Muslim minority communities.

There clearly *is* a problem when it comes to Orthodox dominant societies. In the Balkans, Orthodox and nationalist assertion have often gone hand-in-hand, and been actively or implicitly directed against 'Islam' and Muslim communities. This has been true both at the popular level and that of institutions. It is not clear, however, whether this is related to the nature and impact of Orthodoxy itself, or to (a) collective memory of domination by, and conflict with, the Ottoman Empire; (b) the Communist suppression of religious aspirations and identities; (c) political circumstances and manœuvring by domestic and/or outside actors.

- Considerable similarity exists between the situation and fate of immigrant Muslim communities on the one hand, and indigenous ones on the other. Differences would appear to be mainly political in nature. For both, the real or imagined problems which emerge or are brought onto the scene by members of the dominant society are similar, although this happens in wholly different circumstances and for different reasons. It may also be noted that one of the differences which clearly did exist, namely the greater extent of secularisation among Europe's old indigenous Muslim communities, has begun to be levelled by political events.

- In Europe political activity by immigrant Muslims has emerged first, and has been more intensive – even in the absence of acute friction or conflict – in those countries where immigrants could acquire citizenship most easily (in particular, Britain and France). This is natural: citizenship forms the basis on which political activity occurs, and without citizenship individuals tend not to be in a sufficiently strong position to conduct such activities.

- Where there is a crisis in the concept of the nation-state, or if this 'nation-state' is still in some way in the process of definition, as in the Balkans, the problems for the minority group (in this case the Muslims) become more acute. This crisis or process of definition may be about the nature of the state, its legitimacy, its institutions and underpinning principles, or its territorial extent and boundaries. This factor accounts for some of the major differences between, respectively, the Eastern (especially Balkan) and Western European experiences with regard to the Muslim communities.

- It is particularly in the above context that external interference and manipulation of inter-faith relations may become a salient factor. Again, therefore, instances of such external involvement, particularly by non-Muslim actors, as a nefarious factor in Muslim–Christian relations have been most noticeable in the Balkans (and cannot be compared with the kind of role played in Western Europe by Middle Eastern and North African governments and institutions).

- To the extent that any generalisations are possible, the level of awareness and expression of Muslim identity has risen amongst Muslim populations throughout Europe. This has been linked to a variety of factors (in different combinations in Eastern and Western Europe), including those referred to above. One striking phenomenon has been the new and 'independent' way in which many young Muslims (especially in Western Europe) have begun to rediscover Islam: it is sometimes observed that these young people read the Koran 'as if it had been revealed yesterday'. At the same time it must be stressed that the evidence equally shows Islam to be multifarious, in both Western and Eastern Europe. Such differentiation derives from an array of factors, including immigrant or indigenous status, economic status, ethnic background, socio-cultural context, personal conviction, etc. Although it may be modified over time, such differentiation will persist. This means that the future development of Muslim communities in Europe will be as multifarious as their present characteristics and dynamics – a variety which will continue to be shaped by internal as well as contextual driving factors.

5. Approaches of the dominant society: past, present and future

The ways in which non-Muslim dominant societies in Europe, and in particular the political and intellectual elites, have approached the issue of Muslim communities has varied both geographically and temporally. The geographical divide is, not surprisingly, that between 'Western Europe' and 'Eastern Europe'. The temporal one refers to the post-Cold War changes one can observe in the way these elites, in both East and West, are thinking about inter-faith (and inter-ethnic) relations, the relation between state and groups, and the question of group or minority rights.

Traditionally, the Western approach was rooted in a secularised Christian society, assimilation to which was assumed to be the only viable and conceivable way for minority groupings to develop. Indeed, the necessity of adherence to this model was held to extend to all members of society, regardless of their religious or ethnic background (see section 2.2 above). In France, this was formulated as the principle of *laïcité*. Elsewhere, even though the precise form in which the principle was given shape might vary (with some states being more closely identified with a particular religious confession), the essence also remained that of a 'civic society', i.e. a society where all individuals related to the state as citizens, in a way regulated by law and the constitution which guaranteed the safeguarding of their rights *vis-à-vis* each other and the state. Evidence of instances where this ideal was breached do not diminish the strength of the conscious or implicit convictions underlying this principle. The assumption was that, if the principle of a civic society (whether or not expressed as *laïcité*) were to be safeguarded and upheld, it was not desirable to single out groups as being 'different', and to accord them special treatment or special rights.

In Eastern Europe (with the exception, of course, of Greece), Communist rule did recognise differences, indeed labelling different 'nationalities' and 'cultures'. In Bosnia, Muslims were even recognised *as* a nationality. Yet there was no question that overall control and domination was exerted by the authoritarian political system. This meant a repression of autonomous expression on the part of such groups, and usually a repression of religious expression, whether Christian or Muslim (the main exception being Poland, where the Church retained a relatively powerful position in society).

In the 'New' Europe, clear shifts have been occurring in these attitudes. In both East and West, the debate on liberalism as a moral and political organising principle, and the implications which the implementation of liberal principles have for the treatment of minorities, has expanded but remains unresolved. It is, indeed, a vexed issue. The traditional interpretation of liberalism, with its focus on individual freedoms and civil rights, and the separation of church and state or state and ethnicity, sits uncomfortably with demands for the recognition of differential group rights, especially when certain conventions and rules within such ethnic and/or religious groups may be seen as conflicting with liberalism's basic principles. Equally, however, a recognition has gained ground that this traditional liberal interpretation does not offer a solution for some of the increasingly obvious (and potentially destabilising) problems which minorities may face. As Kymlicka has argued: 'It has become increasingly clear that minority rights cannot be subsumed under the category of human rights.'[21] The fact that traditional human rights simply do not address some of the key issues relating to the position or grievances of cultural minorities, has meant that such issues have 'been left to the usual process of majoritarian decision-making within each state. The result . . . has been to render cultural minorities vulnerable to significant injustice at the hands of the majority, and to exacerbate ethno-cultural conflict.'[22] Kymlicka's is one of the only systematic attempts so far to reconcile liberal theory with minority rights. He starts from Rawls' stipulation that 'justice requires removing or compensating for undeserved or "morally arbitrary" disadvantages, particularly if these are "profound and pervasive and present from birth"'. If it were not for certain group-differentiated rights, he argues,

> the members of minority cultures would not have the same ability to live and work in their own language and culture that the members of majority cultures take for granted. This . . . can be seen as just as profound and arbitrary a disadvantage as the inequalities in race and class that liberals more standardly worry about.[23]

This case is strengthened by 'the way that liberals implicitly invoke cultural membership to defend existing state borders and restrictions on citizenship'.[24] Even Kymlicka, however, while making

a compelling case that 'group representation is not inherently il-
liberal or undemocratic',[25] remains rather vague on the precise ways
in which such a reconciliation might be implemented, and on the
limitations to which it might be subject. While the issue has crept
onto the intellectual agenda, therefore, and while group rights of
some sort – including the rights of Muslim communities in Europe –
clearly need addressing, the debate has not yet achieved complete
clarity, let alone a resolution.

In Western Europe, it would seem that there has been a trend
(which in fact started well before the end of the Cold War) towards
the acceptance of group rights, both in general and with regard to
Muslim communities. The extent to which this has developed, however, has varied strongly. France is perhaps the most striking example
of a dominant society retaining its adherence to the principles of
secularism and the civic state in their traditional liberal interpretation (however much reality might diverge from this ideal because of
the de facto dominance of Christianity, albeit secularised). Sweden,
on the other hand, while still largely de facto difference-blind, has
adopted a number of policies granting what are in effect differential
rights. The situation in Belgium and the Netherlands is different
again, because of the organisation of dominant society and polity
themselves into ideological/confessional 'pillars', even if Islam has
not quite yet achieved equal status to the other pillars.

In Eastern Europe, the search for post-Communist organising
principles of society and polity is on-going. The approaches towards
cultural minorities (ethnic or religious) has varied considerably. On
the whole, the turn away from authoritarianism has engendered an
enthusiasm among the intellectual and part of the political elites for
the liberal principles elaborated in the West, and therefore varying
degrees of reluctance to expand group rights (including for Muslim
communities) as opposed to individual civil rights. The extent to
which elites and governments have recognised the problematic
moral and practical issues involved in the non-acknowledgement of
group grievances and demands, has varied, as has their willingness
to act on such recognition.

In this volume, these debates are reflected perhaps most strik-
ingly by the diametrically opposite approaches of, on the one hand,
West European authors Sander and House (in their chapters on
Sweden and France, respectively), and, on the other, Najcevska,
Simoska and Gaber, in their chapter on the Republic of Macedonia.

The former are the most explicit advocates of diluting the secularist, 'difference-blind' principles underpinning West European polities (especially the French model) in order to accommodate the differential group rights (or needs) of the Muslim communities. The latter make a strong plea for precisely the secular, civic society approach of legally protected individual rights, that France exemplifies.

The future development of these debates, and of the approaches and policies which result, remains an open question. The factors listed in the previous section will continue to influence both philosophical and practical trends, whether at the level of the elites or in the dominant societies at large. Yet precisely because of the prominence of practical factors and considerations (as opposed to philosophical debates) in the influences on, and implications of, the evolution of inter-faith relations in Europe, it seems worth considering another of Kymlicka's conclusions. His discussion of the desirability or otherwise of acceding to ethnic and national minorities' demands for polyethnic rights and representation is directly applicable also to the case of Muslim communities in Europe. In response to fears of the majority society about threats to their own polity's cohesion, Kymlicka observes:

> The demands of immigrants and disadvantaged groups for polyethnic rights and representation rights are primarily demands for inclusion, for full membership in the larger society . . . People from different national [or other minority] groups will only share an allegiance to the larger polity if they see it as the context within which their . . . identity is nurtured, rather than subordinated.[26]

Apart from 'national' identity (although often related to or part of it), the key components of communal identity beyond the family and the clan or region, are arguably language and religion. Accommodation by the dominant society of the needs of Europe's Muslim communities – as Muslims and, particularly in the case of Eastern Europe, also as members of a different linguistic and/or ethnic group – therefore would seem to be a necessary ingredient of the creation or maintenance of stable polities and social cohesion. It must be stressed, however, that the search for such accommodation should be conducted in a spirit which recognises the need for socio-cultural coherence and security of the dominant society, as much as that of the Muslim communities. This is of special relevance in Western Europe where Islam is mostly a recent and originally immigration-based presence. Indeed, any advocacy (academic or otherwise) of minority rights which is not formulated in those terms, will find little hearing among the dominant society which it is aimed at.

Notes

1   The author is grateful to Hugh Miall of Lancaster University, as well as Tim Niblock, for reading and commenting on this chapter.

2   J. Nielsen, 'Muslims, Christians and loyalties in the Nation-State' in Nielsen, *Religion and Citizenship in Europe and the Arab World* (London: Grey Seal Books, 1992), pp. 1–6, p. 1. A very good brief history of the Muslim presence in Western Europe to the 1950s can be found in Nielsen, *Muslims in Western Europe* (Edinburgh: Edinburgh University Press, 1992), pp. 1–7.

3   Nielsen, 'Muslims, Christians . . .', p. 2.

4   *Ibid.*, pp. 2–3.

5   F. Clark, 'Religion and State in Europe' in Nielsen, *Religion . . .* , pp. 39–56, p. 39.

6   *Ibid.*, pp. 44–50.

7   Nielsen, 'Muslims, Christians . . .', pp. 4–5.

8   T. Khaldi, 'Religion and Citizenship in Islam' in Nielsen, *Religion . . .* , pp. 25–30.

9   N. Ayubi, *Political Islam* (London: Routledge, 1991).

10   J. Piscatori, *Islam in a World of Nation-States* (Cambridge: Cambridge University Press, 1986).

11   Khaldi, *op. cit.*, pp. 29–30.

12   M. Anwar, 'Muslims in Western Europe' in Nielsen, *Religion . . .* , pp. 71–94, p. 92.

13   Nielsen, *Muslims in Western Europe*, Chapter 10.

14   *Ibid.*, p. 151.

15   *Ibid.*, p. 159.

16   *Ibid.*, pp. 165–6.

17   *Ibid.*, p. 166.

18   H. Poulton, 'Changing national identity of Muslim minorities in Bulgaria, Greece and FYROM (Macedonia)', paper presented to the *Conference on Muslim Communities in Post-Bipolar Europe* (Amman, Jordan, September 1994).

19   Enver Hoxha went further than any other East European Communist leader in banning religious practice, destroying mosques and churches, and officially fostering atheism.

20   A point made by Hugh Miall.

21   W. Kymlicka, *Multicultural Citizenship: A liberal theory of minority rights* (Oxford: Clarendon Press, 1995), p. 4.

22   *Ibid.*, p. 5.

23   *Ibid.*, p. 126.

24   *Ibid.*, p. 127.

25   *Ibid.*, p. 151.

26   *Ibid.*, pp. 189–90.

PART II
EASTERN EUROPE

2

Islam and Ethnicity in Eastern Europe: Concepts, Statistics, and a Note on the Polish Case[1]

Bogdan Szajkowski, Tim Niblock and Gerd Nonneman

1. Introduction: the concept of ethnicity and the religious factor

This chapter seeks to contribute to an understanding of the factors which have shaped the Muslim communities of Eastern Europe. Such an understanding must start with an analysis of how the religious dimension has interacted with other dimensions: social, economic, cultural and political. Of critical importance here is the link between religious identity and ethnic identity.

For two reasons, the assertion of a link between Islam and ethnicity may initially seem surprising. First, Islam has traditionally been a religion which draws in people of many different cultures and races. It has shown a remarkable ability to imbue its followers with a consciousness of their oneness within the Islamic *umma*, and has emphasised the irrelevance of differences in skin-colour, language and race.

Yet religious identity and ethnic identity have in fact often been bound together in a dynamic relationship in Muslim communities, especially around the fringes of the Islamic world. A good example of this, taken from the eastern rather than the western fringes of the Muslim world, can be taken from Malaysia. Hussein Mutalib, in his recent book on Islam and ethnicity in Malaysia, tells us that

both Islam and ethnic nationalism are forces of central significance in Malay culture and identity. Islam is not only the faith
of the Malays; it serves also as one of the core foundations upon
which their self-identity is based.[2]

Islam is, of course, not alone among world religions in having
contributed a religious basis to the identities which have underlain
ethnic groupings. To take an example from Christianity, this time
relating to sectarian differences within the one religion, the intertwining of religious and ethnic factors is evident in the communal
groupings of Northern Ireland. The two communities of the province have different origins: 'native Irish' and Scots-Irish. Yet it is
religious persuasion (Catholic or Protestant) which has provided the
core around which each community has constructed its identity.

The second cause for surprise in the assertion that Islam and
ethnicity in Eastern Europe are closely interrelated stems from a perception of the character and origins of some of the Muslim groupings
of Eastern Europe. It is clear that at least some of these groupings
share a common racial origin with non-Muslims in the surrounding
areas. The Bosnian Muslims are an obvious example of this (in so far
as most of them are descended from Slavs who were converted to
Islam in Ottoman times), as also are the Bulgarian Pomaks. These
may, therefore, appear to be cases which suggest the autonomy of
the religious factor, i.e. that religious identity has not interacted with
ethnic identity but has overridden it in creating a separate communal
identity.

To respond to this point, it is necessary to consider the meaning
and content of 'ethnicity'. The theoretical literature on ethnicity
has emphasised that there are both objective and subjective elements
in the concept. The objective elements cover characteristics which
are actually held in common: perhaps kinship, physical appearance,
culture, language, etc. (some combination of these characteristics,
but not necessarily all, would have to be present in order for a group
of people to qualify as an ethnic grouping). The subjective elements
rest on the feeling of community. What is important here is the
representations which a group has of itself, whether or not those
representations are actually correct. The group may purvey a historical narrative of its origins, possibly claiming common ancestry,
which may be largely fictitious. Yet 'myths can be potent and it is the
group's representations of itself that are important'.[3]

Theorists differ in the emphasis which they give to objective as against subjective elements. Geertz, for example, places emphasis on the objective elements, seeing kinship and culture as constituting natural attachments which determine the formation of ethnic identities.[4] Barth, on the other hand, stresses the subjective elements, contending that ethnic groups can only be understood in terms of boundary creation and maintenance. In the latter terms, a common culture is not a defining characteristic of an ethnic grouping; it may in fact come into existence as a result of a particular grouping asserting its own position. Cultural features, Barth maintains, are used by ethnic groupings to mark the groupings' boundaries.[5] Similarly, notions of kinship can be projected and/or constructed so as to give greater body to the feelings of commonality within the grouping.

The approach to ethnicity which emphasises subjective elements is the more valuable of the two approaches when examining the relationship between Islam and ethnicity in Eastern Europe. The dynamics of communities in Eastern Europe have been shaped by people holding a conviction that they share a common fate with others, and that they must act together if their individual interests are to be protected. To enquire into the kinship links which underlie such groupings would be complicated and perhaps sterile. Cultural factors are important, but the most critical aspect here concerns the significance which individuals subjectively attach to the different parts of their cultural heritage. It is the subjective elements which require the closest examination.

The assertion that Bosnian Muslims are of Slavic descent and enjoy a common blood kinship with the members of surrounding communities, therefore, is not necessarily relevant to an understanding of the identity and dynamics of the Bosnian Muslim community. The absence of exclusive kinship links does not imply the absence of an ethnic grouping; nor should the commonality of the religion lead to the conclusion that the grouping is 'purely religious'. In the perception of ethnicity which has been put forward above, the religious factor can play a crucial role in the cultural infrastructure which creates and maintains an ethnic grouping. It can act as a 'repository of memories', giving the grouping its feeling of distinctiveness and its rationale for separate existence. Added complexity stems from the system of socio-political organisation implemented under the Ottoman Empire, viz. that of the *millets*. As mentioned in the first chapter, every *millet*, or non-Islamic religious community, i.e. the Jews and the Christians, was left to organise its own life. This included education as well as worship. The non-assimilative nature of this system allowed a degree of distinctiveness to remain between the communities, and helped provide a basis for subsequent confusion between the concepts of citizenship, ethnicity and religion.

2. Difficulties in estimating the size of Muslim communities in Eastern Europe

The attempt to estimate the size of different Muslim communities in Eastern Europe is, of course, a valuable exercise in itself. It does, however, have a further advantage: the exercise throws into relief some of the problems encountered in examining the relationship between Islam and ethnicity in the region.

For a start, it should be said that the Muslim peoples of Eastern Europe are among the least researched of the world's Muslim groupings. This poses problems in the gathering and presentation of relevant statistical information. There is not even agreement on nomenclature or on who can be included as 'Muslim groupings'. In Bulgaria, for example, are Turks and Tatars necessarily Muslims, and do these national categories overlap with Pomaks (Bulgarian-speaking Muslims)? In Romania, should 'Muslim gypsies' be deemed a community, or should it be subsumed within the category of 'Rumelians'? In Albania, how does the division between Ghegs and Tosks impinge on the communal identities of the Muslim population? Furthermore, what impact did the policies pursued by Communist governments have on the religious affiliations of populations? As will become clear also from subsequent chapters, instances of changing self-identification are not uncommon; in the case of Albania, this is true even for the Muslim–Christian distinction.

It is hardly surprising, therefore, that there is considerable confusion over the numerical strength of the communities, individually and collectively. Are we talking about 9 million Muslims in Eastern Europe, or is the more accurate figure 6 to 7 million? Is it intellectually defensible to contend that the Muslim population of Albania in 1982 stood at 2,110,000, or 75 per cent of the population,[6] despite the fact that the Albanian regime had by then been (for 15 years) conducting deliberate policies aimed at the elimination of any vestiges of religion? What of those who, before 1967, identified with the religious values of Islam and who subsequently abandoned them? Should they be dropped from the statistics for Muslims (assuming one could find out how many there were), or retained on the grounds that they still formed part of a community which was covertly Muslim?

Tables 2.1 to 2.8 (at the end of this chapter) present statistics which were published in various sources during the 1970s, 1980s and early 1990s, giving the numbers of Muslims in Eastern European countries. Reliable new figures since the end of the 1980s are few and far between, in part because the state of flux in the post-Communist era has made the statistics even more volatile than before. In any case, the objective in presenting the statistics is as much to focus attention on the difficulties in arriving at the truth, as it is to give at least some idea of the size of these communities. The statistics cover the Muslim communities in Albania, Bulgaria, Czechoslovakia, Hungary, Poland, Romania, Yugoslavia and Greece. Sources for the data, including page numbers, are shown in the first column, while the second column gives the names by which a group is identified by a particular source. Some sources give the year to which a figure corresponds; whenever available, this is given in the subsequent columns. The penultimate column gives figures which are not related to specific years. The final column gives the most recent total number of Muslims as stated by the source in question.

Even a cursory look at the figures shows substantial discrepancies in the estimates which have been made. These discrepancies are of the following order: for Albania, about half a million; for Bulgaria, some 700,000; for Hungary, over 100,000; for Romania, nearly 300,000; for Poland, some 330,000; for Greece, about 25,000; and for Yugoslavia, 2.5 million. Only in the case of Czechoslovakia do the two available published sources (one from 1984 and one from 1986) arrive at the same figure. Some of the sources ignore altogether the Muslims in four out of the eight (then Communist) Eastern and Central European countries.

A close examination of the material presented in these sources reveals that the figures often cannot be verified by available demographic data. In the case of two Muslim minorities on which some independent demographic data are available, the figures provided by the sources are at variance with these data. The United Nations *Demographic*

Yearbook for 1983 published statistical information on the ethnic composition of Romania, listing the number of Tatars in the country as of
5 January 1977 at 20,508.[7] Weekes, however – who also gives 1977 as
the basis for his data – lists the number of Tatars as 25,000.[8] An even
larger margin of error exists in the case of Polish Muslims. Figures
of 15,000, 22,000 and 333,000 are given by three different sources
quoted in Table 2.5. However, two independent Polish sources, the
national daily *Kurier Polski* of 10 April 1984 and the Roman Catholic
weekly *Tygodnik Powszechny* of 18 December 1983 and 16 October 1984,
have reported the total Muslim population of Poland to be between
2,500 and 3,000 (excluding foreign students and embassy staff). In
the case of Greece, some sources claim that there may be over 100,000
Turkish-speaking Muslims in Western Thrace alone (compared to
other figures giving a total of around 120,000 for all Muslims in Greece).

There are two main reasons for the differences and discrepancies
which have been outlined above. The first stems from the conceptual
difficulties which have already been alluded to: the problem in determining what categories to employ and how each is related to others.
Without a general acceptance of how the populations can usefully be
classified, the bases on which different sets of statistics are drawn up
will vary. The most critical problems here are found in the overlap
between religious affiliation and ethnic identity. Additional difficulties arise from the variations in self-identification already referred to,
as well as from government-enforced changes in official classification (as for instance with the Turkish-speaking population in Greece).

The second reason is that the data needed for making reliable
estimates have not been available. Many of the estimates have depended on censuses which were taken before World War II, sometimes as
early as 1926 (Bulgaria), 1930 (Hungary) and 1934 (Czechoslovakia).
Furthermore, it should be pointed out that the basis of such censuses
was often native language, rather than religion or perceived nationality. Since the censuses were taken there have been substantial movements of people as a result of the redrawing of the borders of almost all
of the Eastern European states. A number of the sources have ignored
the significance of the latter changes, simply adding an appropriate
percentage increase in population figures to the pre-war statistics.

In addition, there may also be political reasons for massaging
the figures: Muslim communities may well wish to posit higher estimates about their own populations than a government concerned
about national integrity may be prepared to admit.

There were of course censuses in Eastern European countries while they were under Communist rule, and these did include questions relating to the nationality of the respondents (most notably in Albania, 1955; Bulgaria, 1965; and Romania, 1977). However, no questions pertaining to religious affiliation were permitted. In addition, it should be remembered that 'contentious' national affiliations, such as gypsies (of whom some were Muslims), were not always included, as in the Bulgarian census of 1965.

The motivations which led Eastern European governments to omit religious affiliation from censuses are well known. Ostensibly it was to emphasise the separation between church and state; in practice it was to downplay the significance of religious belief. In the case of Albania, the state's rejection of religious beliefs and activities was made explicit in the 1976 constitution, article 37 of which proclaimed that 'the state recognises no religion whatsoever and supports atheist propaganda for the purpose of inculcating the scientific materialist world outlook in people'. Any indication of the continued strength of religious affiliations would, of course, have risked discrediting the policies pursued by the governments concerned – showing that these policies were proving ineffective.

The census material on Yugoslavia tended to be rather more useful (with regard to estimating the size of Muslim communities) than that on other Eastern European countries. While maintaining the ban on religious affiliation being listed in censuses, the Yugoslav authorities did in some censuses allow citizens to declare themselves as Muslim in ethnic/national terms. In the 1948 census, Yugoslav citizens were permitted to declare their nationality as Muslims. In the 1953 census, 'Muslim' was omitted as a category, while 'Yugoslav ethnically undetermined' was added. Most Serbo-Croatian-speaking Muslims in Bosnia-Hercegovina declared themselves to be 'Yugoslavs'. In the 1961 census, a 'Muslim in the ethnic sense' category appeared, and the majority of Muslims in Bosnia-Hercegovina declared themselves .as such.[9] Finally, in 1971, the census included a category of 'Muslims in the national sense', and most Muslims in Bosnia-Hercegovina identified themselves with that category. Details of the population numbers from the census are given in Table 2.9.

The changing nomenclature employed in the Yugoslav censuses reflects the difficulties encountered in classifying the Muslim population, and also a transition in attitudes. This transition was a consequence of three factors: the abandonment of 'Yugoslavian' as

a satisfactory approach to inter-ethnic relations; the increasing political consciousness of Muslims within Yugoslavia; and the growing
status of Muslims in the political establishment.[10] The census results
showed that large numbers of Bosnians did regard 'Muslims' as an
appropriate category for the description of their identity.

In effect the Yugoslav government (through to the break-up of
the Yugoslav state) recognised Bosnian Muslims as one of the ethnic
groupings of which Yugoslavia was composed. It is significant that
the designations 'Muslims in the ethnic sense' and 'Muslims in the
national sense' did not comprise all the Muslims in Yugoslavia. It
excluded, for example, the Albanian and Turkish minorities.

Censuses taken in the 1990s also have offered less than categor-
ical evidence about precise numbers. The December 1992 census in
Bulgaria (see Table 2.2, and Chapter 6) probably strongly understated
the number of Roma (gypsies) and did not clearly identify the Pomaks.
In the Republic of Macedonia (see Chapters 3 and 4), controversy
remains over whether the number of ethnic Albanians has been
adequately reflected in the 1994 census, partly because, according to
many Albanians, the government would have wished to understate
their strength, and in part because of 'census-resistance' among
Albanians (related to the above accusation).

Is it possible, then, to say anything meaningful about the numbers of Muslims in Eastern Europe? We would argue that it is, in very
broad terms, provided that the *caveats* about the varying meanings
of the label, and the uncertainty of some estimates, are reckoned
with. Taking the 'least bad' and most recent estimates, it would seem
possible for practical purposes to put the total number of Muslims
(however defined) in Eastern Europe at some 7 to 8.3 million. They
are concentrated mainly in former Yugoslavia (mainly in Bosnia,
Kosovo and Macedonia), Albania, and Bulgaria – in that order.
Smaller communities are found in Greece and Romania; while in
Hungary, Poland and former Czechoslovakia they number no more
than a few thousand each.

3. A comparative note on the Muslim minority in Poland

The Polish Muslim minority is very small. It does, nonetheless, merit
taking as a case study, especially as its current small size often deprives

it of academic attention. This is a pity both because of the intrinsic interest which attaches to its history and dynamics, and because it illustrates well the linkages which exist between Islam and ethnicity in the shaping and dynamics of Eastern European Muslim communities.[11]

Muslims in fact constitute one of the smallest religious groups in Poland. Polish estimates of their numerical strength vary, but the figure of 'less than 3,000 practising believers' put forward by *Tygodnik Powszechny* on 18 December 1983 is probably accurate. This figure excludes the several thousand students and other visitors from Islamic countries who are temporarily resident in Poland. The overwhelming majority of Polish Muslims are Tatars. (The term 'Tatar' means 'archer'. The name today applies to several related but spacially disparate peoples. Modern Tatars cannot be regarded as direct descendants of the Tatar Mongols of Manchuria who overran much of Eurasia in the thirteenth century. They are distant scions of the Turkic-speaking Volga-Kama Bulgars, to whom they owe their Islamic heritage.)[12]

The Tatars arrived in the Lithuanian part of the Kingdom of Poland and Lithuania in the 14th century.[13] According to a 15th-century Polish historian, Jan Dlugosz, many thousands of them were taken prisoner by the Lithuanian Duke Witold in 1397 during his expedition on the Volga river, and were subsequently relocated with their entire families to his lands. Over the next three centuries, many more Tatars followed the earlier arrivals. Following a succession of famines, epidemics, internal clashes and feuds in their native khanates, a considerable number of Tatar nobles left their houses and resettled in Polish lands. Most settled around the Lithuanian capital Vilna, but others went to the foothills of the Tatra Mountains in southern Poland (Podlasie) and in the Lublin regions. Renowned and experienced warriors, they served mostly in special Tatar units with either the royal forces or the local magnates' own private armies. Legally enjoying the same privileges as the Polish nobility, they were given vast estates. Those of more humble origin established themselves in villages and small cities, becoming known as excellent horse breeders, horse traders, gardeners, horticulturists and artisans.

A census ordered in 1631 by King Sigismund III listed more than 100,000 Tatar settlers in Poland. The last important colonisation scheme involving Tatars was started in the late 17th century by King

John Sobieski. Unable to pay his Tatar officers their salaries, overdue for more than three years, Sobieski decided to give them properties from the state-owned estates in Podlasie.

The Tatars enjoyed religious tolerance and maintained contacts with Islamic centres abroad. Many Tatar customs became part of Polish tradition, especially among the Polish nobility. The traditional long robes (*kontusz*), fur caps (*kolpak*) and curved swords (*karabela*) were imitations of the garb worn by the Crimean Tatars.[14]

The Tatars lost their language, most likely sometime in the 17th century, and began using the local Polish Byelorussian dialect. Although most Tatars lived in their ethnic enclaves, they became Polonised through inter-marriage and the changing of values. This process was without doubt accelerated by the increase of religious intolerance towards the end of the 17th century, one indication of which was the prohibition on the construction of mosques.

After the third division of Poland in 1795, when the Polish state ceased to exist, the Tatars joined the Poles in the fight for the country's independence. They played an important part in Bonaparte's Russian campaign and in the two national uprisings against the Russians in 1830 and 1863. For this they were bitterly persecuted by the Czarist regime.

Later, during World War I, the Tatars fought in the Polish Legions. Their patriotism was acknowledged and admired by Poles and non-Poles alike. When, in 1918, Poland regained its independence and statehood, only a small number of Tatar enclaves in the north-eastern provinces remained within the Polish borders. The total population of Tatars varied between 6,000 and 8,000. In 1925, the Socio-Cultural Association of Tatars was formed with headquarters in Warsaw. The association published *Rocznik Tatarski* (Tatar Annals) and *Zycie Tatarskie* (a periodical on Tatar life). Between 1936 and 1939, a Tatar cavalry squadron existed in the Polish army.

In 1936 a special legal act permitted the formation of a Muslim Religious Association. According to its provisions, the 19 Muslim parishes were placed under the religious supervision of a *mufti*. Each community was built around a parish council with an *imam* at its head, and each had (as a rule) its own mosque and an appropriate religious cemetery.

During World War II, most of the Tatar intelligentsia was exterminated by the Nazis in retaliation for the Tatar detachment's strong resistance against the invading German armies in September 1939.

After the war, only two Tatar enclaves (Bohoniki and Kruszyniany) remained within the borders of Poland. As a result of the redrawing of the Polish boundaries, the other enclaves became part of the Soviet Union. Some Tatars from the former Polish territories were resettled in the recovered lands in western and north-western Poland. This of course meant that a vital part of their religious and cultural heritage – mosques, cemeteries, schools, etc. – were left behind. Only the two above-named communities (both in north-eastern Poland) still had mosques and traditional burial grounds. Other Tatars, dispersed in about eight localities in various parts of the country, had no designated places of worship and lacked organisational structures. This had a substantially negative impact on the preservation of religious and ethnic values, and accelerated further the Polonisation of the Tatars.

It was only in 1969 that steps were taken to rebuild the organisational structure of the Muslims in Poland. That year, the Polish government permitted the holding of the first post-war Congress of Polish Muslims, which created the Muslim Religious Union of Poland. Led by a five-man body called the Muslim Board, which was headed by a lay person, the Union became the 'spokesman' on behalf of this proud but dwindling minority.

In 1971, the Office for Religious Denominations in Poland created a new legal framework of religious work among the Muslims. Since then, the mosques in the two oldest Tatar enclaves (Bohoniki and Kruszyniany) have been restored with grants from Arab countries in the Gulf. In September 1984, a foundation stone was laid for the construction of a new mosque in Gdansk-Oliwa, the first to be erected in Poland for 192 years. In addition to fulfilling the usual religious functions, this mosque now has a library and facilities for the teaching of Arabic.

Today, most Polish Muslims live within six parishes: Bialystok, Bohoniki, Kruszyniany, Gdansk-Oliwa, Szczecin and Warsaw.[15] The largest is the Bialystok parish, with an estimated 800 members. The parish in Gdansk-Oliwa in the early 1990s had approximately 270 members, and that in Warsaw 300. The six administrative parish units control four Islamic cemeteries, two of which are located in Warsaw. In cities without Islamic cemeteries, the municipal authorities designate special sectors in the local cemeteries to be reserved for Islamic burials. There are no Koranic schools in Poland and thus the Muslims use, for religious purposes, a dialect which is a mixture of the Polish and Byelorussian languages with some vocabulary taken from Turkish and Arabic. Since 1969, a national congress of the Muslim Religious Union has been held every five years. The congress is attended by delegates from each of the parishes; from those participating it elects the Highest Collegiate (the governing body) of the Union.[16]

Nowadays, most of the Tatars in Poland can hardly be distinguished from other Poles. Mixed marriages have contributed visibly to the obliteration of typical Tatar features. Yet the tiny Muslim minority is still in existence. Its survival, in a predominantly Roman Catholic country ruled for forty years by a polity whose ideology was avowedly atheistic, is remarkable.

4. Conclusion

The factors which have shaped the Polish Muslim community are not unlike those which have shaped other Muslim communities in Eastern Europe. The interaction between Islam and ethnicity has provided the crucial dynamic which has maintained communities. The significance of the Islamic factor has remained even when the practice of religion has been minimal (in the case of the Polish Muslims, there have been times when the only distinctively Islamic practice remaining has been the separate place of burial). The Islamic factor has asserted itself through constituting a repository of memories, memories which give unity to the community, mark its boundaries and give it a separate identity.

So powerful has the Islamic factor been, indeed, that it has effectively been able to create new ethnic groupings, by providing the common link which has enabled groups of people to establish a distinct identity and to cohere as a community – in a manner which goes beyond the simple defence of their religious practices, institutions and structures (which may, or may not, have retained their vitality). This has been the case with the Bosnian Muslims.

One important lesson for the future may be drawn from the case of the Polish Muslims. The Tatars have historically made a substantial contribution to the Polish/Lithuanian state, and indeed have helped to establish and buttress the independence of the Polish nation. For much of this period they retained a strong awareness of their own cultural distinctness, and throughout have kept a feeling of their own separate identity. This provides a useful model of how

Muslim communities can relate to the wider national communities of which they form part in Europe: retaining their own culture and identity, and contributing positively to the wider community. The ability of Muslim communities to do this, and the likelihood of their doing it, depend on the political and economic frameworks which surround them. It is up to European societies to ensure that such frameworks are in existence; they have much to gain from it.

Table 2.1

Comparative Statistics on the Muslims in Albania

Source	Name given	1971	1977	1982	1990	Data for which no year given	Last total estimate
1. Vucinich '69 p. 236	Sunnite Muslims Bektashis Total					800,000 200,000 1,000,000	1,000,000
2. Weekes '78 p. 500	Albanian (Gheg-Tosk)		1,750,000				1,750,000
3. *Gazetteer* p. 977	Muslims					1,763,000	1,763,000
4. Kettani '86 p. 26	Muslims	1,580,000		2,110,000			2,110,000
5. Shaikh '92	Muslims				2,275,000		2,275,000

Table 2.2

Comparative Statistics on the Muslim Minorities in Bulgaria

	Source	Name given	1977	1982	1990	1993	Data for which no year given	Last total estimate
1.	Vucinich '69 p. 236	Turks					700,000	
		Pomaks					180,000	
		Muslim Gypsies					120,000	
		Tatars					5,000	
		Total					1,005,000	1,005,000
2.	Ramet '84 p. 25	Muslims					800,000	800,000
							1,000,000	1,000,000
3.	Irwin '84* p. 218	Turks					700,000	
		Pomaks					120,000	
		Tatars					5,000	
		Muslim Gypsies					120,000	
		Total					945,000	945,000
4.	Weekes '78 p. 501	Turkic	749,000					
		Rumelian	739,000					
		Tatar	10,000					
		Muslim Gypsies	175,000					
		Total	1,637,000					1,673,000

41

[Table 2.2 continued]

	Source	Name given	1977	1982	1990	1993	Data for which no year given	Last total estimate
5.	Gazetteer pp. 982–4	Muslims					1,207,000	1,207,000
6.	Kettani '86 p. 31	Turks and Tatars		1,050,000				
		Pomaks		370,000				
		Gypsies		280,000				
		Total		1,700,000				1,700,000
7.	Shaikh '92	Pomaks			300,000			
		Turks			870,000			
		Muslim Gypsies			450,000–750,000			
		Total			1,620,000–1,920,000			1,620,000–1,920,000
8.	Popovic '93	Pomaks				150,000		
		Turks				600,000		
		Total				800,000		800,000
9.	Ilchev and Perry '96†	Turks				700,000		
		Muslim Roma				300,000		
		'Bulgarian Muslims' (Pomaks)				200,000		
		Total				1,200,000		1,200,000

* Irwin quotes Vucinich as his source.
† These figures are presented as tentative estimates.

42

Table 2.3

Comparative Statistics on the Muslim Minority in Czechoslovakia

Source	Name given	Data for which no year given	Last total estimate
1. Ramet '84 p. 25	Muslims	2,000	2,000
2. Kettani '86 p. 49	Muslims	2,000	2,000

Table 2.4

Comparative Statistics on the Muslim Minority in Hungary

Source	Name given	1949	1985	1990	Data for which no year given	Last total estimates
1. *Gazetteer*	Muslims				105,000	105,000
2. Kettani '86 p. 48	Muslims	3,300	6,000			6,000
3. Shaikh '92 p. 92	Muslims			3,000		3,000

Table 2.5

Comparative Statistics on the Muslim Minority in Poland

Source	Name given	1972	1982	1990	Data for which no year given	Last total estimates
1. Ramet '84 p. 25	Muslims				15,000	15,000
2. *Gazetteer* pp. 382–4	Muslims				333,000	333,000
3. *Kurier Polski* and *Tygodnik Powszecha* '83/'84 (see text)	Muslims				2,500–3,000	2,500–3,000
4. Kettani '86 p. 48	Muslims	15,000	22,000			22,000
5. Shaikh '92 p. 197	Muslims			3,000		3,000

Table 2.6

Comparative Statistics on the Muslim Minority in Romania

Source	Name given	1971	1977	1982	1993	Data for which no year given	Last total estimates
1. Vucinich '69 p. 236	Tatars					21,000	
	Turks					15,000	
	Total					37,000	37,000
2. Ramet '84 p. 25	Muslims					35,000	35,000
3. Weekes '78 p. 519	Turkic		173,000				
	Rumelian		148,000				
	Tatars		25,000				
	Total		346,000				346,000
4. *Gazetteer*	Muslims					188,000	188,000
5. Kettani '86 p. 47	Muslims	50,000		65,000			65,000
6. Shaikh '92 p. 200	Muslims					52,000	52,000
7. Popovic '93	Muslims				50,000		50,000

GOSHEN COLLEGE LIBRARY
GOSHEN, INDIANA

Table 2.7

Comparative Statistics on the Muslim Minorities in former Yugoslavia

Source	Name given	1971	1977	1981	1991	1993	Data for which no year given	Last total estimates
1. Vucinich '69 p. 236	Ethnic Muslims						1,300,000	
	Albanians						900,000	
	Turks and Gypsies						180,000	
	Total						2,380,000	2,380,000
2. Ramet '84 p. 25	Muslims			2,000,000				2,000,000
3. King p. 272	Muslims	1,218,732						1,218,732
4. Weekes '78 p. 527	Bosnian		1,744,000					
	Albanian (Gheg-Tosk)		1,389,000					
	Gypsies		833,000					
	Turkic		176,000					
	Rumelian		176,000					
	Total		4,142,000					4,142,000
5. Gazetteer pp. 982–4							4,192,000	4,192,000

[Table 2.7 continued]

Source	Name given	1971	1977	1981	1991	1993	Data for which no year given	Last total estimates
6. Kettani '86 p. 30	Bosniac Muslims			2,340,000				
	Albanians			1,730,000				
	Turks			120,000				
	Gypsy Muslims			100,000				
	Total			4,290,000				4,290,000*
7. Shaikh '92	Muslims				4,500,000			4,500,000
8. Popovic '93	Muslims					well over 3 million		well over 3 million

* Kettani also mentions that in addition 'there are also several thousand Muslims who identify themselves as Croatians, Serbians, Macedonians, Circassians, etc.'

Table 2.8

Comparative Statistics on the Muslim Population of Greece

	Source	Name given	1981	1993	Data for which no year given	Last total estimate
1.	Alexandris '88	Turks Pomaks Athigani Total	55,000 43,000 22,000 120,000			120,000
2.	Shaikh '92	Muslims			over 120,000	over 120,000
3.	*Kathimerini* 28/2/93	Turks Pomaks Athigani Total		54,000 36,000 24,000 114,000		114,000
4.	Popovic '93	Muslims		130,000–150,000		130,000–150,000

Table 2.9
Population of Bosnia-Hercegovina

Communities	1948	1953	1961	1971	1981
Total	2,565,277	2,847,790	3,277,935	3,746,111	4,125,000*
Serbs	1,136,116	1,264,372	1,406,053	1,393,148	1,320,000
Serb-Muslims	71,991	–	–	–	–
Croats	614,123	654,229	711,660	772,660	758,000
Croat-Muslims	25,295	–	–	–	–
Muslims (ethnically undetermined)	788,403	–	–	–	–
Yugoslavs (ethnically undetermined)	–	891,800	275,883	43,796	326,280
Muslims (in the ethnic sense)	–	–	842,247	–	–
Muslims (in the national sense)	–	–	–	1,482,430	1,630,000

Source: B. Szajkowski, 'Muslim People in Eastern Europe', Journal, Institute of Muslim Minority Affairs, vol. 9, no. 1, January 1988, p. 115.
*The 'total' figures do not add up to the totals of the figures in the columns.

Notes

1   In addition to the sources referred to in subsequent footnotes, the following have also been drawn on:
     World Muslim Gazetteer (henceforth: *Gazetteer*) 3rd edn (Delhi: International Islamic Publishers, 1985); A. Alexandris, 'Oi Mousoulmanoi tis Ditikis Thrakis' [The Muslims of western Thrace] in *Oi Ellinotourkikes Sxeseis 1923–1987* [Greek–Turkish Relations 1923–1987] (Athens: Greek Institution of Foreign and Defense Policy, Gnosy, 1988); S. Balic, 'Eastern Europe: the Islamic Dimensions', *Journal Institute of Muslim Minority Affairs*, vol. 1, no. 1 (Summer 1979), pp. 29–37; I. Ilchev and D. Perry, 'The Muslims of Bulgaria' (Chapter 6 in this volume) J. Krejci, 'What is a Nation?' in P. Merkl and N. Smart (eds.), *Religion and Politics in the Modern World* (New York University Press, 1983), pp. 29–43; A. Popovic, *L'Islam Balkanique* (Wiesbaden: Harrassowitz, 1986); A. Popovic, 'Les Communautés musulmanes Balkaniques dans la période post-communiste', paper presented to the Conference on Islam in Europe, St Catherine's College, Oxford University, 5–7 April 1993; H. Poulton, *The Balkans: Minorities and States in Conflict*, 2nd edn (London: MRG Publication, 1993); H. Poulton, 'Changing National Identity of Muslim Minorities in Bulgaria, Greece, and FYROM (Macedonia)', paper presented to the *Conference on Muslim Communities in Post-Bipolar Europe* (Amman, Jordan, September 1994); P. Ramet (ed.), *Religion and Politics in Soviet and East European Politics* (Durham, NC: Duke University Press, 1984); F. Shaikh (ed.), *Islam and Islamic Groups: A Worldwide Reference Guide* (London: Longman, 1992); P. Shoup, *The East European and Soviet Data Handbook* (Columbia University Press, 1981); P. Sugar (ed.), *Ethnic Diversity and Conflict in Eastern Europe* (Santa Barbara: ABC-Clio, 1980); W. Vucinich, 'Islam in the Balkans' in A. Arberry (ed.), *Religion in the Middle East*, Vol. 2: *Islam* (Cambridge: Cambridge University Press, 1969), pp. 236–52; *Wielka Encyklopedia Powszechna* [Great Popular Encyclopedia] (Warsaw: PWN, 1962).
2   H. Mutalib, *Islam and Ethnicity in Malay Politics* (Oxford: Oxford University Press, 1990), p. 1.
3   E. Ben-Rafael and S. Sharot, *Ethnicity, Religion and Class in Israeli Society* (Cambridge: Cambridge University Press, 1991), p. 6.
4   C. Geertz, 'The Integrative Revolution: Primordial Sentiments and Civil Politics in New States' in C. Geertz (ed.), *Old Societies and New States: the Quest for Modernity in Asia and Africa* (New York: Free Press, 1963), pp. 105–57.
5   F. Barth, 'Introduction' in F. Barth (ed.), *Ethnic Groups and Boundaries* (London: George Allen & Unwin, 1969), pp. 9–38.
6   A. Kettani, *Muslim Minorities in the World Today* (London: Mansell Publishing, 1986), p. 26.
7   *United Nations Demographic Handbook, 1983* (New York: United Nations, 1985), p. 719.

8   R. Weekes (ed.), *Muslim Peoples: A World Ethnographic Survey* (Westport, Connecticut: Greenwood Press, 1978), pp. 499–527.

9   R. King, *Minorities under Communism: Nationalities as a Source of Tension among Balkan Communist States* (Cambridge, Mass.: Harvard University Press, 1973), p. 212.

10 Z. Irwin, 'The Fate of Islam in the Balkans: A Comparison of Four New State Policies' in P. Ramet (ed.), *Religion and Politics in Soviet and East European Politics* (Durham, NC: Duke University Press, 1984), p. 214.

11 Much of the material on the Polish Tatars which is given here is taken from B. Szajkowski, 'Muslim People in Eastern Europe', *Journal Institute of Muslim Minority Studies*, Vol. 9, 1988, No. 1, pp. 103–18.

12 Weekes, *op. cit.*, p. 395.

13 The Duchy of Lithuania was, in 1385, united with Poland under a common King, Wladyslaw Jagiello. The union lasted until the partition of Poland in 1795.

14 Few contemporary Poles know that the name of the traditional Polish light cavalry, the Ulans, comes from a Tatar captain in the Royal Cavalry, Adam Ulan. He was raised to the nobility in 1681 and founded a long succession of Tatar officers commanding these formations named after him.

15 A number of Tatar families live in other cities: Eblag, Zielona Gora, Wroclaw Cracow and Gorzow Wielkopolski. These small groups also form part of one of the parishes.

16 The meeting of the National Congress of the Muslim Religious Union which was held in Bialystok on 10–11 March 1984 was attended by some 80 delegates.

3

CITIZENSHIP, STATUS, AND MINORITY POLITICAL PARTICIPATION: THE EVIDENCE FROM THE REPUBLIC OF MACEDONIA

Robert W. Mickey

1. Introduction[1]

In 1995, Macedonia's ethnic relations were in crisis. A stand-off between a large minority community of ethnic Albanians and an insecure, ethnically Slav Macedonian[2] majority was threatening to unravel the new Republic of Macedonia. But rather than anomalous, the crisis is fairly representative, in form and content, of other inter-ethnic tensions in post-communist Europe's multi-ethnic states.

While this volume concerns Muslim communities in Europe, it is important to emphasise that in this case, the salience of religion as a source and fuel of conflict is surprisingly low. Although the Albanian minority, the focal point of ethnic conflict in Macedonia, is predominantly Muslim, and although other Islamic communities with significant grievances are present in Macedonia as well, this stand-off concerns the group status of Albanians as a large minority, i.e. the question about who 'owns' Macedonia.

Of course, this question of status is not a new one. During the forty-odd years of the Yugoslav federation, balances of power among various nationalities were in part regulated by conferring on them first-, second-, and even third-class status. But as new states emerge from the federation, the question, transformed, remains dangerous. A political stand-off rather than a struggle for the securing provisions for minority protection, the issue of status drives Albanian political participation in Macedonia. Although this participation is affected by a number of other variables, including substantive and symbolic aspects of citizenship, the demand to achieve status as a 'partner-nation' of Macedonia, above and beyond other ethnic minorities, is the overarching goal of ethnic Albanians, and informs all other demands and much of the nature of their participation. Given the country's precarious internal and external environments, this parti-cipation is the key to the country's stability. Failure to resolve the status stand-off could lead to Macedonia's implosion. Despite ambigu-ities surrounding its reputed benefits, status matters. And, as will be demonstrated below, the question of status conferred on larger minorities is indicative of a region-wide problem.

2. The *Macédoine* salad

For the past millennium, the region known as 'Macedonia', which includes the present-day Republic of Macedonia, as well as parts of Greece, Serbia, Bulgaria, and Albania, has been a highly valued, and much fought over, strategic point of transit between West and East. Today, Macedonia (population 2.1 million) is home to more than 400,000 ethnic Albanians (approximately 23 per cent of the total population), as well as about 80,000 ethnic Turks, a small but significant community of Slav-speaking Muslim Macedonians (*Torbeshi*), and several thousand ethnic Roma, Serbs, and Vlachs.[3] Highly concentrated in western and north-western Macedonia along the Albanian and Kosovo borders, the Albanians have been set apart from Slavs and others by their history, language, and traditions. Organised in tightly-knit clans and following their own centuries-old 'custom' law, most Albanians speak Macedonian, but members of other ethnic groups do not speak Albanian. Albanians, like the Turks in Macedonia, are predominantly Muslim. Unlike the Turks, how-ever, who are largely assimilated into the mainstream of Macedonian society, Albanians have remained fairly isolated socially.

The remainder of Macedonia's population (approximately 66 per cent) are Macedonians, a relatively new Slav-Orthodox nation-ality which began to develop at the turn of this century and which was consolidated after World War II under the encouragement of Tito. Of Macedonia's four neighbours, only Albania has recognised the existence of the Macedonian people (and then only half-heartedly). Macedonians perceive threats from Kosovo and Serbia, are alarmed by the treatment of fellow Macedonians in Bulgaria and Greece, and lament their inability to defend themselves. Serb minorities within Macedonia are a possible lever to be used by Serbia to destabilise the country. Macedonians also perceive real prospects of economic collapse (spurred on by Greece's embargo and the UN blockade against Serbia, Macedonia's largest trading partner) and the subsequent introduction of an international protectorate (in which the first UNPROFOR (now UNPREDEP) deployments are feared to be only a scouting force). It is understandable, therefore, that Macedonians feel highly insecure as the titular nationality of an extremely weak state. The 'threat' posed by Macedonia's ethnic minorities provides an internal counterpart to this treacherous external environment.

Heavily discriminated against in the former Yugoslavia, poorer, and even more poorly educated, Albanians in Macedonia reacted to Macedonia's independence with a sense of impatience and opportunity. They hoped that an independent republic, free from anti-Albanian manipulations emanating from Belgrade, would be able to redress Albanian grievances and construct a truly multi-ethnic civil society. The Albanian Question, however, has complicated matters. With more than half of ethnic Albanians living outside Albania proper, the demise of Yugoslavia seemed (and for many still seems) to present an opportunity for the creation of a Greater Albania, which would include western Macedonia and Kosovo (Serbia's overwhelming Albanian province, where 2 million Albanians live under what can be termed little else than Serb repression). This 'opportunity' led to demands in late 1991 and early 1992 for Albanian autonomy in western Macedonia. Although these demands were later retracted, for Macedonians they were tantamount to secession, and therefore civil war, and exacerbated their fears of Macedonia's implosion.

The issues upon which Albanians have sought remedy are several, but are common to all larger ethnic minorities (e.g. Serbs, Hungarians, and Russians) in post-Communist Europe. They have called for much wider access to Albanian-language secondary- and higher-level education. Also, Albanians have clamoured for the right to use their language in official fora, on identification cards, and in parliament. This concern over use of language extends to the area of cultural production, where Albanians have called for increased programming in the Albanian language in state-subsidised media (radio, newspapers, and television). More controversially, they argue that Albanians be represented proportionally (according to their percentage of the population) in all administrative posts, and demand passage of strong local self-government legislation so that they can better manage the affairs of municipalities in which they predominate.

3. The question of status in the former Yugoslav federation

Ethnic Albanian leaders voice these and other demands, but the all-encompassing demand is that of a special status within the state. Status is both the rationale for other demands, and the ultimate goal. The roots of this question lie in the former Yugoslav federation.

With the ratification of the 1974 Yugoslav federal constitution, six 'Nations of Yugoslavia' were recognised as the constituent elements of the federation: Serbs, Croats, Slovenes, Bosnians, Montenegrins, and Macedonians. As the titular nationalities of the federation's six republics, these 'nations' held special powers in federal representative bodies, and had to be consulted over decisions involving the future of the republic. Each held the right to secede. Other ethnic communities, including ethnic Albanians and Hungarians, had the status of 'nationalities'.[4] These nationalities were granted expanded educational and cultural rights, but did not possess their own titular republics or provinces. For instance, although a predominantly Albanian Kosovo was declared an autonomous region within the Serb republic, it was never designated by nationality but instead 'bespoke the Albanian-Serbian terrain'.[5]

At the level of the republics, Yugoslavia's minority communities were often granted special rights. In the autonomous region of Kosovo, ethnic Albanians were given the leading administrative positions, and the constitution of the region included sections outlining specific rights for ethnic Turks. Meanwhile, until 1989, when a Serb-led crackdown on minorities began, the constitution of the Macedonian republic in its preamble gave special recognition to its Albanians and Turks as minorities who shared the state with Macedonians: Macedonia was the 'state of the Macedonian people and the Albanian and Turkish minorities'. Here, Albanians and Turks were granted a special status above and beyond that of other minorities, such as Roma, Serbs, and Vlachs. This constitution also included specific articles outlining the equality of rights held by Albanians and Turks living in Macedonia. While this equality of rights was of course not consistently applied in practice (e.g. in the sphere of minority-language education), Albanians and Turks perceived that the constitution's preamble granted them a sufficient status in the federal republic of Macedonia.

In 1989, pressure emanating from Belgrade in the face of increased tensions in Kosovo, and the decision by the then party boss Slobodan Milosevic to manipulate ethnic tensions for his own political gain, led Macedonian leaders to modify the republican constitution's preamble. The revised preamble described the Macedonian republic as 'the national state of the Macedonian nation'. It was then used in debates to justify the government's refusal to make improvements in minority-language education.[6] This change in constitutionally granted status, especially in combination with the Serbs' crackdown in Kosovo, was seen as a major loss of power by Albanians and Turks.[7]

As Macedonian politicians moved cautiously toward declaring the republic's independence in the autumn of 1991, discussions on the soon-to-be state's constitution focused quickly on the issue of status of the country's ethnic groups. The preamble to the new constitution, which was passed by the *Sobranie* (Macedonia's parliament) on 21 November 1991, declares that

> Macedonia is established as a national state of the Macedonian people, in which full equality as citizens and permanent co-existence with the Macedonian people is provided for Albanians, Turks, Vlachs, Romanies and other nationalities living in the Republic of Macedonia.[8]

While this formulation placed 'ownership' of the Macedonian state squarely in the hands of the ethnic Slav Macedonians, the body of the constitution provided a relatively progressive array of minority rights on a host of issues. However, Albanian MPs refused to vote on the constitution's ratification, and even recommended to the international community that it not recognise Macedonia because of the phrase 'national state of the Macedonian people'.

This formulation was a compromise between Macedonian nationalist demands for a purely national state, in which minorities would not be favourably mentioned (if at all) in the preamble, and Albanian leaders, who demanded that the state be defined purely as a civil state. The compromise, like most other controversial issues in Macedonia, was brokered by ethnic Macedonian moderates, led by President Kiro Gligorov who, then and now, have wielded the most political power in the country.

Ethnic Macedonians argued that they are entitled to hold the highest status in the constitution because, unlike minorities, they have no 'kin-state' to whom they can appeal for help, no land of their own to which they can return. Their argument here corresponds with that of other majorities in Europe.[9] Moreover, Macedonians argue that Albanians cannot hold an equal status because they would 'aspire to have their own state and [the right to] secede', equal status gives a group the grounds for a future claim to self-determination.[10] Here, parallels to the Yugoslav federation are apparent in the minds of most Macedonians: in this perception, changes in the present preamble are not to be distinguished from calls for autonomy in their potential danger to the stability of the country. Albanian politicians argue that their status as a mere 'nationality' precludes their ability to prevent the government from fundamentally altering the nature of the state to the Albanians' detriment. Here, they mention most often the example of a Macedonian nationalist government which seeks to form a federation with Bulgaria.[11]

4. The Albanian demand for 'partner-nation' status

Since the constitution's ratification, Albanian political leaders have continued to demand that its preamble be modified to grant Albanians a special status within the Macedonian polity. They argue that the preamble of the constitution should grant the Albanians a partner-nation status with the Macedonians. Various parties and streams within the Albanian political community in Macedonia disagree on tactical approaches to securing this status, as well as on other goals. However, they all agree on the need for this improvement in their group status.

4.1. *The rationale for the demands*

Albanian leaders argue that they deserve this co-owner status for several reasons.[12] These arguments bear close attention: how minorities argue for their status reveals important clues about their perception of what status confers.

First, they argue that their substantial share of the country's population entitles them to a status greater than that of other ethnic minorities.[13] Before the 1994 census, these leaders argued that ethnic Albanians comprised from one-third to four-tenths of the population. The more radical of these (as well as Albanian diaspora groups in the United States and elsewhere) even claimed that Albanians out-numbered ethnic Macedonians.[14] In fact, the Albanian community's boycott of the 1991 census, on orders of Albanian leaders, only enhanced the validity of these claims (as they well understood), given the ensuing ambiguity, both domestically and internationally, over the size of the Albanian community.[15]

The presence in predominantly Albanian towns in western Macedonia of tens of thousands of Kosovar Albanians, who had fled Kosovo since 1991, also fuelled perceptions of a burgeoning Albanian community in Macedonia. However, after the 1994 European Union-sponsored census, in which the Albanians (grudgingly) took part, only about 23 per cent of the registered citizens of Macedonia declared themselves to be of Albanian origin. Since October 1994, when census figures were released publicly, Albanian leaders have continued to argue both that the census was not carried out properly, undercounting the Albanian community by up to 50 per cent, and that in any case, 23 per cent clearly justified a special status within the state.[16]

Second, Albanian leaders argue that because of their compact, historical settlement in western Macedonia, they deserve a special partner-nation status. Albanians claim their ancestors lived in this area for centuries before the arrival of the Slavs.[17] Albanians began moving east into the geographic territory of Macedonia early in the nineteenth century, and by displacing local Slavs they settled mostly along the western rim of what is now the Republic of Macedonia. During World War II, most of this area was absorbed by the Italian protectorate of Albania. After the war, most Albanians in Yugoslavia were included in the autonomous province of Kosovo-Metohija. However, north-western and western Macedonia, though predominantly Albanian, were not added to this province when it was drawn up because these areas were considered 'traditional' Macedonian territory. Significantly, 'there was some feeling that the Albanians might be more effectively controlled if they were administratively separated.'[18] The fact that this area of Macedonia bordering modern-day Albania and Kosovo has been settled predominantly by Albanians for centuries is used by Albanian leaders to support the case for their 'ownership' of this land, which, once it became included in an independent Republic of Macedonia, certainly justifies their securing a partner-nation status with the 'newer' ethnic Macedonians.

Third, Albanians argue that their positive historical contribution to the region, and the state, of Macedonia warrants an improved status for their community. A peaceful indigenous people, often living in mixed villages and towns with ethnic Macedonians, Turks, and others, Albanians have, it is argued, contributed to the development of the Macedonian state. Mohammed Halili, a prominent Albanian politician and Minister without Portfolio in the current governing coalition, goes so far as to note that Albanians joined ethnic Macedonians in the fight for independence against the Turks in 1903.[19]

Finally, it is important how this demand for partner status is *not* articulated. Unlike claims for higher status made by other minorities in Eastern Europe (see below), Albanian politicians in Macedonia do not root their demand in international legal standards related to minority protection and promotion. While, as will be discussed below, the viability of doing so is unclear, it is significant that Albanian leaders do not attempt to buttress their claims with such international provisions. Theirs is not a rights-based argument, but a power-based one. The most important, and perhaps most compelling, argument concerns their numerical strength. Albanian leaders argue, and many seem to agree, that numbers translate into political power. Whether, and under what condition, this argument can win the day for an improvement in status for the Albanian community will be explored below. For now, it is enough to emphasise that the numbers game is one deftly played by all sides.

4.2. *The benefits conferred by status*

Why Albanian leaders feel they deserve partner-nation status is clearer than the benefits conferred by this status. Albanian and Macedonian politicians, as well as international observers, do not fully agree over what this status brings the groups which possess it. Perceptions of these benefits, however, are just as important as any 'real' benefits status may confer, as status plays a crucial role in political debates over a number of issues.

The key Albanian understanding of partner-nation status is the notion of joint decision-making. Analogous to co-owners of an enterprise, co-owners of a state must reach all important decisions by consensus. Thus, Albanians argue that an equal status with the state's titular nationality gives its possessor the right to continuous consultations, both formally and informally, on the most important decisions facing the state. For the Albanian community, the largest threat in this sense is Macedonia's entry into a confederation of other Slavic states (as Slobodan Milosevic, as well as some Bulgarian leaders, have advocated). In the words of Arben Xhaferi, a leader of the more radical Albanian faction, partner status would allow Albanians to veto Macedonia's 'slide into Orthodox alliances'.[20] Albanians suggest that Macedonia's whole method of state- and local-level decision-making would be altered by a partner-nation status. The parliament, for example, would feature modified majority-rule voting procedures, an agenda developed only by consensus between Albanian and Macedonian parliamentarians, and mutual vetoes on issues of concern to either nationality.[21]

Albanian leaders also agree that partner-nation status implies a right to the proportional representation of ethnic Albanians in important state institutions based on their share of the population. Chief among these are the police, the Interior and Foreign ministries, local administration offices, the armed forces, and the judiciary.[22] These changes are seen as especially important, given the extreme paucity of Albanians in these and other institutions.[23]

Albanians consider the loss of important rights to be caused by the revocation of partner-nation status (when in 1989 the republic's constitutional preamble was revised). For example, the use of Albanian language in official fora (such as the parliament) has been curtailed, as has the public use of the Albanian flag. More important, they argue, has been the precipitous decline in the enrolment since the 1980s in Albanian-language primary and secondary education.[24] Conversely, Albanian politicians claim these and other rights are implied in partner-nation status, and would be reintroduced were this to be secured. Some of these rights are, it is argued, implied in various articles in the body of the constitution; therefore, the desired change in status would lead to these articles finally being fully activated.

How the matter of the Albanians' status has functioned in political debates since the late 1980s reveals both the benefits of status in practice and how Macedonians perceive what status confers. As was mentioned earlier, the lowered status of Albanians in the revised 1989 preamble was successfully employed in discussions to limit investments in Albanian-language education. Since independence, Macedonian MPs in parliamentary debates again and again return to the Macedonians' 'ownership' of the state to defeat Albanian objections to draft laws concerning citizenship, language use, education, as well as all aspects of the politics of symbols (the state seal, the composition of banknotes, etc.). This argument is based on legal as well as political grounds. More than referring politically to the preamble, some Macedonian MPs charge that certain proposed provisions are actually unconstitutional, as they are in conflict with the notion of Macedonians as owners of the state.

Moreover, the present constitution's preamble, which establishes Macedonia to be the 'national state of the Macedonian people', is used to interpret restrictively all constitutional articles related to minority rights provisions. For example, in the on-going crisis over the establishment of an Albanian-language university in Tetovo (the political and cultural centre of Albanians in western Macedonia), Macedonians claim that the constitutional provision allowing minorities to 'establish private schools at all levels of education, with the exception of primary education, under conditions determined by law' does not, after all, apply to higher education.[25] Macedonian policymakers rightly point to the lack of the necessary laws regulating the establishment and accreditation of such institutions. However, they add, even were such regulations in effect, such a university would not be allowed. When prodded, they invoke the preamble as their trump card.

There is, therefore, an implicit agreement among Macedonians and Albanians over the power of the preamble. While Macedonians affirm this power in debates over nation- and state-building controversies, their argument against the need for a change in the status of Albanians undercuts it. First, they argue that Albanians do not need or deserve a partner-nation status, especially given the relatively progressive constitutional provisions related to minorities.[26] Second,

Albanians need not worry about the preamble for it is non-operational relative to the body of the constitution.[27] In this argument, the preamble fulfils an important nation-building task for an insecure (and relatively new) titular nationality, but at the same time has no negative bearing on minorities residing in this 'national state'. As a fallback, Macedonians plead that even if it were advisable to do so, the present political situation precludes their ability to open up the constitution to revision.[28]

Finally, most Macedonian politicians add that to grant such a status to the Albanians would be suicidal for the state: analogous to granting them territorial autonomy, such status would 'lead to Bosnia'.[29] Here, Macedonians infer similar benefits of partner-nation status as those mentioned by Albanians. For example, echoing the Albanians, Petar Goshev, the president of the Democratic Party, has spoken of the dangers of modified majority rule and mutual vetoes inherent in partner-nation status.

This discussion raises a number of important issues, as well as possible counter-arguments to the notion that the battle for status is essential, rather than epiphenomenal, to Macedonia's inter-ethnic relations. As has been argued above, evidence for the importance of status can be found in public discussions about a variety of issues of concern to minorities, especially Albanians. In these discussions, Macedonians invoke their 'senior partner' status to reject Albanian demands. It could be argued, however, that these arguments had little bearing on the *outcomes* of these debates: given their numerical superiority, Macedonian MPs would (and will) prevail; therefore, the rhetorical devices with which they buttress their arguments, such as status, matter little.

However, this counterargument underestimates the importance of these rhetorical stances in shaping the range of options which a polity views as possible. The clearest example of this fact becomes apparent when one considers the overriding import of the Yugoslav federation's legacy on Macedonia's political actors. This legacy is in most senses a negative one – the lessons which these actors believe they have learned from the federation are cautionary tales, especially when devising efforts to regulate tensions in multi-ethnic states. Whether positive or negative, however, this legacy shapes, and thereby limits, the scope of possible actions to manage Albanian–Macedonian tensions. Both Albanian and Macedonian understandings of what partner-nation status would mean follow fairly closely the conflict regulation procedures built into the 1974 federal constitution's attempts to manage inter-republican relations.[30] Probably for the foreseeable future this set of 'lessons' will guide both Albanian and Macedonian conceptions of how to manage their own situations within Macedonia.

A key difficulty here is assessing the weight to be given to the preamble relative to the body of the constitution, as well as the weight of the constitution relative to other sources of group legitimation and power. In standard constitutional practice, items contained in preambles are considered 'formally symbolic rather than legally binding' as compared to language in the 'operative text' (or body) of the constitution.[31] However, in the Macedonian case, as well as with those of other former Yugoslav republics, 'the traditional rules of constitutional interpretation . . . have been reversed: the preamble both states and reinforces constitutional nationalism despite the protections of the operative text.'[32] The trend in constitutional practice of formerly Yugoslav republics is apparently consistent with the federal Yugoslav case: Hayden points out that 'the renowned "right to secession" in the 1974 [Federal] Constitution was contained only in the "Introductory Part" but was treated as if it were one of the operative articles.'[33]

Even in a situation in which a preamble is operative, it is possible that articles in the main body could outweigh the preamble in importance, thereby reducing its relevance for the granting of status. As was mentioned above, Macedonian constitutional provisions are relatively progressive, such as article no. 7 (guaranteeing official use of minority languages on the local level in areas where minorities are numerous), nos. 44–48 related to minority-language education, and article no. 114 on strong local self-government.[34] Further, backing off from a declaration that Macedonia is a unitary and national state (qualms not shared by, for example, the framers and ratifiers of Romania's post-Ceausescu constitution), the preamble also declares Macedonia to be a 'civil and democratic' state and provides for 'peace and a common home for the Macedonian people with the nationalities living in the Republic of Macedonia'. Article 2 supports this by stating that the 'sovereignty of the Republic of Macedonia derives from the citizens and belongs to the citizens'. Clearly, the Macedonian constitution is a messy compromise of competing civic and national tendencies. Where the balance lies is not so clear.[35]

However, due to the contemporary politics of constitutional interpretation, this ambiguity does not work in favour of the Albanians. The Macedonian parliament largely conducts this interpretation through its consideration of draft laws. Macedonian parliamentarians, often eager to score points by outbidding one another in appearing patriotic (or, at a minimum, to protect themselves and their parties from charges of selling out the state to ethnic minorities), interpret constitutional articles from a national rather than civic posture. The most recent example of this trend has been the modification of parliamentary procedure to forbid the use of minority languages in parliamentary discussions (reversing a right granted but rarely used in the pre-1991 era). Macedonian politicians, and in particular Parliamentary speaker Stojan Andov (a possible successor to President Kiro Gligorov), have invoked article 7 of the constitution, which declares Macedonian to be the official language of the state. Here, article 7 is interpreted broadly, through the preamble, to preclude the use of minority languages in a parliamentary setting. For Albanians, it is apparent that status cannot be derived inductively through the pasting together of various liberal interpretations of constitutional provisions. Rather, since such interpretations can be reversed by political winds and undermined by the preamble, the attainment and maintenance of equal status with the Macedonian nation can only occur with an alteration of this preamble.

It is worth exploring the importance of the constitution in granting group status relative to other, extra-constitutional sources of power. Macedonians often argue that the real demonstration of Albanian power is their representation in parliament (18 Albanian MPs out of a total of 120) and the four-party governing coalition (in which they have four ministers). Here, a large minority community is able to mobilise virtually the entirety of its voting population to elect its 'own' members of parliament (as well as councillors and other positions at the local level). This successful ethnic mobilisation guarantees not only strong parliamentary representation, the Macedonians argue, but also a position in governing coalitions, which brings with it great input on policy matters.

Albanians reject this argument, and point to the fact that on issues of concern to them, and to other minorities, they are always outvoted by a coalition of Macedonian parties. In the previous parliament, governing and opposition parties came together to defeat

Albanian positions. Albanians refer to this rather predictable situation of (ethnic) majority rule as 'systematic outvoting'. For Albanians, political representation without success is of almost no value. This view has been expressed in practice through a series of walk-outs from the parliament. These began with the vote on the ratification of the referendum, and have occurred intermittently since then. At the time of writing (April 1995), two of three Albanian political parties with seats in parliament were 'boycotting' parliamentary proceedings in protest against various decisions (including the decision to ban the use of minority languages on the parliamentary floor).

If parliamentary representation does not meet the Albanian desire for an upgrade in status, neither does Albanian participation in the governing coalition. The ministries directed by Albanian politicians are among the least influential: culture; development; labour and social policy; and one minister without portfolio. Moreover, these and other ministries are almost completely bereft of Albanian staffers. In cabinet discussion, Albanians complain, their views rarely hold sway, nor are they able to redress political losses suffered in parliament.[36]

4.3. *Conclusion*

From the discussion above, a few points should be summarised. First, group status is a predominant issue in relations among ethnic groups. Out of the Yugoslav experience, minority communities, and especially larger minority communities, vie for greater status relative to other groups. Albanians in Macedonia feel they deserve partner-nation status for several reasons. In the context of their own insecurities as an embattled nationality in a weak state, Macedonians are just as adamant that 'ownership' of the state resides with them. In light of Albanian ambitions regionally for a complete nation-state of Albania, these Macedonian concerns are all the stronger. Second, it is clear that the constitution, through the preamble, confers group status as well as reinforcing national interpretations of other constitutional provisions. Third, the power inherent in what is, at least numerically, very significant Albanian political participation does not compensate for the (perceived) lack of appropriate status conferred by the constitution. What remains unclear is how Albanian political participation is structured around the issue of status; why this participation is crucial for the state's stability; and how the issue of status functions regionally.

5. Albanian political participation

Three main parties represent Albanians living in Macedonia: the Party for Democratic Prosperity (PDP); the National Democratic Party (NDP); and the Party for Democratic Prosperity of Albanians (PDPA). From 1990 until 1992, all significant community power was held by the PDP. During this period, the Albanian community was fairly homogeneous politically. While various streams of opinion on the national question existed within the PDP, the political community remained quite stable. In late 1993 these differences erupted, and since that time control over power has become an (almost) open game.

Several factors account for this increasing heterogeneity. First, Albania, the kin-state to this community, precipitated splits by weighing in on the side of the more radical elements (those calling for the creation of a parallel society, and even secession). This interference from the kin-state was in part due to a confused and confusing competition for control over the Albanian 'diaspora' between Albania's President Sali Berisha and the Albanian leader in Kosovo, Ibrahim Rugova.[37] Second, as the Yugoslav wars dragged on, Macedonia remained in an economic stranglehold between north and south, and little progress was made on key Albanian grievances. These have combined to cause increasing impatience for immediate results on the part of the Albanian leadership. Third, a number of more radical Albanian activists from Kosovo, many of whom were born in Macedonia, have returned to lend their organisational acumen to the radicals (and to secure leadership roles for themselves).

As a result of this increasing heterogeneity, the Albanian community is vulnerable to the dangerous logic of ethnic outbidding. Radicals in the PDPA and NDP have captured much of the PDP's political base, and threaten to overwhelm the more moderate PDP leadership.[38] Consequently, the PDP has taken more strident stands on many issues in order to dilute the drawing power of the radicals (and, given the organisation of interests in the Albanian community, the moderates' appeal to Tirana is almost as important as their appeal to the Albanian electorate in Macedonia). PDP support for a highly controversial and extra-legal Albanian-language university in Tetovo is only one symptom of this increased competition.

Demands for status as a partner nation is another. Radical leaders of the PDPA and the NDP, most importantly Arben Xhaferi (PDPA), have placed more pressure on both rival Albanian leaders to call for an improvement in status. Xhaferi proposes an 'historical agreement', or 'treaty', between the two ethnic groups. In the absence of such a restructuring of politics along group lines, he threatens to take the Albanian community 'underground'.[39] Macedonia's Albanian-language press, now a forum for open debate where a Pravda-like unanimity once reigned, more frequently echoes such arguments.[40] Two changes are important to note here. First, moderate Albanian leaders are being pushed into demanding a change in status almost in the manner of an ultimatum. Second, the radicals are articulating an expanded notion of a status improvement, one in which a grand bargain between the two groups continues as an on-going process of negotiation, similar to Lijphart's notion of consociational democracy.[41] These changes in emphasis raise the stakes in the battle for status, and may limit the manœuvring room available to the Albanian leadership in their dealings with Macedonian counterparts.

This manœuvring room is crucial, not only for the survival of a moderate Albanian leadership, but for the survival of Macedonia itself. The republic's stable instability up until now has depended on the presence of the Albanian parties in the country's governing coalitions.[42] Until the last elections, which anti-government Macedonian parties boycotted, thus allowing the governing coalition to sweep the parliament, these coalitions would have collapsed without the 18 to 22 MPs of the PDP and NDP. This participation, as noted above, brought influence, but not influence perceived as significant enough to effect Albanian goals. Pressures on these parties to withdraw support for the coalition account for the very tenuous nature of this support – parliamentary walkouts by Albanian MPs occur regularly. Until recently, these walkouts threatened to undermine the government, and were often met by compromises from the Macedonian side. In effect, they functioned as a somewhat clumsy and dangerous conflict regulation mechanism. If a consensus emerges among Macedonian parties which obviates the need for Albanian participation in the governing coalition, walkouts and other Albanian threats of withdrawal of its support will become ineffective, and Albanian moderates, and radicals (now represented in the parliament), may resort to more dangerous actions.

Albanian participation in the government not only holds together the state against the significant and vociferous Macedonian opposition, but it provides a crucial back-channel for dialogue between Albanian leaders and the President and Prime Minister.[43] It also bestows international legitimacy upon Macedonia as a potentially viable multi-ethnic state. An Albanian 'exit' may lead to disastrous consequences for the state's tenuous peace. A resolution of the issue of status is therefore vital.

6. Status of large minority communities: the regional view

The issue of status in Macedonia is not unique to the region of post-Communist multi-ethnic states. It may be more salient in Macedonia, given the country's overall fragility, but debates over minority status are present elsewhere, and in forms strikingly similar to the Macedonian context.

Serbs in Croatia, the largest among several minority groups, challenge Croatia's constitution[44] on the grounds that it is exclusivist in its favouring of the Croat nation and its granting of second-class status to non-ethnic Croats. Ethnic Hungarians in Slovakia and Romania point to those states' constitutions as similarly exclusivist, symptomatic of Hayden's 'constitutional nationalism'. Ethnic Russians in the Baltic republics and in Central Asia voice similar concerns.

But Hayden and other commentators would have us believe that these debates, all of which centre upon the status to be bestowed or withheld on these states' largest minority communities, amount to a majority's concept of a national state and a minority's favouring of a civic state (that type of state favoured by most liberal Western commentators). Unfortunately, this is a mischaracterisation of what is actually occurring. As was demonstrated above, Albanian perceptions of what status confers amounts to their endorsement of an ethnically-organised state. This is evidenced most baldly in calls for proportional representation in civil service posts and even firm management. In this model, Macedonia enshrines and reifies membership in ethnic communities, and organises the state's management along an on-going agreement among the two largest ethnic groups. This has little similarity to a civic state in which ethnicity plays little or no role in state formation and maintenance beyond the guarantee of individual rights for all.

This minority endorsement of an ethnically organised state is not limited to Macedonia. Serbs in Croatia call for an historic agreement with Croats, over the heads of other minorities. Similarly, Hungarians in Slovakia and Romania have called intermittently for 'partner-nation' status, equal with that of ethnic Slovaks and Romanians, respectively. This approach was even for a time endorsed by the Hungarian Foreign Ministry.[45] Russians, supported by an overwhelmingly powerful kin-state, have made even larger claims on their new home-states.

It can be argued that these minorities are (a) frightened about the future and are responding to initial nationalist articulations of state formation; (b) simply opportunistic, and vary their demands according to the relative power they hold (inside and outside the state); (c) both. Leaderships of large minorities are, in fact, both frightened and opportunistic. But the sources of their calls for ethnically organised states do not alter the fact that these minorities are often not calling for 'civic' states. A realisation of this fact, as this chapter has attempted to demonstrate for the case of Macedonia, is crucial in approaching the management of ethnic tensions in the Balkans and elsewhere.

7. Conclusion

Reducing ethnic tensions by settling disputes over status is easier said than done. Status is the greatest interest to contestants in ethnic conflict. Concern over status supersedes 'conflicts over needs and interests'.[46] Minorities search for guarantees of better treatment in the present and standing in the future. Majorities, on the other hand, fearful of their loss of ownership of the state, foreign intervention, and incessant minority 'demands' based on ever-elastic notions of equality, attempt to provide themselves with a constitutional firebreak which secures their own future. In contrast to issues of material interest, conflicts over symbols and status 'are not readily amenable to compromise . . . Whereas material advancement can be measured both relatively and absolutely, the status advancement of one ethnic group is entirely relative to the status of others.'[47] In the Macedonian case, as elsewhere, a more promising path is to reduce the salience of status by making incremental progress on other issues subsumed under it. In so doing, more credit may be given to moderate ethnic leaders within their own political communities and the dangerous logic of ethnic outbidding may be reduced. Ethnic majorities in states such as Macedonia must realise their own responsibilities in overcoming this logic if their own interests in a stable future are to be secured.

Notes

1   Parts of this paper draw on R. Mickey and A. Smith Albion, 'Success in the Balkans? A Case Study of Ethnic Relations in the Republic of Macedonia' in *Minorities: The New Europe's Old Issue* (New York: Institute for East–West Studies, 1994).

2   Hereafter, 'Albanians' will be used to refer to ethnic Albanians residing in the Republic of Macedonia, while 'Macedonians' will be used to refer to ethnic Slav Macedonians. When ambiguities arise, whether concerning Albanians in Albania proper, or concerning citizens of the state of Macedonia, 'ethnic' will precede each term.

3   These figures are drawn from the census conducted in the summer of 1994. Figures are for the numbers of registered citizens only. Excluded, therefore, are possibly more than 100,000 ethnic Albanians from Kosovo now living in western Macedonia.

4   The term used was *narodnosti*, meaning 'nationalities' or 'peoples'. Until 1963, these communities were called 'national minorities'.

5   The official name was 'Autonomous Province of Kosovo-Metohija'. See G. Brunner, 'The Status of Muslims in the Federative Systems of the Soviet Union and Yugoslavia' in A. Kappeler, G. Simon and G. Brunner (eds.), *Muslim Communities Re-emerge: Historical Perspectives on Nationality, Politics and Opposition in the Former Soviet Union and Yugoslavia* (Durham: Duke University Press, 1994), p. 190.

6   Milan Andrejovich, 'Resurgent Nationalism in Macedonia: A Challenge to Pluralism', RFE Report on Eastern Europe, 17 May 1991, p. 27.

7   Author's interviews with Albanian and Turkish politicians, 1993 and 1994.

8   Constitution (1991).

9   See below for a fuller discussion of status in a regional context.

10   Interview with Vladimir Mostrov, deputy minister for education, April 1993.

11   Muhammed Halili, quoted in *Borba* (Belgrade), 19 November 1992, reprinted in FBIS, 10 December 1992, p. 51. Ilijaz Halimi, president of the more radical ethnic Albanian NDP party, suggested that Albanians have been denied nation status deliberately so that Macedonians will have a free hand to enter into such arrangements. Interview, 28 March 1993.

12   This section is based on the author's interviews with Muhammed Halili, Arben Xhaferi, Naser Ziberi, Ilijaz Halimi, Esref Aliu and many other leading ethnic Albanian politicians in Macedonia from 1993 to 1995.

13   'This [position] is justified simply by the larger number of Albanians in Macedonia'; see Abdulnaser Sinani, 'The Albanians: the number one factor of stability' in *Flaka e Vellazerimit*, 28 January 1995.

14   Xhafer Krasniqi and Sinan Kamberaj, '400,000 Albanians in Macedonia Vote on Autonomy Plan', *Illyria*, 13 January 1992. This argument relied on the notion, much in favour in much of the region, that a Macedonian ethnic consciousness does not exist. This argument is clearly dangerous,

for in a region in which states are conceived of on national rather than civic terms, it suggests that Albanian and Bulgarian (or Serbian, or Greek) irredentism are logical courses of action.

15   For details on the census, see R. Mickey, 'Unstable in a Stable Way', *Transition*, Vol. 1, No. 1 (30 January 1995), pp. 36–40.

16   See complaints about census preparations by Muhammed Halili in *Mac-News*, 21 September 1994.

17   P. Prifti, *Socialist Albania Since 1944* (Cambridge: MIT Press, 1978), p. 224.

18   S. Palmer and R. King, *Yugoslav Communism and the Macedonian Question* (Hamden, Conn.: Archon Books, 1971), p. 175.

19   Interview printed in FBIS, 10 December 1992. This was the famed (but illfated) Iliden Uprising (which began on the Day of Saint Ilia), now enshrined by Macedonians as the cornerstone in the development of the Macedonian nation free from Ottoman rule.

20   Interview, June 1994.

21   *Ibid.*

22   Interviews with Ilijaz Halimi (April 1993) and Arben Xhaferi (June 1994).

23   Arben Xhaferi, for example, claims that only 2 per cent of positions in Macedonia's state administration are held by ethnic Albanians. More important at the time of the interview, Xhaferi claimed that only one of 192 staffers at the state statistical office which administered the census was Albanian. Interview, June 1994.

24   For example, by the end of the 1980s, the number of Albanian children attending secondary school fell by almost 50 per cent. Hugh Poulton, *Minorities in the Balkans* (London: Minority Rights Group, 1989), p. 27.

25   See remarks made by Minister of Interior Ljubomir Frckovski from an interview published in *Zeri* (Pristina) and quoted in *Mac-News*, 15 April 1995.

26   For example, compared to Bulgarian, Romanian, Albanian, and Slovak constitutions, all states with significant minority populations, the Macedonian constitution scores well. See Mickey and Smith Albion, *op. cit.*

27   Interview with Petar Goshev, president of the Democratic Party, June 1994.

28   Interviews with Dr Gordana Siljanovska-Davkova, Minister without Portfolio and a key member of the constitution's drafting committee, June and December 1994.

29   Interview with Petar Goshev.

30   See S. Ramet, *Nationalism and Federalism in Yugoslavia: 1962–1991*, 2nd edn (Bloomington: Indiana University Press, 1992).

31   R. Hayden, 'Constitutional Nationalism in the Former Yugoslav Republics', *Slavic Review*, Vol. 51, No. 4 (Winter 1992), p. 657.

32   *Ibid.*, p. 658.

33   *Ibid.*

34   Provisions for local self-government have not yet been enacted, no thanks to the requirement of a two-thirds vote in the parliament for passage of legislation on local government.

35 Some Albanian commentators concur, suggesting that the constitution is 'neither citizens' nor national'. See Reshat Chahili, 'When the Constitutional "Rights" are Dwindling through the Laws', *Flaka e Vellazerimit*, 4 April 1995.

36 Interviews with Albanian ministers, spring 1993 and summer 1994.

37 See R. Mickey, 'Unstable in a stable way', *Transition*, Vol. 1, No. 1 (30 January 1995), pp. 36–40.

38 For election results, see *ibid.*, and the articles by Fabian Schmidt in *Transition*.

39 Interview with the author, June 1994.

40 'The goal of the Albanian political subject should be the advancement of the political-legal status. The request for a constitutional status should present a permanent engagement and process' [emphasis added]. Reshat Chahili, 'When the Constitutional "Rights" are Dwindling through the Laws', *Flaka e Vellazerimit*, 4 April 1995. Abdulnaser Sinani articulates similar views in 'What kind of changes will the Constitution bring ?', *Flaka e Vellazerimit*, 8–9 April 1995.

41 See *ibid.*

42 See Mickey and Smith Albion, *op. cit.*, n. 1.

43 See *ibid.* for examples of the use of this back-channel in crisis management.

44 See Hayden, *op. cit.*, pp. 657–8.

45 Hungary's Deputy Foreign Minister, Ivan Baba, quoted in S. Engleberg and J. Ingram, 'Now Hungary adds its voice to the ethnic tumult', *New York Times*, 25 January 1993.

46 D. Horowitz, *Ethnic Groups in Conflict* (Berkeley: University of California Press, 1985), p. 187.

47 *Ibid.*, p. 223.

4

MUSLIMS, STATE AND SOCIETY IN THE REPUBLIC OF MACEDONIA: THE VIEW FROM WITHIN

Mirjana Najcevska, Emilija Simoska and Natasha Gaber

1. Introduction

In Europe today we are witnessing many cases of escalating tension between Muslim communities and the rest of the population. The problem is how to define the 'Muslim issue' so as to evoke a constructive response. The writers of this chapter believe that, in policy terms, it is most fruitful to define the category 'Muslim' in religious terms, as opposed to confusing it with ethnic or political definitions: only thus, it is argued, can civic society develop or be maintained. Civic society is composed of individuals who relate to each other through law. The most important function of law in this context is to protect social pluralism – the right of the individual to be different – and to protect every member of society. Among other things, the chapter will contend that only in the context of such a social framework – civil democracy – can the relationship between the Muslim and the state be at its best, for in such a context religious differences are non-political and the notion of citizen is freed from religious connotations. In the framework of general civil rights and personal freedoms, the Muslim religion can enjoy the same treatment as other confessions since everyone has the freedom and right to believe in what he or she wants.

In this chapter, attention will be focused on the case of the Republic of Macedonia, which illustrates the issues particularly well. The question of inter-faith relations is, of course, not solely a matter of law. Social, and above all political, dynamics may strongly affect such relations, for instance with the political use of myths about the 'Muslim threat'. In the following section, the constitutional and legal structures will be described, and the case for a 'civic society' approach argued. In section 3, the problem of myth creation and its impact on society will be discussed. At the time of writing, the authors were all at the Centre for Ethnic Relations in Skopje.[1] They could therefore draw on the result of surveys undertaken by the Centre over the years. In the final part of the chapter, a summary is given of the results of the 1993 survey on national and confessional differences in the Republic of Macedonia.

2. Legal structures and the case for the 'civic society' approach

2.1. Institutional and constitutional structures

Institutionally, relations between the state and the religious communities in Macedonia are conducted through the government's Committee for Relations with the Religious Communities. As a governmental institution, this is responsible for official contacts with the religious communities, for mediating in disputes between religious communities, for helping to deal with issues that arise from such contacts, and for acting as a contact point with other social institutions. Committees with similar concerns are also formed at municipal level, although these tend to act only on an *ad hoc* basis when needed.

From the juridical point of view, relations between the state and the religious communities in Macedonia are covered by the Constitution and by various other laws and by-laws. In the Constitution, the state is defined exclusively as a civic state. In accordance with this, Article 19 of the Constitution emphasises that all the religious communities without exception are separated from the state and are equal before the law. No religion is described as being special or official. The provision for citizens' rights and freedoms with respect to religion are covered by the chapter on citizens' basic rights.

Article 9 of the Constitution states: 'the citizens of the Republic of Macedonia are equal in their freedoms and rights, regardless of . . . religious beliefs.' Article 19 guarantees the freedom of religion and stipulates that the Macedonian Orthodox Church and the other religious communities and groups are free to establish religious schools and other social and charitable institutions, according to a procedure laid down by law. According to Article 54, freedoms and rights of citizens can be limited only in specific cases determined by the Constitution. Freedoms and rights cannot be limited on grounds of religion.

One of the laws elaborating on the provisions of the Constitution is the *Law on the Legal Status of the Religious Communities* in which religious affiliation is defined as the private affair of the individual (Article 1). This law states that all religious communities have equal legal status (Article 3) and that they are separate from both the state and schools (Article 3). Article 6 stipulates that no one's rights may be restricted due to membership of a particular religious community and that, on the other hand, no one may enjoy special rights and privileges or special protection because of such membership. According to this Article, religious identity or membership of a religious community do not constitute a basis for regulating the citizen's obligations towards the State as laid down in the Constitution, laws and by-laws. Religious communities are free to have their own press and to issue other publications, to carry out religious instruction and to collect donations. A religious community's activities must not be used for political purposes or to spread religious intolerance, hatred or discord.

The above rules are protected by Criminal Law, which defines as offences any breaches of the law on equality of citizenship where people are discriminated against because of their religion (Article 50); and causing 'religious hatred, discord and intolerance' (Article 134/ 18).

2.2. *The rationale for a 'civic society' approach to inter-faith relations*

These laws show that the legislators have been applying the basic concepts of international laws regarding the protection of citizens' rights. What is the rationale behind this?

First, if, with regard to religion, citizens were to be treated as 'groups' (as was typical under the previous, socialist political system), then the problem would be put *a priori* into a political framework, possibly prejudging a political solution. This would obstruct the development of a primarily juridical approach – which after all offers the best chance of resolving the issues. That is why the term 'Muslim' is only used here in the sense of 'individuals belonging to the Muslim confession'. In this sense it does not imply some special fixed group but rather individuals who are by this specific criterion identified as different from other individuals.

Second, this problem has special features in Macedonia because most Muslims there are also members of the Albanian minority. This often obscures the demarcation line between minority rights and rights pertaining to adherence to different religions. The law provides for these two sets of rights to be treated distinctively but in practice the two notions are often confused.

The Constitutional order recognises the existence of national minorities in Macedonia (among whom are ethnic Albanians, ethnic Turks and Roma – 'Gypsies' – the latter both Muslim and of other religions) and establishes a special regime for the protection of their ethnic and national rights. This regime is more far-reaching (in both extent and depth of coverage) than that for protection of religious rights and freedoms. The issue is covered by the Preamble to the Constitution, by the fundamental values stated in the Constitution in the provision for the basic rights and freedoms of the individual, by guarantees protecting cultural rights and by the organisation of state authority.

Third, in Macedonia and the Balkans in general it is necessary to separate national or ethnic affiliation from religious confession in assessing eligibility for citizenship (we believe, incidentally, that this principle would merit being applied more widely in Europe). For the historic heritage and collective memory of a nation are of inevitable importance in the identification and regulation of relationships among different ethnic and religious groups living on the territory of a particular state.

Fourth, in the Republic of Macedonia, the two-fold and quite distinct identification of Muslims, as belonging to the Muslim *religion* on the one hand, and to any particular nationality on the other, is an inevitability because of the variety of ethnic groups on Macedonian territory that are oriented towards Islam – Turkish Muslims, Muslim Roma, Albanian Muslims and ethnic Macedonian Muslims.

Successful relationships among different religious communities in the Republic are evidence that treatment of this issue in the Republic's legislation has been relatively satisfactory. In social terms and in the interaction between people of the various faiths, research data show that there has traditionally been a high degree of religious tolerance – although there does appear to be evidence of a very recent trend towards greater confessional prejudice (see section 3). The relative adequacy of the current legislation is also shown by the fact that even in the period of political transformation, no special requests were made for changes to the legal framework regulating the specifically religious aspects of community relations (as distinct from ethnic minority questions).

This should not be interpreted as suggesting that relations are ideal, but only as indicating that the methods adopted for tackling the issue are moving in the right direction.

Although the law may provide for equal treatment of all confessions, distortions may nevertheless occur in the practical implementation of the law. Because the majority of the population is Christian Orthodox, the Orthodox church in fact receives special treatment. Orthodoxy is the only confession named directly in the Constitution[2] (although it is not designated as having any special competence or privileges). In the euphoria of political transformation and the abandonment of imposed atheism, it is easy to fall into the trap of going to the other extreme, that is of an enforced return to Orthodoxy. This is a particular risk in view of the interrelationship between the Orthodox church and the Macedonian national cause. Any attempt by the Orthodox church to shape the Macedonian nation could end in a clash, particularly with Islam which is the second most prevalent religion in Macedonia.

2.3. *The Muslim position*

Some negative indications in respect of the above can already be detected, for example, in the change of name of the Islamic Community of Macedonia to that of the Islamic Community *in* Macedonia. Also, despite the existence of the laws described above, under the aegis of the multi-party system some political parties defining themselves with reference to Islam have started operating (for instance, the Bosnian Muslim Party for Democratic Action, which is registered in the republic). These parties aim at dissolving the national and ethnic specificity of Muslims, ignoring all ethnic differences and creating a Muslim 'melting-pot'.

One particular problem arises from the Muslim community in Macedonia itself, namely the linguistic isolation policy of ethnic Albanians. While there are Muslim Macedonians and Turkish Muslims in Macedonia, Muslim clerics are elected who speak no Macedonian, or speak only Albanian. Similarly, in the *Madrasas* (special schools for the training of Muslim clerics), there are many more Albanians than Turks or Macedonians. This phenomenon of linguistic self-isolation which extends throughout the Albanian community in Macedonia provides fertile ground for manipulation of information and for the spreading of misinformation.

Another problem is the social isolation of Muslim women, especially among ethnic Albanians. More generally, some gender-related practices run counter to widely accepted rules of conduct on equality of the sexes and freedom and rights of the individual. Some of these practices contradict the provisions of the laws of the Republic of Macedonia – particularly the law on inheritance – or state policies, such as the population policy which aims at preventing overpopulation and its effects on child health.

Nor is Macedonian society immune from cases of Muslim discrimination against non-Muslims. The other side of that same coin is that, although Muslims have lived in Macedonia for centuries and play an active part in Macedonian society, there nevertheless remains, for some, a latent tendency to identify with an Islamic 'supra-nationality'. Today this is not much in evidence because of the disorganisation of the Islamic community in the Balkans (resulting particularly from the dissolution of Yugoslavia and of the Islamic structures that existed there), but it remains an undercurrent.

Clearly, while concern for the rights and difficulties of Muslim citizens is justified, equally any society and state will require all its citizens, for their part, to fulfil their civic obligations. This also holds for the Republic of Macedonia. Centrally, the question of 'loyalty' comes in here, emotionally loaded as it is. It is perhaps a truism that any group's or people's loyalty to the state grows in proportion to the rights they enjoy. It must be stressed, however, that this dynamic will only materialise when those rights are properly formulated, guaranteed and protected by the laws of the country. What is more, such formulation, guarantee and protection are the safest means by which this issue can be moved out of the volatile political sphere and into the realm of law.

What, then, do the Muslims of Macedonia feel about their position and the state? A good indication of this may be gleaned from the data of recent surveys on the subject of loyalty to the state among the population of the country. Most of the debate in the Republic has centred on interpretation of 'rights' and 'obligations' (loyalty). The results of the survey were predictable: 91 per cent of Muslims said that they do not have enough rights; 53 per cent of the Orthodox group of respondents thought that 'the others' have enough rights while the remaining 47 per cent thought that they have too many rights. (However, since in Macedonia's case, most of the Muslims are ethnic Albanians and most of the Orthodox Christians are ethnic Macedonians, it should be remembered, when analysing the answers, that people do not always make a distinction between their ethnicity and their religion.)

Nevertheless, the data show that most of the Muslims consider themselves to be 'second-class' citizens because of their ethnic and religious identity. This provides fertile ground for political manipulation. Indeed, the Muslim population has from time to time been targeted by political activists and encouraged to use different forms of political pressure (such as boycotting obligations towards the state). Naturally, the reaction of the majority of the population is to consider such actions 'disloyal', so widening the gulf between the two groups. It is clear, however, that the apparent 'disloyalty' stems more from a sense of inequality – thus indicating that the integration of the Muslim communities has not been as successful as it might have been. This also provides broad scope for religious feelings to be used for political ends. This is not a new phenomenon but it is one which adds to the sources of religious conflict new to this region. There remains a need, then, to address this problem. The solution will at least in part lie in ameliorating the perceived inequalities, but this would still need to happen within the context of a civic society, where, moreover, any myth-mongering is avoided.

2.4. A plea for the separation of religion and politics: the 'civic society' option

It is of course true that there are differences which may set Muslims apart from non-Muslims in the same society, although differentiation within the Muslim population, and differentiation on the basis of non-religious criteria, may be at least as, if not more, important. It does mean, however, that there is a potential for 'differential iden-tification' both on the part of Muslims themselves and on the part of the rest of society. The extent to which this will become an issue will generally depend on contextual factors such as domestic and/ or international politics, economic developments etc. But it points up the importance of being aware of this potential, and therefore of an approach which is able to ameliorate and if possible pre-empt the undesirable consequences which may be associated with it, in terms of inter-faith friction and socio-political instability.

Even in countries where the state is explicitly secular and where there is no official or state religion, citizens, or more specifically Muslims, still tend to be categorised de facto by their religious affili-ation. Their attendance at special schools, and generally their social and cultural mores – even if they do not themselves insist on special arrangements – effectively mean that they are to varying degrees set outside the mainstream of social life and opportunities. Their reli-gious identity is thereby transferred from the private to the public sphere. Where, in mainly Christian/secular countries, the threat of xenophobic or anti-Muslim sentiment or acts leads to the institution of special measures to safeguard the rights of the Muslim population, this often has the effect of pushing them further into social isolation and a stronger assertion of religion-based differences. The situation, therefore, is almost inevitably problematic. The matter is even more complex in countries which do have an official religion, and takes on a special dimension when there are several official religions which play a role in the structure of the state and particularly in the educational system.

A peculiar case is where conditions are created for the 'Islam-isation' of some parts of the population to avoid their identification as ethnic minorities. This was the case for some time in Bulgaria, and in Greece it still applies to ethnic Turks: as a group they are labelled 'Muslims' on the basis of a partial misinterpretation of the Treaty of Lausanne of 1923. The fact that the Pomaks and Roma (who con-stitute quite different ethnic groups) are also Muslim is thereby ignored.

It is argued here that the least bad way to approach the issue of inter-faith relations, and the relations between religious denomina-tions and the state, is precisely the 'civic society' approach referred to earlier, where all citizens relate to the state and have their rights protected through law, and where civil democracy can function on that basis. It is in the spirit of civic society to keep religion within the private sphere where it is a distinction only at the individual, not the collective, level. It is true that this very civic society makes exemptions and enables politicisation of the Muslim religion. This is not particularly new: it happened before with the treatment of the Jews in Europe. Yet the essence of civic democracy is to proclaim all the differences that exist between individuals as non-political, so declaring every member of the nation an equal participant in the people's sovereignty. In this regard, Muslims should not be asked to sacrifice the privilege of adhering to a confession in order to gain the privilege of general human rights. Yet the authors believe that any measure aimed at removing religion from the private sphere weakens the state's ability to respond to demands for equal treatment from the diverse religious communities. Whenever this principle is abandoned, the state is put in the position of having to balance the interests of the different confessions. This leads to the 'measuring' of the real rights of those communities which in turn generates further conflict. Then the various political parties embroil themselves in the debate, offering solutions. The only real answer that we can find is to return religious confession to the private sphere. In the framework of the world as a global village, allowing any one confession to dominate can be a factor for destabilisation and destruction.

In the industrialised countries of Western Europe, the nature of the Muslim presence is different from that in countries such as the Republic of Macedonia, where the Muslim element of the population has been part of society for centuries. As, in the West, the presence derives mainly from immigration, a number of special characteristics are attached to it. Issues of immigration policy, rights of immigrants as distinct from the indigenous population, and the variation within the immigrant population in terms of long-term aims (integration? assimilation? re-emigration?) all complicate the picture. Significant sections of this Muslim population, certainly initially, were not particularly interested in asserting religious differences in the public arena, being more concerned with other goals (economic betterment, return, or indeed, for many, assimilation). Despite this, both formal and de facto categorisation of Muslims takes place in these countries, both from below (the Muslim and non- Muslim population alike) and from above (officialdom). This results from a variety of factors, including the 'visibility' factor referred to above, political and international dynamics, and the fear and/or reality of anti-Muslim sentiment and acts.

Such categorisation, whatever the causes, creates a conducive environment for positioning these individuals *vis-à-vis* the country of domicile as a collectivity with articulated interests and requests. This and further self-isolation tend to be followed by the process of substitution of state structures and law with alternatives provided by Islam and its religious rules. It is not surprising that this creates tensions, or worsens already existing ones, both at the socio-cultural and political level.

The underlying difficulty is not unlike that experienced in the post-Communist systems of Eastern Europe. The authors of this chapter would argue that the experience of countries where Muslims have lived for centuries can be instructive for countries where the Muslim presence is relatively new. Given the wrong policies, Islam can be a challenge to the Western world, to the institutions of Western democracy and to the very concept of civil democracy itself. The positioning of Muslim communities within the general framework of civil democracy and the application of the principles of such democracy are a test for the system, but one without which the system itself may end up seriously damaged, to the detriment of Muslim and non-Muslim alike.

It must be recognised that the sense of inequality among the Muslims of Macedonia, which gives rise to some of the problematic issues referred to, is in part the result of fears that the majority Orthodox community is intent on defining them as a threat and therefore to be contained and controlled. It is true, also, that there have been signs of such a 'mythology' taking hold among parts of the Orthodox population. Indeed, it would appear to have had a nefarious effect in terms of growing confessional prejudice after 1992. It is this issue which the chapter now turns to.

3. The role of myth: between 'Muslim conspiracy' and 'endangered Orthodoxy'[3]

A phenomenon evident in all the former Yugoslav republics in the last few years has been the enormous exploitation of mythology for political purposes. It is well enough established that political myths appear at times of radical transition. They are phenomena that feature 'a time or a site which is betwixt and between'.[4] Naturally, their content and effect vary according to local history, national psychology and so on, but they are a proven stimulus for political action.

In theory, Macedonia provides a perfect medium for such a practice: its history lends itself to it; it is both a multinational and a multiconfessional community; and its present position is uncertain.

To a large extent, Macedonia has avoided falling into the trap of being guided by myth-producing policy. Like other countries embarking on independence, it did of course experience a certain revival of the unavoidable element that Burke calls 'a political memory of a society', manifesting itself as 'national romanticism'.

However, more recently elements of a familiar scenario have surfaced which, although not originating from official policy, still risk causing some disturbances and whose impact should not be ignored.

Although its origins are much wider, a particular 'story' has been propagated in this region at various times for political purposes. This is the myth of 'endangered Orthodoxy' and the 'Muslim conspiracy'.

Several questions need to be addressed in this context. Are there elements in Macedonian political culture, past and present, which make it fertile soil for such myths to redirect political life? Is the apparent image of a confrontation between Islam and Orthodoxy an authentic, internal phenomenon, or is it an imported ideology? Finally, what are the present attitudes, values and prejudices of the population?

As mentioned above, one of the main problems relates to the specific historical and present political milieu in Macedonia and the elements which make it suitable for the application of a political mythology of this kind. For this purpose, without elaborating too much on the question of myth as a phenomenon, we must outline at least one of its features.

The myth's basic function is evidently to appear whenever certain political solutions are 'not convincing enough', and an additional, irrational, mythological verification is needed. In other words, myths are needed at times when the people's strong emotional support is required, whether this is to initiate, to strengthen or to break down certain political conceptions. Macedonia's history provides at least two elements that lay it open to the use of political mythology as an instrument.

First, in the recent past, in the communist period an authoritarian value model often needed, and drew strong support from, a suitably tailored mythology. This had two obvious features: one was the principle of explanation through the dichotomy of 'heroes' and 'enemies'. The myth of 'the enemy' is not limited to communist societies – many of the older democracies were built with its help – but in this particular context, it may have special consequences.

The other characteristic of this period with respect to the political culture and socialisation was the emphasis on socio-centric orientation. The attitude that 'all that is ours is good' always and everywhere stimulates the cohesion of the community, but it easily risks being transformed into an attitude affirming that 'everything that is not ours is bad'. In a multinational and multiconfessional community such as that of Macedonia it inevitably leads to an ethnocentric political culture. In this case, it turned into a paradox: the ethnocentrism became a product of a system which officially paid most attention to values such as national and confessional tolerance, brotherhood and unity. The attitude towards 'the other' that emerged was naturally directed towards the other nationalities or confessions.

Secondly, the country's history, in which it was always a victim of various interests, rather than an active participant, has produced a strong sense of being endangered, of struggling to survive in hostile surroundings and to preserve a national identity in the face of powerful propaganda. In this context, the above-mentioned ethnocentrism can have dangerous implications if it becomes part of political culture.

People do not easily overcome the sense of being endangered, especially if the context does not change. This provides ample opportunity for long-term manipulation for various ends. In such cases, in order to create a specific political atmosphere and channel it in the desired direction, three elements are needed: 'the victim', 'the enemy' and the 'defender'.

Since 1992, some attempts have been made to create such an atmosphere, using the myth of the 'Muslim conspiracy' as the 'enemy', and the 'endangered Orthodoxy' as the 'victim'. As mentioned earlier, the myths regarding the endangered Orthodoxy have been well tested in this region. Historians will have observed that they always appear when the struggle between Western and Eastern interests intensifies, whenever the arrows of the political compass which show the opposite sides of the world have to be 'balanced'. Macedonia has been caught between these two interests for a long time; the 'salvation and protection' offered by the Orthodox world, and the ideology which originates from it, have been frequently used in propaganda efforts among the population.

Two questions are particularly relevant in this context: why have such phenomena intensified recently and why should the Muslims be used as an instrument?

In answer to the first question, the period since 1992 has been particularly suited for the practice of such a method. The global and regional context has played a great part in this. The fact that the present is referred to as the 'post-bipolar world' does not mean that European bipolar interests are really past at all, and it most certainly does not mean that the 'poles' have stopped reflecting on this region. More specifically, myths which include different confessions or nationalities as victims and enemies usually appear at times when the national identity is being endangered in some way. The Republic of Macedonia has experienced this in a particularly acute way: at a time when most of the world has been concerned with what name the republic should be given, the people feared that their nation might simply disappear. They were also disappointed that basic rights as asserted in international law (and confirmed in the Badinter report's recommendation that the republic be recognised) seemed to function for everyone except them.

Against this background, all that was required was an adequate enemy. In a country with a high proportion of Muslims it was not very difficult to find proof of the 'threat'. The demographic structure and trends produce additional 'arguments', viz. that one day the Muslim population will outnumber the Orthodox one, which would be easily 'swallowed'. It was also not difficult to use both Muslims and Orthodox Christians as instruments, both populations being already sensitised to the current situation. Ethnic and confessional prejudices can always be found among groups, and any serious incident can be used as the triggering argument.

Further, confessional unity is much easier to manipulate than national unity, for two reasons: first, national groups – certainly in the case of Macedonia – are already subject to an internal differentiation; they comprise people with different political views and differing degrees of tolerance for other nationalities, including people who prefer to see themselves as 'citizens of the world'. This makes the 'nationality' less reliable as an instrument for manipulation. In contrast, the religious identity produces an image of unity 'without options', which people relate to more easily. Secondly, the expression of one's religious denomination has recently become fashionable – not for religious reasons, but as a reaction against the former system where the religion was not treated as a positive value. Both issues have contributed to making Orthodoxy an attractive element for political marketing. Since in marketing there must be a 'competitor', the myth of the 'encroaching Islam' has been used.

This had a considerable impact on the citizens, as illustrated by the results of a 1993 research project on 'The National and the Confessional Distance in the Republic of Macedonia', undertaken by the Centre for Ethnic Relations in March 1993, and which the Centre has been able to compare with those of similar surveys in previous years. An extensive summary of these results is given in section 4 below. For now, some comments will suffice to support and illustrate the arguments presented here.

The most significant results are those which illustrate the 'closing in' of the confessional groups on themselves, which has increased in the last few years. Indeed, even the increase in the single year since 1992 was striking.

Perhaps one of the most interesting examples is that of attitudes towards mixed marriages, as families are the microcosm in which all wider social relations are reflected. Over 70 per cent of both the Muslim and the Orthodox respondents thought that marriages should remain within the same faith (although less than half was negative about crossing the *ethnic* divide). In 1992 only 20 per cent of the Orthodox population had indicated their opposition to interfaith marriages (and those were mostly members of the older generation and those with devout religious beliefs). In fact 'nationality' as a factor had diminished in importance compared with religion. The reasons for the sharp rise of anti-Muslim prejudice in this area among Orthodox Macedonians (from 20 per cent to 74 per cent) clearly are *not* religious in nature, as the data also show that a mere 30 per cent of the nominally Orthodox population can be termed devout.

Similar prejudice can be observed in other respects, albeit not as strongly – but then it had been almost absent the previous year.

The very suddenness of this development would seem to indicate that it might be superficial. Other survey results appear to confirm this (thus, less than 30 per cent said they felt any emotional hatred for the other group and less than 20 per cent would ever consider an armed confessional or ethnic conflict).

A most interesting point is that over 60 per cent of both groups interviewed were aware that inter-confessional problems arise in large part as a result of political manipulation. This they blame partly on the political parties, partly on the extremists on both sides and to a great extent on the interference of the other countries. Paradoxically, then, even the victims of the myth are somehow aware that they have been used as instruments. Still, the Orthodox Christians now feel a danger from the Muslims which they cannot explain – a fear mirrored among the Muslims. This adds to the impression that the observed intolerance has been 'taught' rather than springing from direct experience.

Even this brief review of the data shows that religion has been *introduced* as a new factor in the relations among citizens. Specific political events and activities inside and across the country's borders (which there is not space here to detail) equally support this. The term 'introduced' is used advisedly, for several reasons. First, it is implausible that in the time-span of a single year so many people could suddenly turn into true believers, exhibiting a specific type of behaviour in the name of a particular religious dogma. Indeed, the Centre's research has shown that most of the Orthodox population do not even know the basic doctrine of the Orthodoxy they identify with and are ready to 'defend'. Their attitude is one of defending something which they feel is part of their cultural identity, which they often cannot distinguish from their nationality. The feeling of being endangered and the attitude of defence automatically produce the same effect, for the same reasons, on the 'other side'. This is the usual scenario: the first step is for a community to close in on itself, regarding the others 'strange' and alien; later a more hostile attitude develops; and finally, serious tension between the two groups develops, which, at a suitable moment, can easily be transformed into a direct conflict in which both sides may well be forced to turn to someone else for a solution. This latter point leads to the second reason for thinking that the 'religious factor' was, at least in part, artificially introduced. Creation of a conflict in the country has been the aim of many – a conflict, of course, which would appear to have been produced from inside as a logical result of exising intolerance. The rationale for such aims is widely recognised:

such conflict would demonstrate that the country cannot solve its problems alone, and that it needs to ask for outside 'help'.

Since, in the mythological construct employed towards such ends, this time the Muslims are painted as 'the enemy', it should be expected that salvation, on the part of the majority Orthodox population, is sought in the Orthodox world. If at the same time the country is sufficiently socially and economically exhausted, this provides an additional argument against its ability to exist independently – fuel for the argument that it should be put in someone else's grip. The final step is then to introduce the mythical 'defender' – again in the guise of Orthodoxy.

What is argued here, then, is that the myth of the 'Muslim conspiracy' and 'endangered Orthodoxy' is in large part a new import as far as the Republic of Macedonia is concerned, but one with very damaging effects on the social fabric and inter-faith (as well as inter-ethnic) relations in the country. Given the domestic economic situation and the regional and international context referred to, it is perhaps not surprising that it has gained ground among some of the population. This remains a paradox, given that (1) Macedonia has in fact in many respects been a *victim* of the Orthodox world; (2) it was once partitioned among three Orthodox countries, under the supervision of a fourth, the largest, whose interests have not changed much; (3) it never had any traditional friends among the Orthodox countries; and (4) Macedonian Orthodoxy itself has never been recognised by the national Orthodox churches in the Eastern European countries.

Fortunately, there remain some reasons for hope. First, those members of the population who are actively engaged in the transmission of these myths are not yet sufficiently numerous to be able to cause any radical disorder; most citizens still believe in dialogue, peace and tolerance as offering the only solution. Nevertheless, this myth-based ideology should not be ignored since it is introducing a new and potentially potent source of possible tension – religious intolerance – with consequences that cannot be predicted.

Secondly, religious intolerance does not have historical roots in the country, in the sense that it has never been a source of direct, aggressive conflicts. It has been used only (as it is now) as an accompanying instrument for efforts at regional political consolidation, to nudge the country towards one of the sides of the European 'bipolar' world, the Eastern Orthodox one. It emerges at times when the West appears indifferent to the complexity of regional relations in this part of the Balkans.

The Republic of Macedonia is a point where three civilisations meet: those of the West, the Eastern Orthodox world, and Islam, worlds that have for centuries used the game of 'victims, enemies and defenders' in all conceivable combinations. One can only hope that when (and if) 'post-bipolar' Europe takes root, such myths will not be necessary to keep the poles and the people apart.

4. 'The National and Confessional Distance in the Republic of Macedonia': a summary of the 1993 public opinion survey

What follows is a summary of the main results of a survey carried out by the Centre for Ethnic Relations in March 1993. The same questions were put to two samples of 500 people each (one Macedonian Orthodox and one Muslim, mainly Albanian). The project focused on the existence of prejudices among the population and the forms which such prejudices most often take. It also surveyed the political sympathies and attitudes to political questions in the two population groups. This was the tenth such survey – one having been undertaken in each of the previous years.

The first result to note, is that among the Orthodox population, only some 30 per cent could be classified as devout. Among the Muslim population this proportion was thought to be somewhat higher, although no precise data are available.

Nevertheless, attitudes towards members of the other faith appeared to have grown more negative than this proportion would lead one to expect. Areas where questions about inter-faith social relations were asked, concerned marriage and relationships, friends, employers and teachers.

Among the Orthodox population, 75 per cent would not marry a person of different confession and almost all of these rejected the idea of a mixed marriage with Muslims (only 8 per cent referred to Catholics as a 'non-desirable combination'). Among the Muslim population, 78 per cent would not choose a non-Muslim partner (57 per cent singled out Orthodox Christians, and a smaller number did so with Catholics). As a general rule, more than 70 per cent of both populations think that marriages should occur only between people of the same *religious* persuasion. However, only just over 45 per cent (again of both populations) favour *ethnically* homogeneous marriages.

It must be pointed out that this level of religious, as opposed to 'national', prejudice as measured in 1993 was a dramatic increase over the level measured in 1992. It was in fact the first time that the Macedonian Orthodox population exhibited a high confessional prejudice. Only one year before, just 20 per cent of this part of the population disapproved of relationships with people of non-Orthodox confession. These were mostly members of the older generation and those with devout religious beliefs. It is quite obvious that the reasons for the rise (to 74 per cent, with particular discrimination against Muslims), are not religious in nature: that much should be clear from the finding about the low level of devout religiosity.

The same trends can be observed with respect to choice of friends, work colleagues and neighbours. The discrimination is not manifested to the same extent in these areas, but in earlier years there had been virtually no sign at all of the religious denomination being a factor that interfered with social roles and relations.

At least 75 per cent of both groups do not object to working for a private employer of a different nationality. They differed greatly, however, in their responses to the question of whether it was good for pupils to be taught by a teacher of a different nationality. Seventy per cent of the Macedonians said the nationality of the teacher did not matter. But 75 per cent of the Albanians objected strongly.[5]

The results on attitudes towards the religious institutions are also instructive. In answer to a question about the influence of the Macedonian Orthodox Church on inter-ethnic relations, 67 per cent of Orthodox Macedonians said they thought the influence was positive while 26 per cent had no particular opinion on this issue. Nineteen per cent of the Muslim respondents thought the Church's influence was positive while 63 per cent saw it as negative.

In contrast, 91 per cent of the Muslim group thought that the Islamic religious community played a positive role in inter-ethnic relations, while 64 per cent of the Orthodox sample thought the community's influence was negative and 30 per cent had no particular opinion.

There are, however, more positive indicators. Over 70 per cent of both groups declared that they did not feel any emotional hatred for the other nationalities or religious denominations. Additional questions which were used for this subject – which cannot be presented here for reasons of space – confirm that we can speak only of a 'distance' which in many ways is rather superficial and which lacks deeper emotional roots or even firm prejudice. In addition more than 80 per cent of both populations would never think of starting a conflict or a 'war' based on confessional or ethnic motives.

Interestingly, both groups were well aware of the misuse of inter-ethnic relations for political purposes and propaganda. Asked which factors they thought worsened inter-ethnic relations (i.e. helped political manipulation), the two groups were more or less in agreement that the social and economic crisis was the main cause, followed, in that order, by extreme nationalism, the non-recognition of the Republic of Macedonia, the political parties, interference by neighbouring countries, the primitive political culture and the role of the religious communities. Specifically, then, over 60 per cent of both groups interviewed were aware that inter-confessional problems arise as a result of political manipulation, which they blame partly on the political parties, partly on the extremists on both sides and to a great extent on the interference of the other countries.

Turning now to attitudes towards the institutions of the state, it is striking that the head of state is viewed in a positive light by most in both communities: 76 per cent of the Muslim respondents and 83 per cent of the Macedonian Orthodox sample consider the President of the Republic to have considerable beneficial influence in inter-ethnic relations.[6] This positive attitude does not extend to other institutions, however: only 47 per cent of both groups have the same confidence in the government's abilities. The parliament was unpopular with 71 per cent of the Macedonian Orthodox sample and with 77 per cent of the Muslims (see below for political party affiliation).

Another question was asked about the new law requiring 15 years of continuous residence in the Republic of Macedonia as a qualification for Macedonian citizenship. Sixty-one per cent of Orthodox respondents agreed with this law, but 29 per cent thought the qualifying period was too short. In contrast, 89 per cent of the Muslims (who, it will be remembered, are mainly ethnic Albanian) said 15 years was too long.

Opinion was similarly divided on the question of the official use of the Macedonian and Albanian languages. Seventy per cent of

Macedonians thought that the Macedonian language should be the only official language and 28 per cent agreed with the solution allowed for in the Constitution: article 7 stipulates that 'in units of local self-government where the majority (or a considerable number) of inhabitants belong to a nationality, their language and alphabet are, in addition to the Macedonian language and the Cyrillic alphabet, also in official use, in a manner determined by law'. In contrast, 84 per cent of the Albanian group thought that all languages should have equal treatment, while the remainder agreed with the above article of the constitution.

No solution has yet been found to the question of design of identity cards. The survey in fact followed vigorous debate in parliament on this issue. The responses were divided as follows: 70 per cent of the Orthodox sample preferred names on identity cards to appear in Cyrillic characters only, in Macedonian transcription when it concerned non-Macedonian names; but 25 per cent thought that the name should appear first in Cyrillic and then in brackets in the owner's native language. Seventy-five per cent of the Muslim (mainly Albanian) respondents preferred their identity cards to be written in their native language only, while 22 per cent were willing to accept their name in brackets in this language after the version in Macedonian.

Turning, finally, to political and party affiliation, the Muslim group proved to be extremely homogeneous with 91 per cent of members supporting the PDP (Party for Democratic Progress, the main 'Albanian' party). In contrast, the Macedonian group was more divided: 19 per cent supported the VMRO-DPMNE (the nationalist end of the political spectrum),[7] 22 per cent the Social Democrats, 7 per cent the Liberal Party and 4 per cent the League for Democracy (not represented in parliament). Twenty-eight per cent did not particularly like any party – an indication of disenchantment with political parties generally – and the remainder supported numerous smaller parties. The majority in both groups support some political party, but in the Muslim/Albanian group opinion is almost unanimous whereas that in the Orthodox Macedonian group is divided in relation to the extent of individuals' national tolerance, reflected in the ideology and values of the party they choose to support.

All of the above results reflect the averages within each group. The survey also helps, however, to clarify the picture of social strata in Macedonian society today. In particular, it can be noted that in the Orthodox Macedonian group, young people (aged 18 to 20) are more critical of state institutions, have negative views about the media and have a stronger feeling of nationhood. At the same time, they are apathetic towards religion and highly sceptical about the principles and values of the older generation.

The older people show greater tolerance in inter-ethnic relations, tending to prefer compromise solutions and the methods adopted by the leading political authorities. Less well-educated groups incline more towards the Macedonian Orthodox Church and show less willingness to communicate beyond their ethnically homogeneous environment. In contrast, the better educated group shows much greater openness and willingness to communicate without prejudice. A similar distinction can be observed between rural communities, on the one hand, and the urban population on the other.

Supporters of the VMRO put strong emphasis on nationalism but at the same time are critical of officialdom and the media, showing as much intolerance towards these as towards the Islamic religious community. The Social Democrats, the Liberals and the politically neutral among the Orthodox Macedonian population show greater acceptance of general policies and greater ethnic tolerance, and tend to follow global trends.

It is difficult to draw conclusions about intra-Muslim (or perhaps more precisely, intra-Albanian) differentiation from the survey results, because of this group's high degree of unanimity. However, it can be said that those who support parties other than the PDP show greater acceptance of the Constitution and legal solutions, have greater sympathy for the government and tend to have better inter-ethnic/inter-faith communication. Similar tendencies can be detected among the younger generation as well as among highly educated people, those with mixed marriages and to a certain extent among the urban population.

Notwithstanding domestic and regional complexities and disturbing recent trends, then, reasons to be hopeful about the future of inter-faith and inter-ethnic relations in the Republic of Macedonia remain. Yet in order for such hopes to be realised, awareness of the threats from myths, regional interference, economic dislocation and perceptions of inequality must be combined with consistent attempts to address those issues, as well as sensitivity to the difficulties involved on the part of those in positions of social or political responsibility. The best domestic framework in which the results of such efforts could be safeguarded, the authors believe, is a 'civic society' and polity, where the opportunity for religious denomination to become the basis for any sort of discrimination, is reduced to the minimum.

Notes

1   Emilija Simoska, previously Director of the Centre, became Minister of Education in November 1994; Mirjana Najcevska is the current Director; Natasha Gaber is a scientific researcher at the Centre.

2   Article 19, paragraphs 2 and 3.

3   This section was contributed by Emilija Simoska, and is based on a chapter previously published under the title 'Macedonia between the myths of "Muslim conspiracy" and "endangered Orthodoxy"' in *The Social, Political and Cultural Role of the Muslim Communities in Post-bipolar Europe* (Skopje: Centre for Ethnic Relations [Institute for Sociological, Political and Juridical Research]), 1993, pp. 95–102.

4   V. Turner, *Myth and Symbol* (Basingstoke/New York: Macmillan, 1968), p. 576.

5   Out of 10,166 primary school classes in the Republic of Macedonia, 2,694 are run in the Albanian language. These have 72,121 pupils and 3,571 Albanian teachers. Only 7,661 pupils completed primary school (a phenomenon arising from tradition and living conditions). Primary school education is also provided in Turkish and Serbo-Croat. At secondary level, there are bilingual and trilingual schools. Five of these have classes in Albanian (accounting for 2,535 pupils) and two have classes in Turkish (16 pupils). Recently the Macedonian government passed a new draft law on secondary education which gives children the right to have classes in their mother tongue and allows the establishment of private secondary schools. According to the Statistical Office of Macedonia, there were 148 Albanian teachers and 19 Turkish teachers in 1993.

6   When opinions are analysed by party preference, the President is shown to be unpopular with 37 per cent of VMRO-DPMNE party voters; see note 7.

7   Internal Macedonian Revolutionary Organisation – Democratic Party for Macedonian National Unity. The data showed a decline in support for this party, compared with the 1990 elections.

5

THE MUSLIMS OF BOSNIA

Alexander Lopasic

1. Introduction and historical background

The Muslims of Bosnia represent a particularly interesting example
of that complicated ethnic conglomerate which formed Yugoslavia.[1]

It should be emphasised that the Bosnian Muslims have remained a part of Bosnian cultural space and contributed toward the
cultural continuity of Bosnia until the present day. But in order to
understand the Bosnian situation, a few words should be said about
the situation before the arrival of Islam after 1463, when Bosnia and
many of her neighbours were conquered by the Ottoman forces.
In addition, it is worth drawing attention at this point to Bosnia's
isolated geographic position: the area was a remote mountainous
region isolated from the sea and important trade routes. It was only
as a result of the Austrian occupation in 1878 that Bosnia became
connected by road and rail to Central Europe, and that the destiny
of Bosnia became influenced not only by Istanbul, but also by
Vienna, Budapest and the rest of Europe. It will also be remembered
that it was in Sarajevo in 1914 that the assassination of Archduke
Ferdinand triggered off the First World War.

Bosnia, as a country, was first mentioned in the work of Con-
stantine Porfirogenit, the 10th-century Byzantine emperor and his-
torian, in his *De administrando Imperio*, and the first known ruler of
Bosnia was Ban Borić (a title possibly of Avar origin) who reigned
in the mid-12th century and who was described as a vassal of
Hungary. This latter point links into the country's later history, as
Hungary became an influential neighbour often intervening in
Bosnian affairs. It was, however, Ban Kulin (1180–1204) who started
the development of Bosnia along lines parallel to her neighbours,
Serbia in the south and the Croat-Hungarian state in the west. It was

during this period that closer links with Rome and the Pope were established (though the first Catholic bishopric had been created between 1081–8, and the Orthodox Church had become established in Southern Hercegovina). During the reign of Kulin, Bosnia became a centre for a Christian sect known as the Bogumils, who, after being persecuted in Bulgaria and Serbia, are believed to have found refuge in Bosnia. We do not have primary documents proving that Bogumils settled in Bosnia, but the geographical vicinity lends credence to the notion. Documentary evidence does exist, however, about the dualistic movement in Dalmatia, from where it moved to Bosnia during the time of Kulin and his successors.[2] In due course, the Bogumils became a kind of national church, under the name of the 'Bosnian Church'.[3]

This was a Christian fundamentalist sect emphasising the relationship between God's perfection and a world full of misery, imperfection and evil. Only an ascetic life could save human beings in this world, while the soul belonged to God, to whom it would eventually return. Bogumils belonged to a large Christian movement in Medieval Europe, including the Albigenses in Southern France and the Waldenses in Italy, but Bosnia, because of its isolation, remained the centre of Bogumil teaching until the 15th century, even though the Bosnian Bogumils were exposed to persecution and reconversion to Catholicism, which remained the official church of the Bosnian state. In due course, however, particularly in the 15th century, the Bosnian Church became part of a newly developing feudal society and some of its leaders began to perform important functions at the courts of kings and feudal lords. Sometimes they were even leaders of diplomatic missions in their names.[4]

Early in the 15th century, after the battle of Kosovo in 1389, Ottoman armies appeared at the Bosnian frontiers and from 1434 the Ottomans kept the fortress of Hodidjed which was the origin of the present capital Sarajevo. In 1470 this settlement had only 30 houses, but by 1516 it had increased to 20,000 inhabitants, largely Muslim; it was one of the urban centres through which Islam spread after 1463, when Bosnia came under Ottoman rule.[5]

Ottoman documents from 1468/69 and 1478 demonstrate that other smaller urban centres like Rogatica, Foča and Visoko, as well as Muslim Tekke (monasteries) in Rogatica and Visoko, were already in existence.[6] Eastern Bosnia thus became the first part of the country to be converted to Islam. This fact remains relevant today: when a large part of Eastern Bosnia came under Serbian occupation, the historical factor became a major issue in peace negotiations in Geneva.

These Muslim towns became not only centres of Ottoman administration and the army, but also of the Islamic way of life. A number of occupational groups, such as soldiers and miners, originally from Saxony, accepted Islam and received a number of privileges. They were followed by elders of local kinship groups who, with their kin-group members, did the same and received confirmation of their traditional status and property.[7]

On the other hand, the role of the Muslim religious orders should not be underestimated. These were established in different parts of the Balkan peninsula and exercised considerable cultural influence on the local population. Two orders in particular should be mentioned: the Bektashi order with its syncretic and popular Islam, and the Hamzevi, founded by the Bosnian shaykh Hamza Bali (died before 1533), which had a very strong social emphasis.[8]

In due course, a Bosnian Muslim community developed whose identity was strengthened by local folklore through tales, folk stories, poetry and customs referring to individual Muslim heroes: Aliya Dzerzelez (well-known from Ivo Andric's short stories), the brothers Hrnjica, Ali-Bey from Lika, and Malkoq Bey; their lives became symbols of this new Muslim identity. An important result of this development was the creation of a Muslim Bosnian elite which produced a number of Ottoman political, military and religious leaders and a wealthy trading class which contributed to the well-being of Bosnia. This was particularly so in the 16th and 17th centuries, a period which saw the climax of Ottoman power. A special hereditary military aristocracy was created, called Kapudans (captains), who had considerable local autonomy and who became, in the 18th century, an important factor in the development of local Bosnian autonomy: the latter increased with the weakening of the central power in Istanbul.[9]

There were a number of revolts against the central government in the 18th century and the Bosnian elite started to lose faith in it. This led to the elite's open revolt against the different reforms of the *Tanzimat* period. This also explains the lukewarm support for the Sultan when Bosnia, as a result of the Berlin Congress in 1878, became an Austrian province. On the other hand, the fact that, after 400 years of Muslim rule, Bosnia came under a Christian administration, put the Muslims in a completely new situation. They were, of course, afraid of losing the privileged position which they had enjoyed for so long. There was some resistance to the Austrian army which suffered some 5,000 casualties (including 1,000 dead).[10]

Muslim leaders used a number of tactics in order to preserve their old privileges, and the Austrian administration moved very carefully as they did not want to upset the existing balance between three religious groups. The first Austrian census of 1879 showed a population of 448,000 Muslims (39 per cent of the population of Bosnia), 496,000 Orthodox (42 per cent) and 209,000 Catholics (18.5 per cent). In addition there were 14,000 Sephardic Jews (originally expelled from Spain) and a number of Gypsies. The Muslim dignitaries approached General Filipović, the commander of Austrian forces, asking him for recognition of the Muslim religious hierarchy.[11]

This was followed by a number of tactical successes and the first Bosnian parliament of 1910 was divided strictly according to religious denominations. The Upper House included dignitaries of all denominations and the Lower House followed the same principles but also included members voted into office by an electorate which had to show a certain level of income. The same principle was applied to town councils. At the same time the first political parties were established; these, too, were based on religious affiliation.[12] They were the Muslim National Organisation (*Muslimanska Narodna Organizacija*) and the Croat Muslim National Party (*Hrvatska Muslimanska Narodna Stranka*) some members of which, much later in 1941, would join the government of Ante Pavelic and his Independent State. The Muslim parties later agreed to form a United Muslim Organisation. Some of its members joined the Serbian Nationalist Movement, including those who, in 1914, would become involved in the assassination of the Archduke Ferdinand.

The period of Austrian rule was characterised by the preservation of the social status quo between the three religious groups and an interesting experiment by the Austrian administrator, Benjamin Kallay, who, between 1882 and 1903, tried to create a Bosnian nation, consisting of all three religious groups. The idea of 'Bosnjak' identity received support from different groups but particularly from some Muslims.[13] They published a journal called *Bošnjak*, with the slogan: 'From Trebinje to the gates of Brod there are neither Serbs nor Croats but Bošnjaks.'[14] This idea retains its importance: it is strongly supported, for instance, by one of today's Muslim parties, viz. the MBO (*Muslimanska Bosnjacka Organizacija*). Kallay's experiment failed because Serb and Croat ethnic identities were at that time already taking shape, but the period between 1879 and 1918 is important as it helped Bosnia to enter the European economic and political system with the emphasis on interdenominational balance which is being so strongly reiterated by Bosnian Muslim leaders in the 1990s.

In 1918, in the newly created state of the Southern Slavs (Kingdom of Serbs, Croats and Slovenes, or *Kraljevina Srba, Hrvata i Slovenaca*), and after 1929 in the kingdom of Yugoslavia, Muslims, following their previous experience, created the political party known as JMO (*Jugoslavenska Muslimanska Organizacija*) which, in the first elections in 1920, received 110,895 votes and won 24 seats in the Belgrade parliament. Two other Muslim parties received only a few hundred votes and won no seats. The aim of the JMO was to represent Muslim interests in the new state, support equality between religious and ethnic groups, and – considered as particularly important – preserve the political integrity of Bosnia in the new state. They also demanded financial compensation for the land which was expropriated from Muslim owners and given to Serb army volunteers who received that land for their war services. The JMO was a regional party representing interests of all Muslims in the Yugoslav state and it succeeded in bringing together most of the Muslim votes, irrespective of social and economic background. In the elections of 1925 the party received 127,690 votes (29.9 per cent of all Bosnian votes) and won 15 seats, becoming the largest Bosnian party. The results of local elections in 1928 gave JMO 31.4 per cent of all mandates. The party demonstrated that Bosnia had its own social and cultural development and that Muslims never identified themselves as Turks, a word often used in abuse by their opponents.[15]

The popular leader of the party was Mehmed Spaho, former president of the Sarajevo chamber of commerce, who proved himself an able tactician and champion of Muslim interests. For a number of years his party played an important role in many a political battle of the Yugoslav parliament. The first years in the new state were particularly difficult for the Muslims, especially in Eastern Bosnia (Višegrad, Rogatica, Čajniće and Foča) where their property was stolen or destroyed, people intimidated, beaten up and even killed by organised groups of Serb political opponents. The JMO demanded reparation for the destroyed property and justice for those injured or killed.[16] There were a number of clashes between the Gendarmerie and the Muslim population in the early years of the SCS state; one of them at Šahovici in Montenegro was particularly bloody.

The Yugoslav state took the view that Muslims were really Slavs who had embraced Islam during the period of Ottoman rule and were, therefore, traitors to their Christian brethren. The JMO tried to balance carefully between the government in Belgrade, mounting Serbo-Croat differences and their own local interests. This may be an important factor in understanding their position in the tragic developments of the 1990s.

During the Second World War, between 1941 and 1945, the Muslims found themselves in a precarious position, as Bosnia became literally a battlefield for three different political movements: (1) the Ustasha state, which tried to mobilize Muslims on its side, offering them special status in the state, where Muslims became an important minority (717,000 Muslims represented 12 per cent of the total population in 1941);[17] (2) the Communists, who began their struggle and organisation of partisan units after the German attack on the Soviet Union in June 1941, and tried to attract the Muslims to their cause of a new socialist Yugoslavia, even forming exclusively Muslim units; and (3) the Chetniks, who took a very hostile attitude toward Muslims but later tried to find a place for them in their political programme. The fact remains that of all three ethnic-religious groups, Muslims suffered the most losses and deprivations. According to Kočović, 86,000 Muslims were killed, representing 7 per cent of the total population of Yugoslavia.[18]

The desperate situation in Bosnia is well described in reports by the German envoy Benzler, who was accredited to the military government in Belgrade. He reported to Berlin in April 1942, saying:

All the incoming information confirms a new wave of refugees moving toward the river Drina and their number in April must be at least 25,000, particularly women and children who managed to cross into Serbia. The reason for the flight is, no doubt, related to a number of killings and destruction committed by Partisans, Ustashe and plundering Muslim militia; it is often enough that the arrival of Ustasha is mentioned, and the whole population is on the move again.[19]

Muslim aspirations for autonomy grew along with the exposure of the local population to raids, killings and the destruction of whole villages. Again it was eastern Bosnia and Sandjak (Plevlje, Čajniće, Goražde, Foča and Višegrad) which took the brunt of the destruction; it was here that Serbian Chetniks killed more than 8,000 between August 1941 and February 1942.[20]

The Muslim population consequently lost faith in the Pavelić regime which nominally controlled Bosnia, and tried to find support elsewhere. This is the background to one of the more bizarre events of the Second World War, namely the creation of the 13th SS Muslim division 'Handjar', recruited in Bosnia and granted a blessing by the former Grand Mufti of Jerusalem, Amin al-Husseini, at the behest of the SS. The main desire of the Muslims was to escape the control of Pavelić and organise a military force to protect Eastern Bosnia.[21] The 'Handjar' division was trained in France; there a revolt took place when the soldiers heard that they would be sent to Northern Bosnia to defend the non-Muslim population against the Partizans. Towards the end of 1944, parts of the division in Northern Bosnia deserted to the Partizans, who by then controlled a large part of Bosnia. Others just fled home, disappointed by the German promises. Muslims of the Cazin area in Western Bosnia succeeded in creating an autonomous movement which in 1943 and 1944 was led by a Partizan deserter, Husko Miljković. Miljković organised a private army of at least 3,000 well-armed men, carefully balancing between Croat authority in the North and Partizans in the South. He was well-supplied with arms by both sides and could rely on the support of a large Muslim population led by a few local Hodjas, but after he was killed in the latter part of 1944, the movement dispersed.

Interestingly, it is in the same Cazin area that in recent years Muslim politician and entrepreneur Fikret Avdić created the largest Muslim agricultural enterprise, which ended in a major scandal with political undertones. Fikret Avdic subsequently became the self-proclaimed president of Bihac-Cazin autonomous Muslim republic, keeping a balance between, and making peace agreements with, Croats and Serbs.

Another autonomous leader was Hafiz Mehmed Pandža from Sarajevo, who enjoyed considerable respect as president of the Muslim cultural association 'Merhamet', and a member of the Muslim religious leadership. He became leader of a Muslim independence movement after spending some time in Sarajevo supporting different Muslim autonomous organisations. At the end of 1943 he left Sarajevo and started a propaganda campaign for Muslim independence, by distributing leaflets in which he proclaimed his independence from the Pavelić regime.[22]

2.   The Bosnian Muslims after the Second World War

In the period after 1945 the position of Muslims remained an important issue. They were certainly recognized as a religious community, as was the case in the first Yugoslavia, but their identity long remained a controversial point. In postwar censuses they were allowed to label themselves 'Non-declared Yugoslavs' until 1961, when they became 'ethnic Muslims'. In 1964 they received the right of self-determination, which they had been demanding. In 1971 they were recognized as a separate nationality;[23] this has provoked considerable polemic in all of Yugoslavia, but particularly in Serbia. The reasons for this recognition may be related to the fact that Bosnia had a core position in the Yugoslav state, and it became the centre of the Yugoslav armaments industry with a number of prestigious military projects, including the huge underground military airport near Bihać, accommodating at least 70 planes and 500 pilots; these played an important role in the first part of the present conflict.

In the first years after the Second World War, Muslim religious organisations were exposed to expropriation of property and other restrictions typical of a communist system. Several members of the 'Young Muslim movement' which had been set up during the Second World War, were sentenced by courts of the newly established Bosnian federal state in 1949. Some of the present Bosnian Muslim leaders were originally members of the movement.[24]

From the 1960s onward Tito's Yugoslavia started to develop political and economic ties with Muslim countries. This enabled the Muslims of Bosnia to establish contacts with these states as well, including cultural exchanges and even participation in the pilgrimage to Mecca. *Preporod*, the journal of the Muslim community, came out in 1969 and started publishing articles on Islam, its teaching and aims. Some of the authors were leading *ulama* from Bosnia and other Muslim countries. A number of mosques were repaired and some built from community sources; some money also came from abroad, including the Gulf states, Libya and Iran.

3. Bosnia after the death of Tito

However, the death of Tito, creator of Communist Yugoslavia, in 1980 created considerable nervousness and uncertainty among his successors. Any sign of nationalism or 'pan-Islamic' expression became strongly censored and attacked. This eventually led to one of the most spectacular trials of Communist Yugoslavia, in which a Sarajevo lawyer, Alija Izetbegović, the current President of Bosnia and Hercegovina, and twelve Muslim intellectuals were charged with 'hostile and counter-revolutionary activities' in 1983. They were members of the Muslim elite and were alleged to be determined to create 'an ethnically pure Muslim Bosnia and Hercegovina'. The main evidence used against the defendants was a pamphlet written by Izetbegović which, in the opinion of the court, supported the idea of islamisation of Bosnia, and that Bosnia should become a part of a unified Islamic state stretching from Morocco to Indonesia, in which all aspects of social and political life would be ruled by Islamic principles. This pamphlet was originally written and published in 1970. It was also translated into English, German, Turkish, Arabic and Farsi.

As expected, the defendants were found guilty and received sentences of between six months and fifteen years, for 'activities against brotherhood and unity of nationalities of Bosnia with the view of destroying Bosnia as a socialist republic and undermining the existence of the Yugoslav state'.[25]

The regime feared that the recognition of Muslim nationality would encourage the Muslims of Bosnia to develop a political ideology and establish political links with other Muslim countries. By recognising Muslim nationality they were acknowledging that Islam is not only a religion but a social and political order covering large parts of the world. Indeed, Izetbegović said that Bosnian Muslims would be only a 'counterfeit nation' if they did not accept their Muslim past and become part of a large and unified Islamic State.[26]

In February 1987 three more Muslims were arrested for 'advocating violence and terrorism in order to establish an Islamic state in

Bosnia'. Their sentences ranged from two to five years in prison. In the second half of 1988, however, all those sentenced were suspended as part of a general amnesty, and the regime hoped to create a more tolerant climate, even though the state-controlled press, particularly in Serbia, continued with its anti-Muslim propaganda.

Bosnia and Hercegovina was the last republic of former Yugoslavia to introduce political parties, and in the Memorandum of August 1991 Bosnia was declared to be a democratic, independent state of three nationalities (Muslims, Serbs and Croats) and other ethnic groups which were living there. It is important to note that the Muslims had by now come to represent the majority: they made up 43.7 per cent of the total population while 31.3 per cent declared themselves Serbs, and 17.3 per cent Croat. Other groups numbered 7.7 per cent. The official Bosnian map for 1991 shows clearly the concentrated presence of Muslims in their stronghold of eastern and north-eastern Bosnia. Western Bosnia, including the north-west and the south-west, is the main area of the Serb population, while south-western and southern Hercegovina is the old domain of the Croats.

There are two important ethnic enclaves: the Muslim enclave of Bihać, Cazin and Bosanska Kladuša in the north-west, and the Croat enclaves of Bosanski Brod and Bosanski Šamac in the north-east. There was a politico-historical background for the Muslim presence in the north-west: in Ottoman days, they represented a cordon sanitaire against the Austrian military frontier.

On account of the radical changes which had taken place in neighbouring Serbia, Slovenia and Croatia, the Muslim population was apprehensive of the dismemberment of Yugoslavia, which was expected to have a profound effect in Bosnia and Hercegovina. The Bosnian republic was based on the principle of balance between the three ethnic-religious groups. This difficult balance was now seriously threatened.

In August 1990 Bosnia passed a new election law and introduced a multi-party system, and the first free elections after the Second World War were fixed for 18 November and 2 December of the same year. A heated debate followed, and Muslims expressed their fear that the multi-party system would upset the precarious balance between the three main communities and their own position as equal partner and the largest community in Bosnia.

The results of the elections demonstrated very clearly the division of loyalties according to ethnic-religious principles. From

240 seats divided between the 'Council of citizens' (130 seats) and the 'Council of counties' (110 seats), the three ethnic parties received 202 seats with the Communists losing relevance. The election results also signalled clearly that the leading Muslim party, the Party of Democratic Action (Stranka Demokratske Akcije, or SDA) with its 86 seats could hardly on its own save the existence of the Bosnian republic. It had to enter into coalition with one of the two other victors in the elections, the Serbian Democratic Party (Srpska Demokratska Stranka, or SDS) with 72 seats, or the Croat Democratic Union (Hrvatska Demokratska Zajednica, or HDZ) with 44 seats.

These two parties followed their own programmes. While these were ostensibly similar (namely, the promotion of their own respective interests), their ultimate aim was different. From the beginning the SDS followed a hard Serbian line, demanding substantial autonomy within Bosnia, and their leader Radovan Karadjic even threatened to leave Bosnia if it became a separate state within a loose Yugoslav confederation. Serbs were not willing, he emphasized, to remain a minority in a 'foreign' state.[27]

The Croat option was to remain within Bosnia and demand the status of an enlarged *millet* (the cultural and religious autonomy which existed in the Ottoman system and gave a religious community complete internal self-rule) with its own administration, control of security and economic resources. It was clear that the HDZ was the likely Muslim coalition partner under certain conditions. Both Muslim and Croat leadership realised that the main threat came from the SDS which received support from Serbia's strongman Milošević and, even more importantly, from the Yugoslav Army which began to move into Bosnia, increasing the already large military garrison. Half of the original Yugoslav Army, about 80,000 men, were originally stationed in Bosnia, and so was 60 per cent of the armaments industry with important air bases in Bihac, Tuzla, Mostar and Banja Luka. The army felt that its battle for control of Bosnia was a battle for its own survival as, by that time, the Yugoslav Army had pensioned off 30,000 of its officers because of lack of finance. This point of view was clearly expressed by the then Chief of Staff, General Panic, who was prepared to leave Bosnia in five to seven years.

By the end of 1991 the number of soldiers in Bosnia was estimated at 200,000 to which must be added 300,000 auxiliary troops. This increased number was the result of troop withdrawals from Slovenia and Croatia in the second half of 1991. This not only increased ethnic tension but created a serious shortage of basic foods like wheat, sugar and oil, which weakened the already fragile economy of Bosnia. The Muslim leadership tried to avoid obvious confrontations, but a scenario of conflict and bloodshed was developing when a loose confederation with Serbia and Montenegro was offered as a solution. The SDS rejected the proposal, demanding instead a centralised federal state like that already in existence in Serbia.

Even the intervention of the EC countries and a meeting of the 'warring parties' in Lisbon in March 1992 achieved little. The Portuguese mediator, a diplomat and former anthropology lecturer José Cutileiro, developed a very detailed and well-founded plan for Bosnia. It was a compromise solution, but clearly underlined the territorial integrity of the Bosnian State with its present frontiers and the existence of three autonomous, ethnic units or cantons, each with its own administration. Muslims who accepted the idea of territorial integrity for one Bosnian State agreed to the plan. Serbs accepted it, as they saw the possibility of developing further the idea of the ethnic cantons, and Croats saw here the recognition of their *millet*.

Developments in Lisbon and later in Brussels confirmed that Tito's state was dead and that its successors were fighting for the best place in the division of the spoils. The ethnic map of Bosnia which Cutileiro presented on 18 March 1992 was the result of these efforts. It failed eventually because of Serbian refusal on the one hand, and some Muslim reservations on the other. Only Croats signed without reservation. All the other subsequent plans by Lord Owen and Cyrus Vance were based on this plan, sequentially diluted and reshaped to adapt to changing circumstances.

4. The independence referendum of 1992

Following the agreement arranged by José Cutileiro in Lisbon, a referendum on an 'independent Bosnia and Hercegovina, a state of equal citizens, Muslims, Serbs, Croats and other nationalities who live there' was fixed for 29 February and 1 March 1992. In the event, 63 per cent of all voters (1,997,664 votes out of 3,199,037) supported the idea of an independent Bosnia consisting of citizens with equal rights. The SDS proclaimed a boycott of the referendum and put up barricades during the night of 1/2 March all around Sarajevo. A number of attacks by Serbian militia organised by the SDS against Muslims and Croats in many parts of Bosnia followed, underscoring Serbian rejection of the referendum and providing an expression of Serbian unwillingness to become 'a minority in a Muslim state'. Muslims and Croats, on the other hand, accepted the referendum as confirmation that the majority of the people accepted and supported Bosnian independence, while Serbs saw this as a sign of Muslim–Croat domination.

Clashes between Muslims and Croats on the one hand, and Serbs on the other, followed, interrupted only by a few unsuccessful truce arrangements organised by the European Community. A few weeks later the Yugoslav army also intervened, and from April 1992 onwards Bosnia and Hercegovina became the now notorious battle-field, with an estimated 200,000 people killed and many more injured. Some 2.7 million people became refugees, forced to seek refuge elsewhere in Bosnia or outside the country. Croatia alone accepted 300,000 of these refugees.[28]

5. Concluding remarks

From 1878 onward, Bosnian Muslims have tried to preserve their own identity and separateness by establishing direct relations with the ruling power in order to receive its recognition or even protection. This began with the Austrians in 1878, and continued with the Serbs and the Yugoslav government from 1918, with the Pavelic regime in 1941, and with the Partizans and Tito's Yugoslavia since 1944/5. The impact of Tito's death in 1980 made itself felt rather late in Bosnia, and the area was the last of the Yugoslav republics to introduce radical changes such as a multi-party system and eventual separation. The Muslim leadership hoped to avoid the conflicts which had taken place in Croatia and Slovenia, but in the end failed to do so. The hope that a Bosnian state might be created, maintaining a balance between Serb and Croat aspirations while offering them an equal position in a new state, with a Muslim majority status, also proved in vain.

Since 1992, the Bosnian Muslim community – the oldest such community in Europe, established at the end of the 15th century – has been fighting for its very existence. It has been exposed to ethnic cleansing, mass killings, systematic rape and total uncertainty for the future. The case of the Bosnian Muslims illustrates the need for basic humanity and basic rules of co-existence in post-Communist Europe. As far as the Bosnian Muslims are concerned, the post-Communist 'new world order' has begun very badly. It touches on the profound question of basic human rights for a community of two million, which for 500 years has tried to secure its existence in perhaps the most unstable part of the European continent.

Whether the recent agreement reached in Dayton, Ohio, in November 1995 will finally put an end to this human tragedy is, at the time of writing, hard to predict.[29]

Notes

1 In addition to the literature referred to in the notes below, it is worth listing some other useful sources and commentary on Bosnia and its Muslims. In alphabetical order, these are: S. Džaja, *Konfesionalität und Nationalität Bosniens und der Herzegowina (Südeuropäische Arbeiten*, No. 80, Munich, 1984); A. Lopasic, 'Bosnian Muslims: A search for identity', *Bulletin of the British Society for Middle Eastern Studies*, Vol. 8, No. 2, 1981, pp. 115–25; I. Lovremović and M. Imamović, *Bosnia and its People* (Sarajevo, 1992); W. Mayr, 'In den Köpfen ist Krieg: Nationalitäten-konflikt in Bosnien-Herzegowina', *Der Spiegel*, 20 January 1992, pp. 152–8, and 'Der Agresor wird belohnt; Frontstadt für die Ewigkeit', *Der Spiegel*, 8 February 1993, pp. 134–9; A. Purivatra, *Jugoslovenska Muslimanska Organizacija* (Sarajevo, 1974); S. Ramet, *Nationalism and Federalism in Yugoslavia, 1962–1991* (Bloomington: Indiana University Press, 1992); E. Wiedemann, 'Kein Teufel kann so schwartz sein: Feindbilder in Bosnia-Herzegowina', *Der Spiegel*, 25 May 1992, pp. 160–2; A. Zulfikarpašić, 'Bosnia between Croatia and Serbia', *South Slav Journal*, Vol. 16, No. 2, 1983, pp. 2–20, and 'Geister der Vergangenheit: Blutbad in Bosnien', *Der Spiegel*, 20 April 1992, pp. 171–2; also, 'Der Gipfel des Horors: Die Hölle von Sarajevo', *Der Spiegel*, 15 June 1992, pp. 156–63. Also generally the journals *Danas* (Zagreb), issues from 1991 onwards; *Oslobodjenje* (Sarajevo), issues from 1991 onwards; and *Preporod. Islamske Informativne Novine* (Sarajevo), issues from 1991 to 1992.

2 S. Ćirković, *Istorija Srednjovekovne Bosanske države* (Belgrade, 1964), pp. 50–69; S. Džaja, *Die 'Bosnische Kirche' und das Islamisierungsproblem Bosniens und der Herzegowina in den Forschungen nach dem Zweiten Weltkrieg*, Beiträge zur Kenntnis Südosteuropas XXVIII (Munich, 1978), pp. 36–42.

3 S. Ćerić, *Muslimani Srpsko-Hrvatskog jezika* (Sarajevo 1969), p. 55.

4 J. Šidak, *Studije o 'Crkvi Bosanskoj' i bogumilstvu* (Zagreb, 1975), p. 100; Džaja, *op. cit.*, pp. 44–77.

5 Ćerić, *op. cit.*, p. 58; H. Šabanović, *Bosanski Pasaluk, Naučno Društvo NR Bosne i Hercegovine*, Djela knj. XIV, Odj. Ist.Fil. Nauka (Sarajevo, 1959), pp. 27–31.

6 Džaja, *op. cit.*, pp. 73–4; D. Čehajić, *Derviski redovi u Jugoslovenskim zemljama* (Sarajevo: Orijentalni Institut u Sarajevu, pos. Izd. XIV, 1986), pp. 21, 60.

7 A. Lopasic, 'Islamisation of the Balkans: Some General Considerations' in J. Scarce (ed.), *Islam in the Balkans: Symposium on Islam* (Edinburgh, 1979), pp. 49–53.

8 Čehajić, *op. cit.*, pp. 166–7, 191–200.

9 H. Kreševljaković, *Kapetanije u Bosni i Hercegovini* (Sarajevo, 1954); A. Lopasic, 'Islamisation of the Balkans, with Special Reference to Bosnia', *Journal of Islamic Studies*, Vol. 5, No. 2, 1994, pp. 169–70.

10 A. Wagner, 'Die Okkupation Bosniens und der Herzegowina 1978' in F. Wiener (ed.), *Partisanenkampf am Balkan*, Truppen-dienst Taschenbücher, Band 26 (Vienna, 1976), pp. 23–33.

11   F. Hauptmann (ed.), *Borba Muslimana Bosne i Hercgovine za Vjersku i Vakufsko-Mearifsku autonomiju* (Sarajevo, 1967), pp. 24–5.

12   R. Donia, *Islam under the Double Eagle: The Muslims of Bosnia and Herzegowina, 1878–1914*, East European Monographs, LXXVIII (New York, 1981), pp. 50–5.

13   *Ibid.*, pp. 10–17, 160–6.

14   Hauptmann, *op. cit.*; Donia, *op. cit.*, pp. 50–5.

15   A. Purivatra, *Jugoslavenska Muslimanska Organizacija* (Sarajevo, 1974), pp. 111–14, 421–2.

16   Purivatra, *op. cit.*, pp. 46–55.

17   F. Wiener (ed.), *Partisanenkampf am Balkan*, Truppen-dienst Taschenbücher, Band 26 (Vienna, 1976), p. 98.

18   B. Kočović, *Zrtve II Svjetskog rata u Jugoslaviji* (London, 1985).

19   L. Hory and M. Broszat, *Der Kroatische Ustascha-Staat 1941–1945* (Stüttgart, 1965), p. 126.

20   S. Čekić, 'Cetnicki zločini u Jugoistočnoj Bosni i Sandjaku, 1941–1943', Supplement to *Preporod*, 15 November 1991, pp. 1–8; E. Redžić, *Muslimansko autonomastvo i 13 SS. divizija* (Sarajevo, 1987), p. 107.

21   Hory and Broszat, *op. cit.*, pp. 154–62.

22   *Ibid.*, pp. 157–9; Redzic, *op. cit.*, pp. 139–43.

23   See H. Poulton, *The Balkans: Minorities and States in Conflict*, 2nd edn (London: MRG Publication, 1993), Chapter 4.

24   I. Sijercic, 'The activities of the "Young Moslems" at the end of the war 1944–1945', *The South Slav Journal*, Vol. 8, No. 1–2, 1985, pp. 65–70.

25   'The Islamic Declaration', *The South Slav Journal*, Vol. 6, No. 1, 1983, pp. 55–89; 'Dr Izetbegovic's Address at the 1983 Trial', *South Slav Journal*, Vol. 8, No. 1–2, 1985, pp. 94–7; S. Ramet, 'Primordial ethnicity or modern nationalism: the case of Yugoslavia's Muslims reconsidered', *The South Slav Journal*, Vol. 13, No. 1–2, 1990, pp. 1–20.

26   *Ibid.*, p. 13.

27   M. Wimmer, S. Braun and J. Spiering, *Brennpunkt Jugoslawien, Der Vielvölkerstaat in der Krise* (Munich, 1991); pp. 103–4, 108–9.

28   For a vivid account of the disintegration of Yugoslavia and the events leading to it, see BBC, *The Death of Yugoslavia* (London: BBC Books, 1995). Also, a useful summing up at the time of the Dayton peace agreement is 'Peace at last, at least for now', *The Economist*, 25 November 1995, pp. 25–9.

29   See *The Economist*, 'Peace at last', *op. cit.*

6

THE MUSLIMS OF BULGARIA[1]

Ivan Ilchev and Duncan Perry

1. Introduction

With the advent of democratisation in Eastern Europe during the
late 1980s, national dynamics in the region began to change.
Resurgent nationalism spread throughout majority populations,
while ethnic awareness grew among members of minority groups,
creating sharper social and ethnic divisions as well as political problems for the new governments of the region. Bulgaria, where some
16 per cent of the population is made up of ethnic or religious
minorities,[2] certainly has not been immune to these developments.

Muslims in Bulgaria can be categorised in three main groups:
(1) the Bulgarian Turks; (2) the Roma (elsewhere also referred to as
'Gypsies'); and (3) the 'Bulgarian Muslims' – also referred to as
'Pomaks', although they themselves resent this appellation.[3] In
December 1992, the Bulgarian government conducted a state-wide
census. The results indicated that 7,271,185 people (86 per cent of
the population) considered themselves to be ethnic Bulgarians. Another 800,052 (9 per cent) claimed to be ethnic Turks, while 313,396
(4 per cent) declared themselves Roma. The remaining 102,684
(1 per cent) were members of different ethnic groups or were not
identified. The total population was put at 8,487,317 – a 5 per cent
drop from the previous census conducted in 1985.[4] It should be
noted, however, that some demographers and others do not consider these results accurate, in part because a large but unspecified
number of Roma and probably some 30,000–35,000 non-Turkish
Bulgarian-speaking Muslims ('Pomaks') chose to declare themselves
as 'Turks' or 'Bulgarians' in the census.

The total number of Muslims in the country is probably at least
1.2 million (16 per cent of the total population), divided into at least

700,000 Turks, 200,000 'Bulgarian Muslims', and, at a conservative estimate, 300,000 Muslim Roma, even if a substantial number of the latter two groups listed themselves in the census as belonging to the former group. About 99 per cent of the Muslims in Bulgaria are Sunni; the one per cent who are Shiite are almost all Bulgarian Turks.[5]

Ethnic Bulgarians (Orthodox Christian) constitute the dominant ethnic group in 24 of the 26 official districts of the country. The two exceptions are Razgrad region, in north-eastern Bulgaria, where the population is about equally divided between ethnic Bulgarians and ethnic Turks, and the Kûrdzhali region of south-eastern Bulgaria, where Turks outnumber Bulgarians two to one. Bulgarian Turks are also found in large numbers in three other districts: Shumen, Burgas, and Silistra.[6] Ethnic Bulgarians live predominantly in urban areas, while there is no sizeable Turkish presence in urban areas aside from Shumen, Kûrdzhali and Razgrad. Roma live throughout the country, while Bulgarian Muslims live predominantly in the Rhodope Mountains and in parts of the Balkan range.

Although at times suppressed during the Communist era, and never promoted, Islam in Bulgaria persisted. Today, it is being reinvigorated in all three of these communities, although the intensity with which this is occurring is difficult to measure. The level of religious feelings is correlated with the level of education: on the whole, those with a university education are the least religious. Interestingly, the level of religiosity among the young generation of Bulgarian Turks differs little from that of the Orthodox youth. Differences in religiosity between the two confessional groups are located in the old generation. For the Muslim population, identification with the Islamic faith does not necessarily mean that they frequent the mosques. In fact, only 15 per cent – mostly elderly people – do so, and only 30 per cent pray more or less regularly.[7]

2. Bulgarian Turks

2.1. *Historical background*

The origins of Bulgaria's ethnic Turkish population are disputed. Many scholars maintain that Bulgarian Turks are the descendants of

Ottomans who came to Bulgaria mostly from the late 14th to the 16th century, after Bulgaria had fallen under Ottoman rule. Others suggest that the majority of Bulgarian Turks are not Turks at all, but Bulgarian Slavs whose forefathers converted to Islam and in the main adopted Turkish language and culture (contrary to the 'Bulgarian Muslims' who only adopted the religion). The matter is academic.[8] What is of importance today is that their descendants identify themselves as ethnic Turks and Bulgarian citizens simultaneously.

Ascertaining the precise demographic and religious breakdown of Bulgaria at the time of liberation in 1878 is impossible. Yet some data are available about approximate distributions and trends. We know that by 1881, many thousands of Turks had emigrated to Ottoman lands, but that despite this a sizeable population remained in Bulgaria.[9] The status of those who stayed behind changed considerably. Whereas under Ottoman administration, even the poorest Turks had, in the *millet* system, greater rights (and some duties) than their Christian neighbours, they now became members of ethnic and religious minorities without any special status in society. Turks gained full and inalienable civil rights and a few won seats in various parliaments throughout modern Bulgarian history, but no Turk ever gained a ministerial position; a few became members of the Central Committee of the Bulgarian Communist Party (BCP). Prior to 1989, Turkish voters were considered to be pliant, easily manipulated by leaders and a 'lawful dowry' in the election frauds perpetrated by the government. Today, Bulgaria's minority groups enjoy the same civil and legal rights as members of the majority – but that does not mean that forms of discrimination and friction are absent.

Some scholars claim that 1.5 million Turks left Bulgaria during the liberation period and another 350,000 emigrated between 1878 and 1912.[10] Following World War I, additional emigration occurred and later, between the early 1950s and 1978, another 300,000 Turks left Bulgaria.[11] Pre-Communist as well as Communist Bulgarian authorities did their best to dilute the influence of Islamic leaders over those who remained. They targeted especially young people, in an effort to imbue them with a Bulgarian national consciousness. They sought to counteract Turkey's effort to extend its influence among Bulgaria's Turks. Thus, Turkish language schools and the faculty of Turkish studies at Sofia University all taught state propaganda. Books written by Bulgarian Turks were published. Yet to the extent that the state was involved in fostering a Turkish cultural identity, it was mainly another avenue to control them by attempting to mould their political thinking. These efforts yielded meagre results, however, as few Turks entered the bureaucracy, and fewer still became members of the Communist Party.[12]

Such policies were in any case interrupted by periodic assimilation campaigns after the Communist take-over in 1944. This explains limited spurts of emigration in 1950–1, and in the late 1950s and early 1960s. During the 1970s, although the state encouraged research concerning Bulgaria's Ottoman past, the country's cultural policy – under the firm guidance of Todor Zhivkov's daughter Liudmila Zhivkova – emphasised Bulgaria's unique historical and cultural heritage in an effort to stimulate Bulgarian national pride.[13]

Late 1984 saw the start of one of the most divisive developments in modern Bulgarian history, in the shape of the assimilation campaign known as 'the revival process', which was directed chiefly against Bulgarian Turks. Involving forced name changes among ethnic Turks, it was the most flagrant and best publicised abrogation of human rights in contemporary Bulgaria. The programme, which also included eliminating Turkish literature from school curricula, banning the Turkish-language media, forbidding the wearing of Turkish dress, prohibiting the observance of Turkish holidays, etc., culminated in the 1989 exodus of some 350,000 ethnic Turks to Turkey, although between 120,000 and 180,000 subsequently returned.[14]

The exodus began following violent demonstrations in northeastern Bulgaria and with Zhivkov's subsequent announcement on television that Bulgaria's borders with Turkey were declared open. It was further stimulated by Ankara's declaration that it would accept all Turks who chose to leave Bulgaria. Turkey, unable to process and accommodate the flood of immigrants, was forced to close the border in August of that year.

Precisely how and why this decision was taken is not known. Those who took part in the deliberations now deny complicity. Yet the main motivation appears to have been to create a homogeneous Bulgaria by either forcing the Turks out of the country or assimilating them. Other factors that are likely to have played a role include (1) fear of the spread of Muslim fundamentalism among Bulgaria's Turks via Turkey; (2) concern that Turkish population growth, outstripping that of the ethnic Bulgarians, could lead to increased

pressure from the Turkish community for a greater say in govern-
ance and even possibly for a federal solution (ultimately perhaps
even bringing moves towards union with Turkey); and (3) a fear of
Turkey itself – the strongest power in the region and one not above
military action in defence of Turkish minorities (as demonstrated by
the 1974 invasion of Cyprus).

Whatever their reasoning, Bulgaria's leaders badly misjudged
the moment. A serious international outcry followed. Indeed, the
difficulties associated with the assimilation programme might be
seen as marking the beginning of the process that culminated in
1990 with the overthrow of Communist rule in 1989. In any case, the
programme had the opposite effect to that intended. It heightened
Turkish ethnic consciousness and led, among other things, to the
founding in January 1990 of the Movement for Rights and Freedoms
(MRF), a political organisation that now effectively functions as the
party of Bulgaria's Turks.[15]

Since the toppling of the Zhivkov regime, the differences
between Bulgarians of Christian heritage and other ethnic/religious
groups have become more pronounced, and individuals' feelings of
identity within each group have strengthened. Similarities within
groups are stressed, while differences between them are imputed
even when there were none before. A sense of exclusivity among
ethnic Bulgarians, ethnic Turks, Bulgarian Muslims, and some Roma
has been developing.

2.2. *The image of the Turks, and inter-communal relations*

Among ethnic Bulgarians (and other peoples whom the Ottomans
conquered but who did not convert to Islam), Turks (and other
Muslims) have a poor image that has been perpetuated in literature,
schoolbooks, works of art, folklore, and elsewhere. The Turks have
typically been portrayed as devious, duplicitous, and rapacious – the
traditional enemy. Even ethnic Turkish children today learn from
Bulgarian literature such as Ivan Vazov's *Under the Yoke* (reputedly
the most widely read Bulgarian novel in the country, recounting
Bulgaria's struggle for independence in the 19th century), that their
forebears were notorious for their cruelty and barbarism. Even the
title makes this point: the word 'yoke' refers to the five centuries of
what is regarded as the Turkish enslavement of ethnic Bulgarians. No

attempt was made until very recently to balance the unfavourable and often inaccurate historical image of Turks – augmented by present-day uneasiness about the presence of a powerful Turkey on the south-eastern border of Bulgaria – with the contributions of Turks to Bulgaria's history, society, culture, and economy.[16] In 1992, textbooks portraying the Turks as something other than villains prompted an outcry from Bulgarian history teachers and many Bulgarian intellectuals, despite the fact that they had been approved by the Ministry of Education.

Part of the difficulty of presenting a different view of the Turks in Bulgarian history stems from the fact that there are no Bulgarian Turkish heroes from which to draw inspiration. There were almost no Turkish intellectuals, important industrialists, or well-known politicians in Bulgaria after 1878, when Bulgaria became a principality under a Christian prince. Those Turks who did not emigrate were concentrated in agricultural regions; no intellectual class emerged. When asked by researchers, Turkish respondents in a 1992 research project could not name a single famous Turk in Bulgaria – not even a mythical figure. Turkish children used to name Vasil Levski, a Bulgarian revolutionary who died at the hands of the Ottomans in 1873, as the hero they knew best.[17] Now, ethnic Turkish children are looking increasingly to Turkey for their inspiration and yet Mustafa Kemal Atatürk, the father of modern Turkey whose memory remains extremely popular in Turkey, was only mentioned rarely when these children were enumerating heroes. Although some of Bulgaria's Turks now identify with figures in the contemporary Muslim world like Saddam Hussein and Muammar Qaddhafi (as leaders who stand up to the non-Islamic powers, thus recalling the Ottoman *Ghazi* tradition)[18] this is not as yet widespread.

Contacts between ethnic Bulgarians and ethnic Turks have traditionally been limited. Many Bulgarians have spent their entire lives without becoming personally well acquainted with a Turk or a Bulgarian Muslim, and vice versa. Bulgaria's Turks were largely invisible outside the regions they inhabited until 1989. Their presence in the mass media before 1984 was minimal and with the 'revival process' vanished altogether. Among those ethnic Bulgarians who have friends in the ethnic Turkish community, there is a general perception that ethnic Turks as a group differ significantly from ethnic Turks as individuals. In general, the Bulgarian perception of the generic 'Turk', formed by memory, education and the media as well as by oral tradition, is negative. Turks, for their part, tend to see Bulgarians as distant or even hostile. On an individual basis, however, members of one group often respond positively to individuals from the other. In these contacts, or lack thereof, it is not religion which is the defining characteristic, but rather, more fundamentally, language and culture.

The highest degree of intolerance is found in north-eastern and south-eastern Bulgaria where there are mixed populations in which ethnic Turks are in the majority, particularly in the countryside. One likely cause of this intolerance is fear on the part of ethnic Bulgarians that they will be economically disadvantaged as a result of being a local minority or that they will ultimately be forced to abandon their homes and property because increasing Islamisation and Turk-ification of the region would make non-Muslims unwelcome. But even in these areas, ethnic Bulgarian negativism is usually displayed toward that amorphous group, 'the Turks', and not toward individual Turks.

This tendency to respect individual members of an ethnic group that, as an entity, is viewed negatively, helps to explain why some Bulgarians openly opposed the assimilation campaign of 1984–9 and why others resisted it passively in their everyday inter-ethnic contacts. Many Bulgarians living in mixed regions condemned the state's edict that Turks change their Turkish-sounding names to Slavic-sounding ones. It was not uncommon for ethnic Bulgarians to avoid using in public the Bulgarian names which ethnic Turks had been forced to adopt, by the simple expedient of using no names at all. In private, Turkish names were used. The name change process, bred out of the state's assimilation strategy, was a searing blow to Turks, perhaps greater than the Communist authorities seemed to realise: by forcing Muslims to change their names to non-Islamic ones, the government was depriving them of part of their identity, part of their religious being. A Muslim's name cannot be separated from the person.[19]

To reclaim their identities, many Turks emigrated when the state opened the border in 1989. Departing Turks sometimes entrusted their valuables to non-Muslim neighbours. Of course there were also Bulgarians who welcomed these departures because they could profit by purchasing real estate and goods at low prices from Turks who were leaving. Others were pleased because a reduction in the number of Turks diminished the 'Turkish threat'. The government, particularly at the local level, often dealt harshly both with those

Turks who left and with those who subsequently returned, denying many of them compensation for the property they had left behind.

In the space of two months, Turkey received more than 300,000 of these migrants. The state strained to accommodate them, but things were not made any easier by the country's weak economy. Many emigrants consequently fell upon difficult times and returned to Bulgaria. Those who fared best, and stayed, had relatives or friends in Turkey to smooth the transition. Those who returned to Bulgaria between 1989 and 1990, seem to associate themselves more closely with the Bulgarian state than with Turkey. This seems to reflect a desire to reintegrate into Bulgarian society, for they generally found it difficult to accept Turkish culture and be accepted into it.[20] Where enmity was expressed by Bulgarian Turks, it was directed toward Communists who drove them out, and not toward the Bulgarian state.

Perhaps the widest divergences between ethnic Bulgarians and ethnic Turks is to be found in the areas of vocation and education. Turkish children tend to define their status in terms of material goods and to stress the need to earn money in the near future. Their career choices are apt to involve manual labour, and they do not seem to value education as highly as their Bulgarian counterparts. This is not surprising, however, given that the Turkish population is largely agricultural and that until recently most Turks lived and worked in tightly-knit ethnic communities. Agricultural populations are usually conservative and resistant to new ideas, especially if the language of educational instruction is not their mother tongue. The net result is that the overall level of education is lower among ethnic Turks than among ethnic Bulgarians.

In part as a result of this, there appears to be discrimination in the labour market. Few Turks or other minorities have benefited from privatisation and market reforms. Economically, Turks in Bulgaria generally did well until recently, when their traditional agricultural economy began to break down. In the Kûrdzhali region, for example, where Turks constituted about 70 per cent of the population in 1992 (this proportion may have since diminished owing to emigration), tobacco-growing, the region's main agricultural activity, is on the verge of collapse. The quality of life there is plummeting, and the rate of unemployment is among the highest in the country.

Because of the economic down-turn, Turks have begun migrating from rural to urban areas and, sometimes, from there to cities in Turkey. (This pattern resembles the mass resettlement of ethnic Bulgarians in the 1950s and 1960s, from rural areas to cities, as part of a government programme of forced industrialisation which required the creation of an industrial work force). Today, some prefer to go to Turkish cities, which seem to offer greater promise of work and a more attractive lifestyle, though assimilation into Turkish society often still proves difficult or impossible, particularly for those with scant education and/or no network of friends or relatives in Turkey. As with the 1989 wave of migrants, many of the more recent ones therefore also return to Bulgaria.[21] Those who fare best in Turkey are usually those with professional training. The returnees tend to be the less well educated. In the aggregate, this situation means that some of the Bulgarian Turkish community's best minds have left, or are leaving, Bulgaria, thereby depriving the community of leaders, and contributing to the state's already large brain drain.

2.3. The Movement for Rights and Freedoms (MRF)

A major change in the Bulgarian political scene occurred with the founding of the MRF. Never before had a party constituted along ethnic lines been part of the political landscape. Moreover, since the Bulgarian constitution expressly forbids such parties, it is anomalous that the MRF gained legal approval. The Constitutional Court and the government evidently decided to allow the creation of this organisation, partially to quell growing street disturbances, partly to respond to pressure from Turkey with which it had steadily improving relations and partly to reduce support for the opposition Union of Democratic Forces (UDF).

During 1990–2, the influence of the MRF among Turks was indeed strong. It won a number of local council seats in the elections of 1991. According to its leader it had 653 mayors, 27 local councils and 1,144 councillors around the country. In the Shumen region five out of 10 local councils were dominated by the movement. In the Ruse region, Güner Tahir became deputy regional director, the first Bulgarian citizen of Turkish origin to hold such a position. The MRF carried 418,000 votes (7.6 per cent of all ballots cast) in the 13 October 1992 election, thus winning 10 per cent of the seats in the National Assembly. Success at the local level was also substantial. The

MRF won 10.6 per cent of the mayoral contests in large communities and 13 per cent in villages. Almost 12 per cent of communal councillors state-wide belonged to the Movement.[22] The political strongholds of the MRF were Kûrdzhali, Silistra, Tûrgovishte, Shumen, Smolian, Dobrich, and Blagoevgrad where many Bulgarian Muslims cast their political lot with the Turks. In districts where there were no Turks or Bulgarian Muslims, the MRF received no support, notably in Vidin, Vratsa, Kiustendil, Mihailovgrad, Pernik, and Sofia. The MRF, then, was able to mobilise nearly all Turkish voters along with some Bulgarian Muslims, perhaps up to one-fourth of this constituency.

The results of the 1992 elections affirmed the MRF as a viable political force. Its importance was enhanced because neither of the other two parties in parliament, the Bulgarian Socialist Party (BSP, heir to the BCP), nor the anti-Communist Union of Democratic Forces (UDF), had enough votes to form a government. The MRF understandably threw its weight behind the UDF, then led by Filip Dimitrov. The MRF leadership, headed by Ahmed Dogan, clearly enjoyed its role as kingmaker.

Yet the MRF was looked upon with suspicion by the majority of Bulgarians. Even the followers of the UDF gave the impression of being uncomfortable with their ally. Several attempts by different political groups to have the Movement banned on constitutional grounds, however, failed. In its statute, the MRF defined itself as 'an independent socio-political organisation established with the view of promoting the unity of Bulgarian citizens, by respecting the rights and freedoms of all ethnic, religious and cultural entities in Bulgaria'.[23] At the party's second conference, however (in December 1993), Dogan called it an 'ethnic party of a national type or national party of an ethnic type' – an interpretation which contradicts the state's constitution.[24]

Generally the relations between Bulgarians and Turks in localities where power is held by representatives of the MRF are tolerable. Of course, local ethnic Bulgarians who traditionally looked down upon the Turks as second-class citizens resent the change. Stories abound of Turkish officials firing ethnic Bulgarians in order to have Turks appointed in their places. The Bulgarian public reacts quite strongly to this, in contrast with its reaction when Turks are being fired in order to appoint ethnic Bulgarians. In several cases local officials have taken steps which have attracted the attention of the media and the courts. In some localities attempts have been made to replace the Bulgarian names of villages, streets and cultural institutions with Turkish ones. Thus far, such attempts have failed to win court approval.[25]

In December 1992, the MRF, dissatisfied with the pace of reform and what it saw as neglect of Turkish issues, allied with the Bulgarian Socialist Party (BSP) to bring down its erstwhile ally, the anti-Communist UDF. When the next government, billed as a technocratic cabinet, headed by Liuben Berov, failed to reform the economy or satisfy MRF demands, it too fell in 1994. Elections were called and the BSP gained power with 43.5 per cent of the vote and an absolute majority in parliament (125 seats). The UDF won only 24.2 per cent (69 seats), while the MRF carried 5.4 per cent of the vote (15 seats), down from 7.5 per cent in 1991. With much MRF member unhappiness about cooperation with the BSP, successor to the Communists, Mr Dogan in 1994 reopened links with the UDF.

The MRF failed to win the Muslim Roma vote in these elections; it also lost in regions which the leadership had thought secure (in the western Rhodopes, for instance, it lost one of the two seats, though there had been no substantial emigration from this region). A number of Muslim votes went to the BSP, another block (around 40,000) to the splinter formations of the MRF.[26] These results seem to indicate that the ethnic issue was not as significant a factor as in the previous election and that other issues dominated voter thinking.

To compensate for the number of pro-MRF voters who left for Turkey, the leadership turned to other Muslims, but with little success.

In addition, a number of scandals over Movement leaders who had Communist pasts, and others over leaders' unfulfilled promises to ease the plight of their constituency, reflected badly on the party. In particular, some of the party's members of parliament have attracted criticism for apparently putting the glitter and money of the capital above their constituents' interests. In 1995, the former chairman of the MRF's Haskovo organisation – of the key men in the party's top echelon – spoke openly about corruption in the leadership.[27] To make matters worse, the organisation's financial situation is tenuous. Its newspaper *Prava i svobodi* stopped publication for some time in 1995 for lack of funds.

The continuing economic crisis hit all Turks hard, but none with more impact than the Turkish population of south-eastern Bulgaria, where no relief seems in sight. Local leaders, mayors and councillors are simply unable to master the economic crisis afflicting their villages and towns. While this is due in part to lack of resources, lack of qualified personnel also plays a role, as do incompetence and corruption (financial scandals, bribes, and nepotism are commonplace in the villages and towns governed by the MRF, although it should be stressed that other officials are equally implicated in this).[28]

Not surprisingly, rifts have opened within the organisation itself, reversing the monolithic image observers had had of the party. While other parties were continually splitting, the MRF had appeared to be an exception. Dissension is now manifest, however. A rival group was formed under Adem Kenan, a founder of the MRF, and in 1993 several prominent members resigned (including several parliamentary deputies and the deputy leader of the party, Sherife Mustafa, who was the only woman in the leadership). Dogan was under siege, criticised by MRF branches for failing to attend to social problems.

The Movement desperately needs trained people to lead it. The 1989–90 exodus, however, included more than 9,000 Bulgarian Turks with university education and, as already indicated, it was generally the more qualified migrants who did end up staying in Turkey. This left the ethnic Turks in Bulgaria with few qualified leaders, a situation that Dogan thinks will persist for another 10 to 15 years. It is in recognition of this situation that pragmatic cooperation with non-Muslims has become necessary, such as in the small town of Ardino in the Rhodopes, where the MRF voluntarily gave eight seats in the local council to ethnic Bulgarians from the Bulgarian Agrarian National Union, in the hope that their higher level of knowledge and experience will help in solving the problems confronting the town.[29]

As a result of conditions in Bulgaria, emigration of Turks to Turkey continues, although now on a much smaller scale. This is likely to continue notwithstanding the measures which both the Bulgarian and the Turkish governments have been taking to discourage it. Even a number of active members of the MRF, disappointed by events in Bulgaria, have left for Turkey, and others are considering following their example. This threatens the party's fortunes even further, shrinking both its electorate and the pool of its actual and potential leaders.[30]

3. The Roma

Roma (elsewhere also referred to as 'Gypsies') in Bulgaria were said to number 313,396 in the 1992 census. This figure is disputed and the actual number might be as high as 600,000 to 800,000 because the census shows only figures for those who defined themselves explicitly as Roma; many Roma chose, however, to declare themselves Bulgarians or Turks.[31] Roma began to arrive in Bulgaria during the 13th and 14th centuries.[32] All Roma in Bulgaria today have a permanent residence, and most live in urban areas, typically in ghettos. Roma living in cities and towns tend to lose group identity, while it is often preserved in villages. To the average Bulgarian, they constitute a homogeneous people, although there are definite lines segmenting the Roma into groups. It is possible to categorise Roma broadly in three different ways, using the sometimes overlapping criteria of religion, life-style, and language. First, they can be divided into 'Bulgarian' or Christian Roma (*Dromisikane Roma*) on the one hand, and the so-called 'Turkish', or Muslim, Roma (*Khorakhane Roma*) on the other. About half of Bulgaria's Roma are usually thought to be Muslims and about half Christians. Some recent statistics in fact list 44 per cent as Christian, 39 per cent as Muslim, and 16 per cent as not religious.[33] Second, they may be categorised according to whether they used to be sedentary ('local/settled') or nomadic. And finally, they can be divided into those who are bilingual speakers of Bulgarian and Romani (the language of the Roma), those who speak only Bulgarian or Turkish, and bilingual Bulgarian/Romanian-speakers such as the *Rudari* (the latter are Christians and consider themselves Romanian; they were treated like chattel until well into the 19th century, and migrated throughout the Balkans; many eventually settled in Bulgaria.)[34]

In a recent survey of Roma, conducted in 69 villages and 56 towns in Bulgaria, on a sample of 1,882 informants, the majority defined themselves as Bulgarian Roma/*Dromisikane* (47.5 per cent). These have long lived a settled existence. 46.2 per cent thought of themselves as Turkish Roma/*Khorakhane* – also on the whole a settled population. In this survey, *Vlax* or Wallachian Roma made up 6.1 per cent of the Roma population, and *Kardarashi* and *Lovari* Roma 1.6 per cent.[35]

Roma nomads were forced to settle in 1958 as a result of government policy. The formerly nomadic *Kardarashi* Roma[36] typically live in a closed, conservative society, tightly controlled by leaders who resolve all disputes internally without help from the state authorities. Associated in the public mind with illegal activities, they have a comparatively high standard of living and see themselves as superior to the other groups of Roma. As Christians, they do not support the predominantly Turkish MRF, fearing that it would eventually make the Roma part of the Turkish *ethnos*. As a partial defence against such assimilation, Romani is now being taught in some primary schools.

There is no strong sense of ethnic unity among the Roma as a whole. Only one's own clan is considered pure Roma, speaking pure Romani. Others are loutish, 'dirty, lazy, and thievish'.[37] Even so, they consider themselves part of Bulgarian society. Indeed many think of themselves as ethnic Bulgarians; this is usually so among Christians with a higher education. Other Roma argue that they are ethnic Turks, in the hope of improving their standing in the community.[38] Many identify themselves in terms of their religion.

But Roma are not readily accepted into Bulgarian society and are generally stereotyped by non-Roma people as thieves, profiteers, and criminals. Most ethnic Bulgarians see a wide gap between themselves and the Roma. The Turks, too, make a clear distinction between themselves and the Roma, even though many of the latter are Muslim.

Traditionally Roma are the group most neglected by the Bulgarian state. In the decades after liberation they stood at the bottom of the social pyramid; their level of education and standard of living were the lowest in the country. Some attempts were made in the 1930s to induce nomadic Roma to settle down. The programme was unsuccessful. During the early years of socialism, which began in 1944, the state allowed Roma to develop programmes to foster their culture. This policy changed in the 1950s when the authorities tried to discourage a Romani identity by attempting to integrate and assimilate Roma into the ethnic Bulgarian community, a policy that remained in effect throughout the Communist era.[39] During the revival period, news about Roma disappeared from the press – just as did anything Turkish.[40] Historically, then, the Roma have long been discriminated against. Since the fall of Communism, human rights abuses have continued despite a democratic sounding constitution.[41]

After the fall of Todor Zhivkov in 1989, the BCP and the Fatherland Front tried to organise a Roma Union as their minion. In response, the Roma intelligentsia established the Democratic Union of Roma, a purportedly non-political organisation dedicated to social, educational, and cultural affairs. This group was very strong initially, but its influence subsequently diminished. Among Roma, political programmes are often determined by the aspirations of individuals; thus, there is little cohesion at the political level, and it is not clear who represents whom. In fact, sometimes Roma leaders do not seem to represent anyone but themselves and their closest kin. Matters are complicated by the fact that Roma often speak dialects that are barely intelligible to other Roma outside the dialect group. This and the inter-group rivalries limit the possibilities for collective action.[42]

Conditions for the Roma have, if anything, worsened since the end of Communism. They probably have the highest birth and mortality rates of any group in the country; their children tend to have more health problems than the children of any other group. Living conditions in towns are worse than in the villages. Roma ghettos lack running water, sewage systems, and electricity. Most Roma acquire little formal education. Unemployment rates are higher among them than among other groups; in some towns as many as 90 per cent are jobless. Even so, the authorities are often slow to provide social assistance. Roma living in towns make their living as unskilled labourers, sometimes working illegally; few find better-paid jobs. Many resort to black-market operations, fortune-telling, and begging. In villages, they do seasonal work and ply traditional trades such as iron-mongering, basket-making, and playing music.[43]

The media reinforce the common image of Roma as good-for-nothings, sometimes singled out by references to skin colour. They tend to sensationalise crimes committed by Roma, while hardly ever discussing the social, economic, and other problems confronting the Roma community. Roma have been scapegoats at times of social, economic, or political crisis, even becoming the object of attacks and 'pogroms'.

Official figures indicate that the rate of crime is higher among Bulgarian Roma than among the majority population. In Bulgaria, as elsewhere in Eastern Europe, the government has failed to cope with escalating crime. It has also failed to prosecute perpetrators of anti-Roma violence, thus encouraging even more violence against them. Ethnic Bulgarians and ethnic Turks, for their part, fear falling victim to organised, brutal groups of Roma who are reputed to steal property and even threaten lives. Yet the Roma see themselves as scapegoats.

Negative attitudes appear to be stronger toward Muslim than toward the Christian Roma. The former are believed more likely to be criminals. Such a distinction is in fact meaningless; the picture differs from region to region. In Sliven, for example, Muslim Roma are the poorest of the Roma in the area and the most likely to commit crimes. In Shumen, it is the Christian Roma who are the worst offenders.

Democratisation in Bulgaria has only nominally enabled the Roma to take part in political processes previously not open to them. The constitution does not allow political parties based on ethnicity, religion, or race (the MRF notwithstanding); and thus no Roma party has been established and sanctioned. Furthermore, the existing political parties are reluctant to let Roma occupy high posts. In any case, the number of Roma with the required education and political experience to qualify for higher positions is negligible. Although some Roma leaders argue that the Roma would like to be integrated into Bulgarian society, Roma intellectuals now increasingly demand that their cultural identity and autonomy be respected. Because of internal fragmentation within Roma leaderships and serious intergroup rivalries between the Bulgarian (Christian) and Turkish (Muslim) Roma, unanimity about methods and goals has remained beyond reach. There are a number of groups representing elements in the Roma community, but no single organisation represents all Roma. Many Roma voted for the Socialists in the 1991 elections, although some cast their vote for the MRF or the UDF. The same pattern was repeated in 1994 and there is a BSP Roma deputy in the parliament.

4. Bulgarian Muslims ('Pomaks')

The group normally labelled 'Bulgarian Muslims' (sometimes also referred to by the resented appellation 'Pomaks'), are the descendants of Bulgarians whose forebears converted to Islam between the second half of the 17th century and the late 19th century. They speak Bulgarian and live in the Rhodope Mountains and in the Lovech area. They constitute a religious group rather than an ethnic minority. Bulgarian Muslims are typically agriculturists who tend to live in isolation from neighbouring Christians. Until recently, they did not identify themselves with ethnic Turks, who in fact did not have a high regard for them.

Since 1913 several campaigns were launched with the aim of assimilating the Bulgarian Muslim population in the Rhodopes, one of the most vicious being one carried out between 1971 and 1973. Until the deterioration of the Bulgarian economy, those in the Rhodope region depended chiefly on tobacco-growing for their livelihoods. This work was done largely by the women; the men often worked in construction, generally in urban areas, or were employed in the local lead and zinc mines. When the Bulgarian economy collapsed, the Bulgarian Muslims in the western Rhodopes were among the hardest hit, because construction was severely cut back and the men had to return home.[44] In addition, their isolation, coupled with the decline of local industry and especially of the to-bacco market, seems to have doomed the region to poverty and social tension. In this depressed environment, Turkish political activism, allegedly supported by the MRF, emerged in the wake of the democratisation processes. A good number of Bulgarian Muslims in this region decided to adopt a Turkish identity and demanded education in the Turkish language, despite the fact that Bulgarian Muslims did not generally speak Turkish. Some of the historical barriers between Bulgarian Muslims and Turks are now beginning to disappear, as both see a mutual advantage in cooperation. Some Bulgarian Muslims seek to associate themselves with the Turks, whose political influence is much greater than theirs. Nevertheless, among others an opposite trend is also becoming visible: a desire to strengthen the Bulgarian Muslim identity as one separate from the Turkish and Bulgarian Christian identities. Finally, as already indicated, some Bulgarian Muslims count themselves as simply Bulgarian.

Bulgarian Muslims living in the central part of the Rhodope area have better economic success than those elsewhere in the region. The population there does not depend so heavily on tobacco-growing or mining (with its ecologically disastrous consequences) as do Bulgarian Muslims elsewhere in the region. In fact, their prospects look relatively bright, because tourism and small businesses are developing and there is a growing timber industry. Nevertheless, the findings show that throughout the region younger Bulgarian Muslims (those between 18 and 30 years of age) are likely to face economic insecurity and unemployment.

Because of their small numbers and the fact that they are generally not politically-minded, are economically disadvantaged and geographically divided, Bulgarian Muslims do not constitute a strong political force. They regard government with suspicion in the light of historical attempts to suppress their religious identity.[45] They risk being gradually overwhelmed and perhaps assimilated by larger groups. The MRF needs their support and is seeking to increase its following among them. Ethnic Bulgarians, on the other hand, may not be willing to relinquish their influence over the Bulgarian Muslims, whom they claim as part of their *ethnos*.

5. 'Islamising Bulgaria': the international connection

With a Muslim population making up some 16 per cent of the total population, Bulgaria has a large stake in the question of whether anything like an 'Islamisation of Europe' is in progress. Xenophobes argue that with the proliferation of Muslim families and the extension of Islamic influence from Turkey among Turks in Bulgaria, as well as efforts by other Muslim states to spread their influence in Bosnia and Macedonia in particular, Bulgaria is indeed undergoing a process of Islamic reawakening. Many ethnic Bulgarians have become alarmed by news of Islamic preachers (*imams*) from Arab countries arriving in the country since 1993. In some places these *imams* or a number of Islamic religious foundations have contributed substantial funds towards the restoration of old mosques or the building of new ones. Even some of the leaders of the MRF have declared their alarm at the process.[46] The basic fear is that those who came are but the first of a wave of religious fundamentalists who would use Bulgaria as a springboard for penetration in Europe.

While it is true that there has indeed been some revival of Islamic identities relative to the Communist period, this, as was already illustrated in the introduction to this chapter, comes nowhere near the kind of development which these fears refer to. By the same token, the basic question of religious rights has also been solved, thereby taking the worst sting out of religiously-based resentment among the Muslims (though not necessarily eradicating other community-based discrimination and friction), and removing any motivation Turkey might have had to intervene.

Under the Communist regime, state propaganda was given over to condemning a rapacious Turkey seeking to co-opt the Turkish population and to subvert the state.[47] Today, that kind of rhetoric is a dead letter. Although Turkey is the main source of Islamic influence external to Bulgaria, the country's leadership is much too preoccupied with breaking into the European Union, dealing with the Kurdish question and solving its other problems, to be interested in subverting Bulgaria. Moreover, given Turkey's poor relations with Greece, a friendly Bulgaria represents at least the neutralisation of the potential for negative behaviour from Sofia (which does, after all, itself entertain good relations with Athens). Thus, while Turkey's influence in Bulgaria has grown significantly since the Communist era, its relationship with Bulgaria is largely constructive.[48]

In July 1995, Turkish President Suleiman Demirel visited Bulgaria and praised the state for respecting the rights of its Turkish minority. Bulgarian-Turkish relations have been steadily improving since 1990. Some Turkish investment in Bulgaria has been in evidence, though considerably less than the nationalists had feared. In 1995, Turkey and Bulgaria were entering into a free trade zone pact, and Ankara has been the prime mover in seeking to create the Trans-Balkan highway. Turkey does not interfere actively in Bulgarian politics, although it seeks to insure that Bulgaria's Turks are well treated (it has also expressed some interest in Roma or Pomak affairs). Indeed, the last thing Turkey's leadership wants from Bulgaria is another large wave of emigrants to tax its already overburdened economy. In short, neither state is looking to disinter history.

6.   Conclusion

While Muslim Turks and Bulgarian Muslims seem to feel that they are part of the Bulgarian polity, they clearly maintain a culture which is in part separate from that of Christian Bulgarians. Roma, on the other hand – whether Muslim or Christian – seem to feel disenfranchised. Until 1984, feelings of ethnic separateness and the strength of religious convictions were declining in all segments of Bulgarian society. Muslims generally regarded Islam as a relatively unimportant feature of their identity. However, following the introduction of the assimilation programme, solidarity among Turkish Muslims strengthened considerably. Since the beginning of democratisation, in 1989, Islam and Muslim customs have experienced a renewal among all three groups. Coupled with the polarisation between minorities and the ethnic Bulgarian majority, this could constitute a potential for confrontation.

The Roma, whether Muslim or Christian, continue to be treated as outcasts from mainstream society, both by ethnic Bulgarians and by Bulgarian Turks. This suggests shared prejudices about the Roma, who are deemed an alien group despite religious affinities with both ethnic Bulgarians and Turks. Bulgarian Muslims, generally isolated and torn between their Bulgarian identity and the faith which they share with the much more numerous Turks, are struggling to maintain the integrity of their *ethnos*.

Ethnic identity plays a part in Bulgarian politics and nationalism is a feature of everyday life. Events elsewhere in the Balkans, especially in the former Yugoslavia, have illustrated just how explosive the nationality issue can be. 'Religion' *per se* comes into this equation less as a belief system than as an element of ethnic/national identification – especially in the face of economic, social and political pressures. Bulgaria's future will depend in part on the depth of the national leadership's understanding of internal ethnic and religious issues. The state now has very little to fear from Turkey. If trouble emerges, it will be as a result of inter-ethnic tension unmitigated by balanced political programmes, improved education, and an informed public.

Notes

1   An earlier version of this chapter appeared in the *RFE/RL Research Report* in 1993, which was in turn based in part on research findings discussed at a seminar held at Radio Free Europe/Radio Liberty on 12–13 September 1992 in Munich. Thanks to Stefan Krause and Alaina Lemon of the Open Media Research Institute in Prague, Senor Cagaptay of the Center for the Study of Nationalism in Prague, and Kjell Engelbrekt of the University of Stockholm for reading and commenting on this chapter.

2   The term *maltsinstvo* (minority), does not have the same meaning in Bulgarian as in English. Whereas the English word refers to an identifiable, homogeneous group that is numerically smaller than the largest ethnic or religious group (the majority) in the same country, its Bulgarian counter-part typically signifies any ethnic or religious group whose rights are guaranteed and protected by international agreements and legislation.

3   The Turks of Bulgaria are of course also Muslims, as are about half of the Roma. The label 'Bulgarian Muslims', applied to those Muslims in a third category, may therefore seem somewhat confusing. As the members of this group resent the term 'Pomak', however, and since the label 'Bulgarian Muslim' has become the accepted one in Bulgaria, it will also be used in this chapter.

4   Republic of Bulgaria, National Statistical Institute, *Rezultati ot prebroiavaneto na naselenieto*, Vol. I, *Demografski Kharakteri* (Sofia: Natsionalen Statisticheski Institut, 1994), p. 372.

5   Among the Shiites are some sects, notably the Kizilbashi, that generally do not have good relations with Sunni Muslims. See *Bûlgarskite aliani* (Sofia: Sofia University Press, 1991).

6   P. Bozhikov, 'Etnodemografska kharakteristika na Bûlgarskoto naselenie', *Guven III* (27 July 1994), p. 372.

7   P. Mitev, 'Vrûzki na sûvmestimost i ne sûvmestimost vûv vsekidnevieto mezhdu hristijani i miusiulmani v Bûlgariia', *Sotsiologichesko izsledovane* (Sofia, 1994), tables 1–10.

8   For various views on this question, see H. Gandev, *Bulgarskata narodnost prez XV vek: Demografsko i etnografsko isledvanie* [Bulgarian Nationality through the XVth Century: Demographic and Ethnographic Research], 2nd edn (Sofia, 1989); E. Grozdanova, *Bulgarskata narodnost prez XVII vek: Demografsko isledvanie* [Bulgarian Nationality through the XVIIth Century: Demographic Research] (Sofia, 1989); and Vera Mutafchieva's review of the first edition of Gandev's book in *Istorcheski Pregled*, Vol. 4, 1973.

9   See K. Karpat, *Ottoman Population 1830–1914: Demographic and Social Characteristics* (Madison: University of Wisconsin Press, 1985), pp. 45ff.

10   See D. Vasileva, *Izselnicheskiiat vûpros v bûlgaro-turskite otnosheniia – Aspekti na etnokulturnata situatzia v Bûlgariia* (Sofia: Centre for the Study of Democracy/Friederich Naumann Schriftung, 1992), pp. 58–9.

11   I. Baev and N. Kotev, 'Izselnicheskiiat vûpros v bûlgaro-turskite otnosheniia sled vtorata svetovna voina', *Guven* III (15 June 1994), p. 19.

12   Little information about minorities in general within the BCP is available. See J. Bell, *The Bulgarian Communist Party from Blagoev to Zhivkov* (Stanford: Hoover Institution, 1986), pp. 131–2.

13   See R. Crampton, *A Short History of Modern Bulgaria* (Cambridge: Cambridge University Press, 1987), pp. 188–9.

14   D. Perry, 'Bulgarian Nationalism: Permutations on the Past' in P. Latawski (ed.), *Contemporary Nationalism in East Central Europe* (London: Macmillan, 1995), pp. 51–7; D. Perry, 'Ethnic Turks Face Bulgarian Nationalism', *Report of Eastern Europe*, Vol. 2, No. 11 (15 March 1991), pp. 5–8.

15   There are two other Turkish parties: the Democratic Party of Justice, which garnered 0.05 per cent in the 1994 elections and the Party of Democratic Change which weighed in with 0.03 per cent.

16   See H. Poulton, *The Balkans: Minorities and States in Conflict* (London: Minority Rights Group, 1991), p. 153.

17   E. Atansova, 'Az i drugiiat. Mitologiia i identichnost' in *Etnicheskata kartina v Bûlgariia* (Sofia: Klub 90, 1993), p. 159.

18   G. Balgoev, 'Sûvremennite religiozni izmereniia v zhivota na Muslemanskoto naselenie ot iztochnite i zapadnite Rodopi', *Etnicheskata kartina*, pp. 86–7.

19   D. Madzharov, 'Adaptatsiiata – Realnost i obrazi', *Etnicheskata kartina*, p. 121.

20   See *ibid.*, pp. 126–36.

21   Most do not receive lands through the restitution process, however, as they did not possess lands prior to 1944.

22   B. Giuzelov, *Elektornalni naglasi i elektoralno povedenie na maltsinstvata v Bûlgariia (1990–1992)* (Sofia: Centre for the Study of Democracy, 1993), p. 21.

23   *Prava i svobodi*, 10 December 1993: Statute of the MRF.

24   *Prava i svobodi*, 3 December 1993.

25   *Kontinent*, 22 June 1993; *Standart*, 17 June 1993 and 8 August 1994; *Duma*, 17 February 1993.

26   The Democratic Party of Justice and the Party of Democratic Change, referred to in note 15.

27   *Demokratsiia*, 5 June 1993; *Trud*, 7 September 1994.

28   See *24 Chasa*, 28 June 1993; *Demokratsiia*, 10 October 1994.

29   *Duma*, 16 June 1993; *Standart*, 31 May 1993.

30   *Standart*, 10 June 1993, 15 June 1993; *24 Chasa*, 14 June 1993; *Kontinent*, 10 June 1993. In the Kûrdzhali region 25 partial elections for mayors have been conducted to fill the places of those who have already left. See *Standart*, 1 August 1994.

31   Interview, 'Bulgaria: Reaching Out to Minorities', *Transition* (28 July 1995), p. 58; and E. Marushakova and V. Popov, 'Roma in Bulgaria – History and the Present Day', *Roma* (No. 38–39) 1993, p. 55. See E. Marushakova and V. Popov, *Tsiganite v Bûlgariia* (Sofia: Klub 90, 1993)

for a comprehensive treatment.

32 Marushakova and Popov, 'Roma in Bulgaria', p. 55.

33 I. Tomova, *The Gypsies in the Transition Period* (Sofia: International Center for Minority Studies and Intercultural Relations, 1995), pp. 22–6.

34 Debates about Roma identity are many-layered and complex; they concern, in addition to the issues mentioned, endogamy, dialect, profession, traditions, and taboos. See L. Troxel, 'Bulgaria's Gypsies: Numerically Strong, Politically Weak, '*RFE/RL Research Report*, No. 10, 6 March 1992).

35 Tomova, *op. cit.*, pp. 22–6.

36 *Kardarashi* speak Vlach Romani (as do the *Lovari* Roma). They are probably descended from the same group as those known in the US as *Kalderash* and elsewhere in Eastern Europe as *Keldelari*.

37 E. Marushakova, 'Otnosheniia mezhdu tsiganskite grupi v Bûlgariia', *Etnicheskata kartina*, p. 7.

38 Balgoev, *op. cit.*, pp. 87–8.

39 V. Popov, 'Bûlgariia i tsigani (mezhduethnicheski otnosheniia)' *Etnicheskata kartina*, p. 21.

40 Marushakova and Popov, *op. cit.*, p. 55.

41 Amnesty International, *Bulgaria, Turning a Blind Eye to Racism* (London: Amnesty International, 1994).

42 Marushakova, *op. cit.*, pp. 13–16.

43 See the article by I. Tomova, in *24 Chasa*, 30 June 1992 ; also Marushakova and Popov, *op. cit.*, p. 57.

44 See Poulton, *op. cit.*, pp. 111–15.

45 I. Atanasov, 'Otnoshenie na naselenieto ot Gotsedelchevsko kûm tsentralnata vlast i organite po mesta', *Etnicheskata kartina*, p. 90.

46 *24 Chasa*, 29 May 1993; *Demokratsiia*, 12 May 1993; *Trud*, 5 September 1994; Interview with MRF deputy, Ivan Palchev, *Kontinent*, 24 February 1993; *Zora*, 26 January 1993.

47 See for example, *Etnicheskiat konflikt v Bûlgariia 1989* (Sofia: Profizdat, 1990).

48 See K. Engelbrekt, 'Relations with Turkey: A Review of Post-Zhivkov Developments', *Report on Eastern Europe* (Vol. 2, No. 17), 26 April 1991, pp. 7–10.

7

ALBANIAN MUSLIMS, HUMAN RIGHTS, AND RELATIONS WITH THE ISLAMIC WORLD

Elira Cela

1. Introduction

Although Albania was since the late 1960s officially an atheist state, a very large percentage of the population may be classified, at some level, as Muslims. In a population of 3.3 million, some 70 per cent are of Muslim origin (Sunni and Bektashi).

The former Albanian Communist regime declared that freedom of conscience is complete and real only when man abandons any religious faith and affiliation, and when he frees himself from the 'opium of religion' which enslaves him spiritually. This clear and fundamental infringement of the freedom of conscience, a basic human and civil right, was incorporated in the Constitution of the People's Socialist Republic of Albania (1975), where religion was declared illegal. Article 37 of the Constitution proclaimed that the state recognised no religion whatsoever. It forbade all religious activities and organisation, while encouraging atheism. Article 55 of the 1977 Penal Code laid down penalties, including the death sentence, for religious activities.[1]

Along with many other elementary human rights and freedoms, the right to free thought, belief and expression were also denied to the Albanians. Freedom of conscience and expression were, in practice, rejected.

The development of democratic processes in Albania paved the way to freedom of conscience, thought and religion. Since 1991 Albania witnessed an upsurge of religious feelings and a rapid decline of mass atheism. The request for abrogation of the articles of the Constitution that prohibited freedom of religion, was among the first demands of the democratic movement in Albania.

2. Legal provisions

The religious revival in Albania has had a dominant impact on social and political life. It constitutes part of the drive towards pluralism so essential to the safeguarding of human rights. Respect for the human rights of individuals and minorities including their right to freedom of thought, conscience, and religious association, requires a positive recognition of the diversity of systems of thought and belief. The new democratic Albanian state adopted the principle that accords freedom and equality under the law to all, whether adhering to the majority faith, minority religions, or no faith at all. In particular, these principles mean that it is the duty of the state, but also of every individual, to work towards the elimination of religious intolerance and to create understanding and respect between people of diverse world views.

The new draft law on 'Religious Communities and Organisation', based on the 1981 United Nations Declaration on the elimination of all forms of intolerance and discrimination based on religion or belief, guarantees the right to freedom of thought, conscience and religion.[2] As such it is meant to become a cornerstone to the restoration of human rights in Albania. According to this law, the Republic of Albania is a secular state. Religious beliefs are separated from the state and equal before the law. So the state is independent of institutional religious control and, in turn, institutional religion is independent of state or political control.

The secular character of the state is not an obstacle to the enjoyment of various religious rights in the religious life of Albania. The separation of the state from religion guarantees freedom and equality of treatment of all religions, and institutional arrangements for redress of grievances help to secure religious freedoms.

Article 8 of the law states that 'no one should become subject to intolerance or discrimination by the state, various institutions, groups of persons or individuals, on the basis of religion or belief.' According to Article 10, hindering or depriving anyone of their right to conduct religious ceremonies is a penal offence.

The law, then, provides for the recognition of human and civil rights and makes clear that it is the duty of the state as well as of every person to defend these rights. It is the human rights ethos which underlies the new law. It is based on values and principles which claim universality, such as the right to respect for, and freedom of, conscience. No one can be discriminated against or persecuted on the basis of their belief/affiliation or the absence thereof. The law seeks to build tolerance and understanding of the diverse religions and beliefs and to eliminate the intellectual and spiritual intolerance which underlay the discrimination and persecution that so frequently disfigured the development of the country and its people.

Article 7 of the law defines the scope of freedom of belief:

> Everyone has the right to freedom of thought, conscience and religion: this right includes freedom to change his religion or belief, and freedom, either alone or in community with others and in public or private, to manifest his religion or belief in teaching, practice worship and observance.

3. Socio-religious realities

In practice, the above legal stipulation gives individuals and groups the right to change their religious affiliation. It is not uncommon in Albania to shift from one religious identity to another. For religious leaders, in particular among the Muslims, this has led to anger and frustration. They are faced with the phenomenon that their own adherents attend worship services of another religious community. Article 7 reflects the recognition that conversion has been quite common in Albania – going back to the era of the Ottoman occupation. In post-Communist Albania, the phenomenon of conversion from Islam to Christianity is occurring again among some young people. What are the main differences between the conversion processes then and now?

While during the years of the Ottoman occupation people were, at least in part, compelled by the invaders as well as by the economic, political and social conditions, at present conversion is a question of personal choice: no one is compelled to change his/her religious affiliation. Also, during the Ottoman occupation mass conversion included almost all age groups. Nowadays, it takes place mostly among young people.

Another characteristic of the present-day youth conversion process in Albania – differing not only from the processes during the Ottoman invasion but also from those taking place in other countries – is that the Muslim youth who seeks conversion to Catholicism in fact usually 'belongs' to Islam only as a result of the family's religious origins. These young people were born and brought up in an anti-religious social environment without mosques, without religious knowledge and without access to the Koran or Islamic teaching.

Some young former Muslims maintain that by changing their faith they had returned to the original religion of their ancestors. Other motives which have encouraged conversion include a liking for Christian culture, fascination with the beauty of Christian churches, with Christian ceremonies, church music, icons, the Italian language (in the case of the Catholic church), etc.[3] In some cases young people convert for utilitarian purposes and for personal profit. Thus some have changed their faith and even their name in order to acquire a visa to go abroad (the Greek Embassy, for instance, issues visas only to Orthodox Christians).

In general, conversion is to Catholicism. Nevertheless, some cases can be observed where both Muslims and Christians convert to newer religions such as the Baha'i faith. Historical experience has shown that a substantial number of those who changed their faith did not undergo a complete conversion experience. They often remained crypto-Catholic or crypto-Orthodox. The question therefore arises: will there be crypto-Muslims among the converted in present-day conditions? Will they be completely devoted to the new faith or will they continue to perform a mixture of religious rites, customs and ceremonies – that is, have a two-fold faith? This depends on psychological and social factors. But it should be noted that family religious tradition plays an important role in this respect.

The moulding of religious psychology is not one which is given once and for all. There are several social factors which exert their influence in this respect. Without denying the role of other factors, it can safely be stated that the family has played, and continues to play, the main role in the preservation and development of religious feeling in Albania.

An emphasis on the role of the family in Albanian socio-cultural dynamics is imperative. The family has been that 'cell' of the Albanian societal fabric that made possible the partial survival of religious customs, rites, feasts, and so on, preserved and observed secretly in the bosom of the family, during the era when they were banned by the totalitarian regime.

Nowadays, too, religion in Albania remains very much a family-related phenomenon. It is a question of personal morality, not especially related to the activity of the economic and political institutions.

4. Popular tolerance and political development

Inevitably, Albanians are not yet very familiar with human rights matters. But their openness and eagerness to put things right again is a hopeful sign for the future. The protection and promotion of the rights and freedoms declared in the human rights instruments is a long-term undertaking, given the complexity of the underlying factors often rooted in complex historical processes.

Norms, judgements, prejudices, superstitions, myths and archetypes whereby behaviour in society is modelled, are culturally transmitted from generation to generation. These norms, judgements and prejudices that condition our ideas about equality among human beings, as well as tolerance and respect for the ideas and feelings of others, are a product of societal forces. This means that in order to eliminate discrimination and intolerance in all its forms, there must necessarily be a change in attitude of the people, which will be a product of the necessary social changes and mental transformations of individuals.

The new freedom and democracy in Albania are still fragile. Many people and political forces are not yet used to, or comfortable with, real democracy, which by definition means tolerance and individual as well as social responsibility. Neither revolutions nor reforms can change attitudes overnight. Such a change can be made possible only after a long and persistent education. Therefore if the international norms concerning human rights fail to penetrate the conscience of each individual, if they fail to embrace what is called public opinion, then one will still be facing discordance with all the ensuing moral and juridical problems. In other words, the democratic political institutions cannot flourish on ground where a civic and democratic culture is missing. Several examples of such a discordance in post-dictatorial Albania can be listed.

It is worth dwelling on a statement issued by the Albanian Helsinki Committee of September 1993. Through the statement the Committee draws public as well as official attention to a number of instances where individuals and organisations appear to have been misinterpreting or indeed contravening the rules on the place of religion. The Committee expressed concern over these matters, as it believed that they imply, on the one hand, a breach of the limit of freedom of belief, and, on the other, a violation of the laws in force.

The statement reads as follows:

1. It has been observed that religious rites are carried out in some state institutions.
2. Courses on Islam are carried out in some schools which are defined as secular by law.
3. The Albanian Television – the only national state-owned TV network – broadcasts special programmes which promote Islam or Christianity, at a time when there are other institutions intended for this purpose.
4. There have been cases where directors of institutions have set religious criteria in employment policies.
5. There are religious societies which stimulate the spirit of religious divisions. Some go so far as to organise sports activities between Muslim children and Christian children.
6. Another concern is that some religious charity societies take advantage of the poverty and low cultural level of some people in order to impose, through gifts and money, either one or the other religion. They go so far as to distribute aid according to religious affiliation: the Orthodox church delivers aid to the Orthodox believers, the Catholic church to the Catholic, and the Muslim community to the Muslim believers. Such an attitude leads to social divisions. Very serious is the situation when aid is used to impose on girls and women the obligation to cover their faces with black veils.
7. Freedom of religion in Albania may be developed and improved only on the basis of the balance between various religions.[4]

Albania has suffered from a lack of human rights education. However, school curricula now for the first time include human rights education as a special subject. This should enable the pupils and students to be introduced to international and national human rights standards and the principles underlying them. The most important ingredient of all in this development, however, must be to see human rights applied and experienced in everyday life. In Albania, currently in the throes of transition to a democratic system, things need to be viewed or done from a new perspective. This calls for an educational process that is aimed essentially at changing attitudes and developing a thinking process conducive to a clear awareness of the intrinsic freedoms of every human being. The information needed does not relate merely to 'human rights' as a legal category, but to the situations in which these rights became an issue and can become a viable proposition. Hence it is necessary not only to include a special human rights content but also to change the approach.

Religious tolerance is a prominent characteristic of the Albanian people. Relations among people belonging to different religions are not only normal, but in many cases even characterised by inter-faith family ties. Close relations between people with different religious affiliations indeed not infrequently crystallise in mixed marriages. Surveys have shown that only few young people consider the question of religious affiliation as a factor determining their marriage. For the majority, feelings of love are the most important. Most tolerant in this respect are Muslims, followed by the Orthodox. This tolerance, which has been passed on from generation to generation, has made Albania an example of harmonious coexistence between different religions. While tolerance meant acceptance by individuals of the right of other individuals to hold different views, the concept of freedom went beyond the situation of individuals: it involved the state and placed heavy responsibilities upon it. The duty to guarantee religious freedom and to guard against discrimination on religious grounds is today prescribed by law.

5. Relations with the Islamic world

Since the demise of communism in Albania, the government has begun to adopt a new policy towards Islamic countries.

All of Eastern Europe suffered economic dislocation in the wake of Communism's demise, but nowhere has the process been more difficult or convulsive than in Albania. As of 1993, 38 per cent of the workforce were without employment. Instead of unemployment benefit, most receive a meagre amount of state assistance, an average of 540 *leks* a month, enough to buy three cans of beer at Tirana's best hotel, the *Dajti*. Foreign investment on the whole has been very slow in coming.

The mass exodus of young Albanians, the breakdown of law and order, the total collapse of the agricultural, commercial and industrial infrastructures – all these factors helped create a situation in which the Albanian population became totally dependent on the outside world for its physical survival.

The fact that the majority of Albanians are Muslim, combined with the fact that the headquarters of the Albanian Muslim Community has now been established, has had an important impact on international relations with the Muslim world. These factors play a significant part in securing economic and political aid and support from the Islamic countries. Towards the end of 1992, Albania made significant overtures to the Arab world. The Albanian President, Sali Berisha, travelled to Saudi Arabia and Egypt and invited the heads of both countries to visit Albania and to support Albania's application for membership of the Organisation of the Islamic Conference (OIC). Albania's accession to the OIC on 2 December 1992, which followed a year of preparation, triggered a sharp political debate. Berisha's move prompted concern that the Albanian leadership was distancing itself from the West as a whole, and from Europe in particular, while moving toward the Islamic countries. The arguments for and against the decision are as varied as they are heated. Critics of the move, which has made Albania the OIC member geographically nearest to Western Europe (Turkey is the only other European member) claim that this is a step backwards for a country that is eager to become a *bona fide* member of the European family of nations, after a century of self-imposed isolation.

President Berisha denied this and stressed that he was pursuing a pragmatic policy by taking into consideration the great potential for assistance, financial and otherwise, from the 1.4 billion people of some 50 Islamic countries. As the instigator and executor of the new diplomatic initiative, the president, who himself is a Muslim, argued that the country had nothing to lose from membership and potentially much to gain, pointing out that OIC member states were likely to offer Albania political and especially economic support. He argued that everything that contributed to the country's development would help expedite its integration into Europe, since what was hindering this process was Albania's poverty and under-development.[5]

It was, indeed, widely accepted among Albanian observers that the decision to join the OIC was prompted by political and economic motives rather than religious ones.

Nevertheless, since Albania's joining of the OIC, a heated debate began between the ruling Albanian Democratic Party and its political opponents, led by the Albanian Socialist Party, over the advisability of moving closer to the Islamic world. Socialist pundits, for their part, say that Tirana's opening to the East runs counter to Albania's geopolitical interests and that both its neighbours and other European nations are suspicious of Berisha's flirtation with the Muslim world. The socialists launched a polemical offensive, charging that by making overtures to the Islamic world Albania was committing political suicide, thereby subscribing to the belief that good relations with Europe and with the Muslim world were irreconcilable alternatives (they were not alone in this: the Democratic Alliance, a new party that had split away from the Democratic Party, also sharply criticised Berisha on this score).[6] Berisha's retort was that Albania 'could become a bridge connecting Europe with the Islamic nations'.

During the parliamentary debate, the Socialist deputies claimed that it was not Tirana but the OIC that had actually initiated the move toward Albanian membership and that it had done so not out of goodwill but for political reasons. They warned that in joining the organisation, Albania might actually be jeopardising its own stability, because anything that facilitated the spread of fundamentalism in the Balkans might help Islamise the conflict there. They stressed that it was necessary to avoid flirting with fundamentalism, not only because this limits the room for manœuvre in Albanian policy, but also because both Islam and the Orthodox Churches are Eastern-oriented. Albania, which is trying to become Western, could be transformed into an arena of conflict. The socialists added that Europe did not need Albania as a bridgehead to the Islamic world, as such bridges had long existed. They also reacted strongly to Berisha's statement that a Bosnian refugee camp, financed by Saudi Arabia, would be set up in Albania.

Several weeks before Albania joined the OIC, the country's leading writer, Ismail Kadare, in an interview in *Zëri i Rinisë*, issued a warning against the rise of Islamic fundamentalism in Albania.[7] He emphasised the Christian aspect of Albanian civilisation not only as the early original religion and civilisation of the Albanians, but also as their traditional culture in the framework of European cultural tradition. According to him, emphasising this historic fact is part of the logic of the new era of democracy and integration of Albania into the European family. The integration does not imply any undervaluation whatsoever of Islam, he went on to argue: on the contrary, the good understanding and lack of conflict between the two religions is an example of tolerance and humane culture. The difficulty of defining the future destiny of Albania in the family of European people, he observed, led to considerable speculation about the religious question and above all about Albanian Islam. Kadare accused 'anti-Albanian circles, especially Serbian', of trying to spread disinformation by presenting Albania not as a European but as an Islamic country.

This campaign, according to Kadare, aims at preparing a new isolation of Albania, a new separation from the rest of Europe. In an assertion clearly inspired by the fear of Islamic fundamentalism, Kadare also claims that it is not sure that the majority of Albanians are Muslim. The Communist regime, he charges, has falsified the figures regarding religious affiliation by overstating the number of Muslims in Albania, in order to justify the detachment from the rest of Europe and to justify the 'friendship' with the countries of the Middle East.

At present there appears to be no reason to fear that Albania is slated to become tomorrow's Iran. Religious tolerance has a long tradition and the overwhelming majority of Albania's Muslims are still non-practising. Today many Muslims in the country make a habit of attending Catholic Church services, apparently because they associate these with the Western civilisation that they strive to be part of. But this could quickly change, especially if the rich Arab countries begin to step up their investments – both economic and religious – in the poverty-stricken Albania and present an Islamic way of life as an attractive option. In such a case, Albanians would quite probably be encouraged to return to practising Islam. In fact, a growing Islamic influence is already apparent in the form of increased activity by Islamic associations and larger amounts of aid from various countries.

The Albanian Muslim Community has relations with the Muslim communities of Saudi Arabia, Kuwait, Libya, Egypt, Lebanon, Tunisia, Morocco, and Turkey, among others. As of 1993 Albania counted 17 Islamic charity associations operating independently of each other. Apart from religious literature, these associations distribute humanitarian aid to Muslim believers. With the funds of these associations they pay the salaries of the teachers for the Islamic schools, such as *medreses*. Thus, for example, the Islamic Centre of Vienna was providing $2,000 every month, to pay the majority of the wages and salaries of the employees of the Islamic institutions and schools. About 80 per cent of the expenses of the Headquarters of the Albanian Muslim Community are provided for by the Islamic Council of the Third World, the Islamic Council for Eastern Europe and by other Islamic associations and organisations.

According to a report on the activity of the Headquarters of the Muslim Community, obtained by the author, some $157,000 were deposited in the Headquarters' account during the period from 14 February 1991 to 15 May 1993, of which about $15,000 was aid from Saudi Arabia, Libya, Turkey and others.

With such foreign aid, ten *medreses* were set up, with 1,058 pupils and 132 teachers. In addition, children were sent to study in the Islamic countries (110 to Turkey, 56 to Malaysia, three to Libya, and two to Egypt).

Some concern may be justified when such aid is used to impose on girls and women the wearing of headscarves, and the conversion of orphanages into fortresses for the training of religious fanatics. But although it is true that some women have resumed wearing headscarves, that some young girls have started to walk in the streets covered by the grey sheet-like 'Islamic' dresses, and that a few unrepresentative *mullahs* have advocated introducing the *Sharia* law to combat Albania's endemic crime, such fears of a lurch to a new extremism do not seem well-founded.

Officials in Tirana have high hopes of further financial and other economic aid from the Muslim world – following the precept that all aid is welcome, whatever its source.

In an interview, Foreign Minister Alfred Serreqi, a Catholic, tried to dispel the notion that Islamic fundamentalism had a chance of gaining a substantial number of followers in Albania now that his country had joined the OIC. He stated:

As far as fundamentalism is concerned, it is a mixture of fanaticism and communist-type political doctrine. For fundamentalism to have a chance in Albania it must have a base, a social stratum with special inclinations: namely toward Islamic fanaticism, which has never existed in Albania. Historically, Albanians have never been religious fanatics. Fundamentalism has no base in Albania, where the Albanian religion is Albanianism.[8]

Joining the OIC was not Albania's first move towards the Muslim world. It had previously succeeded in attracting the support of the Islamic Development Bank (IDB). The bank was willing to invest in Albania and develop cooperation in all areas of the economy, including agriculture, education and transport. The chairman of the Bank noted that an economically strong and stable Albania would be a 'reliable factor' as far as the question of the ethnic Albanians in Kosovo was concerned.[9] This statement added a political dimension to the growing cooperation with Islamic states. Otherwise, for Albanians, drawing closer to these states is important mainly in terms of ameliorating economic conditions in the country.

The support of the Islamic Development Bank is just one example of the growing activity of international Muslim associations in Albania and the increased aid from various Islamic countries. Another example is the construction of the Islamic Educational Centre in Kavaja (a city in central Albania), financed by the Albanian branch of the Islamic Association of the Netherlands and the International Islamic Organisation.

In view of the turmoil and instability in the Balkan region, Albania has increasingly viewed Turkey as its best prospect for patronage and protection. Cooperation between the two countries has increased especially since 1992.[10] There have been numerous visits by high-level state and government delegations, including Turkish Prime Minister Suleyman Demirel's visit in the summer of 1992 and President Turgut Özal's official visit to Tirana from 18 to 20 February 1993. The latter was particularly important for Albania. President Özal offered a fifteen-year economic programme to help rebuild the country and develop tourism and financial institutions, plus additional military cooperation. Turkey provided Albania with economic and humanitarian aid; Turkish humanitarian food aid to Albania between January 1991 and December 1992 amounted to $21.9 million, the highest foreign contribution after Italy's. Turkish businessmen are also busy establishing a foothold in Albania, as was demonstrated in 1993 by the setting up of the Albanian–Turkish joint transportation venture *Alb-Balkan Interbus* and the commencement of flights four times a week between Tirana and Istanbul.

Scholarships have been granted to Albanian students for higher education, both civilian and military, in Turkey. These students, said to number over 1,100, are reportedly twice as numerous as the combined number of Albanian students now studying in Italy, Germany, United States, France and other countries. The most significant of these cooperative ventures was the opening of a Turkish high school in Tirana, financed and built by a Turkish educational foundation. There are also classes in 'religious culture', although the schools are ostensibly non-denominational; teaching is only in English and Turkish.

In pursuing closer links with the Islamic world, President Berisha appears concerned to maintain a certain balance. He has stressed that his country would 'always remain a secular state' but also acknowledged the growing influence of Islam.

As a counterbalance to this influence Berisha is seeking to improve Tirana's already good ties with the Vatican. On 25 April 1993 Pope John Paul II visited Albania, the first pontiff to do so. The Pope, for his part, stressed the neutral nature of his visit to Albania and that the trip was 'a great comfort' to the entire Albanian population. By making this comment, he was indicating that his visit should not be construed as an attempt to drive a wedge between Albania's religious denominations. Indeed, he stressed the need for religious tolerance and harmonious coexistence. He praised the Albanian Catholics for their 'exemplary relations of esteem and respect' towards the Islamic and Orthodox communities. After the establishment in 1991 – for the first time ever – of diplomatic relations between the Vatican and Albania, the Pope's visit allowed Albanian authorities to rebuff accusations that they were becoming too close to Muslim countries.

The situation does, of course, remain in a degree of flux, and so does the balancing act in foreign relations which the Berisha government, or any other, is likely to have to engage in over the next few years.

Notes

1   *Constitution of the People's Socialist Republic of Albania* (Tirana: 8 Nentori, 1977), p. 26.

2   The law has been at the draft stage since 1993 and, at the time of writing, had not yet been passed by Parliament.

3   These and following observations are based on fieldwork undertaken by the author over a number of years after the collapse of Albania's totalitarian system.

4   Taken from the Albanian newspaper *Koha Jonë*, 4 September 1993.

5   *RFE/RL Report*, Vol. 2, No. 7, 12 February 1993.

6   *Ibid.*

7   *Zëri i Rinisë* (Albanian Newspaper), 6 November 1992.

8   *RFE/RL Report*, Vol. 2, No. 7, 12 February 1993.

9   *Rilindja Demokratike* (Newspaper of the Democratic Party of Albania), 26 October 1992.

10   *RFE/RL Report*, Vol. 2, No. 1, 1 January 1993.

8

THE MUSLIM MINORITY IN GREECE

Yorgos Christidis

1. Introduction

Under the Lausanne Convention of 1923 there was a compulsory exchange of Turkish nationals of the Greek Orthodox religion established in Turkish territory and of Greek nationals of the Islamic religion established in Greek territory. The Muslims of western Thrace and the Greeks of Istanbul and of the two small islands at the entrance of Straits, Imvros and Tenedos, were excluded from the exchange. Their legal status was nevertheless defined by the same Lausanne Convention. For the Muslim minority in western Thrace and the Greek Orthodox minority of Istanbul, the convention provided a number of rights in order to preserve their religious and ethnic character. For the Greek population of Imvros and Tenedos, re-named later as Gokceada and Bozcaada, the convention provided for the establishment of a regime of limited autonomy.[1]

The Muslim minority in Greece includes three groups: the ethnic Turks, the Pomaks and the Athigani (also referred to as Gypsies, and reputedly descendants of Christian heretics expelled from Asia Minor during Byzantine rule). Greece distinguishes the minority into three categories: Turkish-speaking Muslims, Pomaks and Athigani. Turkey, which views the Pomaks as Turks, regards the minority as predominantly Turkish.[2]

The minority totalled around 120,000 in 1981. The numeric distribution of the minority, according to Greek sources, was 45 per cent for the Turkish-speaking Muslims, 36 per cent for the Pomaks and 18 per cent for the Athigani.[3] According to more recent Greek data the minority would have fallen to 114,000 by 1993 and was distributed in the three provinces of western Thrace as follows: 42,000 in Xanthi (23,000 Pomaks, 10,000 Turkish-speaking, 9,000

Athigani), 62,000 in Rodopi (11,000 Pomaks, 42,000 Turkish-speaking, 9,000 Athigani) and 10,000 in Evro (2,000 Pomaks, 2,000 Turkish-speaking, 6,000 Athigani).[4] The nature of, and variation in, self-identification among the different sections of this community has not been widely researched. It is clear, though, that it does vary considerably, and that in some village communities, and even within individuals, multiple, or plural, identification can be observed – depending in part on the context which is most relevant at a particular time or in a particular case.[5] There are thought to be some 35,000 Muslims in Athens, and another 15,000 in Rhodes and Chios. The early 1990s also saw an influx of Muslim refugees from Albania.[6]

2. The debate over discrimination

Members of the minority, Turkish and other foreign sources, consistently claim that the minority is facing a number of discriminations. 'The annual human rights report of the United States State Department in February 1991 referred to "a pattern of economic and social discrimination against the Muslim minority in Western Thrace"'[7] – a statement which elicited strong protest from the Greek government. In addition to the larger issues discussed below, the press organs of the Muslim minority in Greece, consisting of ten weeklies and five monthly magazines,[8] have lodged a number of other complaints ranging from delays in obtaining construction permits for houses and Mosques (including permits to restore Mosques), to difficulties in obtaining business and driving licences.[9] Perhaps the key areas of grievance, however, relate to land ownership, citizenship, the status of Islamic endowments, and education.

2.1. The land question

One of the most serious complaints concerns the reduction of the minority's ownership of land. It has been estimated that the minority's share of land holdings in their areas had by 1979 been reduced from 60 per cent to 20 per cent.[10] One of the main reasons for this has been the expropriation of land in the name of public interest.

Bahcheli gives an example of how the expropriation of land affects the minority:

> In May, 1978, 4,000 dunums were expropriated in the Amaranda, Vakos, Triorion and Pamforon villages of Komotini for use as industrial sites; another 4,300 were also expropriated in northwest Komotini in the Yaka region, and 3,000 dunums were expropriated in the same area to establish the proposed Dimocritos University. This last expropriation, in particular, evoked bitter criticism from the Turks, who complained that the land earmarked for Dimocritos University consisted of the prime irrigated farmland. A delegation of Turks submitted topographical plans and evidence to the Governor of Rodopi Prefecture and asked that less productive land in the immediate vicinity be used instead for a university campus. The Turks have also complained that the size of expropriated land far exceeded the need for the stated purpose; it was pointed out that the land area of the University of Thessaloniki is 640 dunums as compared to the 3,000 dunums for the proposed Dimocritos.[11]

Another reason is the reallocation of land. Such reallocation, beginning in western Thrace in 1967, did not benefit the minority as members of the minority received inferior land in exchange.[12]

A third cause, based on a law from 1948, is the combination of adjacent plots in order to create larger, more economical units. The owners of such land are entitled to be compensated by equivalent land elsewhere. According to Bahcheli,

> Turks whose lands were 'exchanged' in this manner have complained that they do not receive land of equivalent value in another area. Furthermore, whereas the initiative to combine parcels of land once rested with a majority of the landowners in the area, since 1974 . . . a change in the application of the law has empowered the governor to start the process.[13]

In addition, it is alleged that the minority is facing difficulties in purchasing land. Poulton finds that its members tend to be denied loans and credits.[14] Bahcheli even claims that 'an existing law has been used to deny Turkish applications for the purchase of land since 1965'.[15] However, Greek data relating to 1991 paint a different picture. According to these data, 285 legal acts of buying and selling land were conducted involving members of the minority in western Thrace in the course of that year. Of these, 169 concerned the transfer of land from Muslims to Muslims, 67 were transfers from Christians to Muslims and 49 from Muslims to Christians. The total surface of land transferred amounted to 1,006,776 square metres. The share of agricultural land in this was 954,367 sq m (439,229 sq m are listed as having been transferred from Muslims to Muslims, 222,558 sq m from Christian to Muslims and 292,580 from Muslims to Christians). The share of transferable land with housing was 52,409 sq m (42,279 sq m are listed as having been transferred from Muslims to Muslims, 10,130 sq m from Christian to Muslims).[16]

2.2. The status of the Islamic endowments

Complaints also abound that the authorities are trying to weaken and control the Islamic endowments (*vakif*) and the office of the Islamic leader (*mufti*). Until the military regime of 1967, muftis were elected by the members of the Muslim minority itself. The military regime, however, altered this practice, decreeing that they would henceforth be appointed by the Ministry of Religious Affairs, thus causing disaffection among the Muslim population. The latter has since been asking for the application of the law 2345/1920 on the election of new muftis. Greek sources argue that law 2345/1920 became 'non-active' with the signing of the Lausanne Convention in 1923; that no new mufti in western Thrace has ever been elected under law 2345/1920; and that, after all, there is no Islamic country where the election of religious leaders is based on popular election.[17] However, the Ministry of Religious Affairs has clearly not always made the right choices: in 1973 a Gypsy (Athigani) Muslim, Ahmet Damatoglu, previously an Imam, was appointed as Mufti of Dhidhimotikon without any qualifications.[18] More recently, in 1985, there was a controversy over the appointment of Meco Cemali, graduate of an Islamic university, as Mufti of Xanthi. Members of the minority challenged his appointment.[19]

Similarly, before the military regime of 1967, the directors of the *vakif* were elected by the Muslim minority. The military altered this practice too, by appropriating for themselves the power to nominate the directors. Later, in 1980, a new law stipulated that each *vakif* should be administered by a group of five, selected by the

Governor of the province, who was also empowered to approve the *vakif*'s budget. Additionally, the law provided that the minority's schools would stop receiving funding from the *vakifs*, receiving funding only from the Ministry of Education. This legislation generated strong displeasure among the Muslims. They protested, asking for its abrogation. The Turkish government also protested. The various provisions of the law have now been deferred by the Greek government.[20]

In 1987 the Greek High Court decided (decision 1729/20 November 1987) to forbid the use of the adjective 'Turkish' in the title of the Turkish Teachers Association of western Thrace (*Bati Trakya Turk Ogretmenler Birligi*), and of the Turkish Youth Association of Komotini (*Gumulcine Turk Genclik Birligi*). In January 1988 members of the minority organised a demonstration in front of the offices of the Turkish Youth Association, to protest against the decision. From the Greek point of view, Alexandris argues that the decision did not aim at disbanding the associations, which can continue operating if they change their titles; and that Ankara's reaction was not justified given the fact that Turkey never permitted the establishment of minority associations that had the adjective 'Greek' in their name.[21]

2.3. *Citizenship*

Another serious complaint relates to citizenship. Members of the minority who leave Greece, even for a temporary period, have been denied re-entry under Article 19 of the Greek Nationality Law 3370/1955. Article 19 states that:

> a person of non-Greek origin who leaves Greece with the intention of not returning, may be declared as having lost Greek nationality.

It is claimed that the law has been used by the authorities to deprive members of the minority of their Greek nationality when they travel abroad.[22]

2.4. Education

In the 1992/3 school term, there were 232 primary schools, 2 secondary schools and two religious schools (*medrese*) serving the minority. The number of minority students were: 9,050 in primary education; 1,602 in secondary education (678 of whom were enrolled at minority secondary schools and medreses, and 924 at non-minority secondary schools).[23]

A number of complaints have been raised concerning educational matters. The first regards the state of primary schools. According to Bahcheli,

> most of these schools consist of dilapidated, one-room buildings, without adequate facilities or equipment. It is common to have one-classroom schools for the first to sixth grades. Under these circumstances, the quality of the education received is very poor.[24]

A second complaint concerns the limited number of secondary minority schools. As Bahcheli points out, it is remarkable that there are only two secondary schools for a population of 120,000.[25]

According to Poulton, the authorities have steadily increased teaching in Greek at the expense of Turkish,[26] although under the Greek-Turkish cultural agreements of 1951 and 1968, Turkish was established as the only educational language for the minority. Alexandris expresses the opinion prevalent in Greece, when arguing that the inadequate knowledge of Greek among the minority has negative implications for their employment: hence the necessity to improve their Greek language ability, for reasons of employment and social mobility.[27]

Although after 1953/4 the Greek authorities began to withdraw specially translated books for the minority schools,[28] using instead books introduced from Turkey, imported Turkish books face excessive delays, resulting in outdated textbooks having to be used. The quality of teachers used in the minority schools is described by some as inadequate as a result of deliberate policies by the Greek authorities. Poulton charges that since 1968 only graduates from the Special Academy in Thessaloniki have been permitted to teach in the minority schools, whereas graduates of teacher-training colleges in Turkey have not been allowed to teach.[29] Greek data give the following number for teachers, employed in minority primary schools, in the academic year 1992/3: out of a total number of 432 teachers, 219 are listed as graduates of the Special Academy in Thessaloniki; 98 as graduates of Turkish colleges; 97 as graduates of religious schools in western Thrace; 11 as graduates of secondary schools (it is not specified if these are minority schools or not); and 7 as graduates of primary schools.[30] This would seem to indicate that some appointments of teachers trained in Turkey have continued to be made, even if the data do not show whether these appointments are post-1968.

The Greek authorities have denied any responsibility for poor facilities and poor education. However, available data show that there has been a reduction in the number of pupils enrolled in minority primary schools over the period 1990–3: from 9,629 in the academic year 1990/1, to 9,050 in 1992/3. At the same time, there has been an increase in the number of minority students enrolled in non-minority secondary schools, during the same period: from 787 in 1990/1, to 924 in 1992/3.[31] Most importantly, according to Oran the illiteracy rate among the Turks in Greece is an estimated 60 per cent, compared with 14.2 per cent for the total population of Greece.[32]

2.5. *Emigration to Turkey*

There has been a continuous trend of emigration to Turkey, although precise figures are lacking. It is estimated that during the period 1939–51 some 20,000 left for Turkey,[33] followed by a further 20,000 in the course of the 1950s.[34] Oran even claims that the number of those who have emigrated to Turkey far exceeds those currently living in western Thrace.[35] As a result of such emigration, the minority population has remained steady for 70 years now, whereas the average annual birth rate of 28 per thousand would normally have led to at least a trebling of the population.

The reasons behind this phenomenon need not be monocausal. Turkish sources cite discrimination as the major reason.[36] Wilson has commented that

> emigration . . . is not necessarily or simply the result of discrimination. Emigration to Turkey could be a natural outcome of ethnic and religious affiliation or of a belief that Turkish cities

provide more opportunities than Greek cities for Turkish-speaking Muslims.[37]

Additionally, historical events such as World War II and the ensuing Greek Civil War of 1946–9 could provide a further explanation for the emigration of the 1940s. Whatever the objective accuracy of the claims of discrimination, however, it seems likely that a *sense* of discrimination, at least, will have contributed to the persistence of the phenomenon.

3. The matter of Ahmet Sadik and Ibrahim Serif

In August 1986, Ahmet Sadik, a representative of the Turkish-speaking Muslim minority in Thrace, was arrested along with a colleague and held for a few days. In a trial held later in Thessaloniki, he was sentenced to two and a half years imprisonment, while his co-defendant, Ibrahim Serif, received a 15-month sentence, on charges of spreading false information and falsifying signatures. They had sent a petition to the United Nations and the Council of Europe alleging a policy of assimilation and forced emigration by the Greek authorities.[38] Both were released pending appeal which was due to be held in December 1988, but was eventually postponed. Ahmet Sadik was elected as a Member of Parliament in the national elections of July 1989, standing as an independent candidate, with some 32 per cent of the vote.

In January 1990, Sadik and Serif were both sentenced to 18 months' imprisonment and three years' deprivation of civil rights. The charges related to an election leaflet distributed by Sadik and Molla Rodoplu, prior to the elections of November 1989. In it they called on Turks to vote for them as independent Muslim candidates standing on a list called 'Trust'. They stated that the main Greek political parties 'spread an atmosphere of terror in the towns and villages' in order to intimidate the minority and gain their votes. Ahmet and Serif were charged under Article 163 of the Penal Code, 'spreading false information' (because of this claim of 'Terror'), and Article 192, which penalises those 'provoking or inciting citizens to acts of violence amongst themselves or to mutual discord and disrupting the public peace', for claiming the existence of a Turkish

minority in Greece.[39] According to Amnesty International there
was no indication that they had advocated violence. In March 1990,
Sadik and Serif were released following appeal. The appeal court
reduced their prison sentences to 15 months and 10 months respectively and allowed them to pay a fine instead of serving the rest of
their sentences.[40] In the national elections of April 1990, Ahmet
Sadik was re-elected MP.

4. The Greek position and fears of Turkish interference

The Greek authorities have denied allegations that they follow a
policy of discrimination against the Muslim minority. Furthermore,
as the Muslim minority enjoys the right of seeking recourse to both
the European Court of Justice and the Commission of Human Rights
of the Council of Europe,[41] Greek sources argue that the use of these
mechanisms could prove whether allegations concerning systematic
discriminations against the minority are real or whether, instead,
they constitute an inflation of a limited number of cases, which are
not the result of a deliberate political decision but rather of social
and economic conditions.[42]

Greek officials find it hard to accept Ankara's concern for the
rights of the minority given the fate of the Greek Orthodox minority in Istanbul. In 1923 the prosperous Greek Orthodox minority in
Istanbul numbered around 110,000. At the end of the 1980s there
were only around 3,500.[43] Hostility and legal harassment by the
Turkish authorities and even physical violence, as in the case of
the anti-Greek riots of 6–7 September 1955 in Istanbul and Izmir,
generated an atmosphere of fear and insecurity for the minority
that led to its near extinction. The fate of the Greek population of
Gokceada and Bozcaada was similar. As a result of open hostility
by the Turkish authorities, the combined Greek population of the
two islands was reduced from over 9,000 in 1920 to under 800 in the
mid-1980s.[44]

Some Greek analysts, as well as much of the political class and
the population at large, view with suspicion and growing concern
Turkey's intentions with regard to the Muslim minority. It is argued
that Turkey is trying to promote a Turkish national character in
the minority and, once this is achieved, will try to promote at an

international level the demand for self-governing and even autonomous status for the minority in western Thrace. Already the idea
of autonomy is propagated inside the minority by various pan-Turkic
magazines, such as *Yeni Bati Trakya* ('New Western Thrace'), *Bati
Trakya Turku* ('West Thracian Turk') and *Sesimiz* ('Our Voice'). It is
alleged that Turkey is using the Turkish Consulate in Komotini (the
administrative capital of one of the three provinces that comprise
western Thrace) and a core of nationalist elements of the minority
to promote its aims.[45]

Many Greek analysts believe that Turkey is trying to use the issue
of the minority as a diplomatic weapon against Greece. Thus Ankara
is attempting to use the minority, it is argued, in order to press
Athens to make concessions on the whole range of issues dividing
the two sides, especially over Cyprus and the Aegean. Furthermore
there is concern that Turkey might attempt to use the minority in
case of a Greek–Turkish war. According to Alexandris, 'the Muslim
minority, following the case of Cyprus, could provide a perfect
pretext for a Turkish "intervention" in western Thrace for the "protection of its Turkish brothers".'[46]

Rejecting this interpretation of Turkey's aims in western Thrace,
Bahcheli argues that Turkey has not had any intention of disputing
'Greek sovereignty in western Thrace. Moreover, despite the widespread abuses of the Turks' rights in Greece, especially since the
mid-1950s Turkish policy-makers have not assigned the issue as much
importance as' the disputes over Cyprus and the Aegean. Greek
anxieties notwithstanding, he concludes, Turkey has shown no interest in challenging the status quo. He adds that among the Muslims
of Thrace there is a widely held belief that

Turkey has not pressured Greece vigorously enough in defence
of their rights. Accordingly, in recent years, the community
has turned to other states, especially Muslim countries, and to
international human rights institutions to publicise their case
to exert pressure on the Greek government. A highly publicised
appeal was made to the ambassadors of the Islamic states in
Greece in 1981 in response to the new law severely restricting
the wakf.[47]

5. Conclusion

Even if the extent of actual discrimination against the Muslim minority in Greece can be vigorously debated, it would appear that there is a significant *sense* of discrimination among sections of the minority. There is no doubt over the sensitivity which the ethno-religious issue has in Greek national political and security considerations – tied, perhaps, to the nation's still recent memory of its national struggle, but certainly, and very specifically, to the regional context of rivalry with Turkey (this itself closely connected to that struggle). The two-way linkage between the position of the Muslim minority on the one hand, and regional relations on the other, remains highly salient. If further evidence of this was needed, it came in the shape of deteriorating relations with Albania in the Summer of 1994, when Greece expelled several thousand illegal (and, by some accounts, many legal) Albanian migrants in retaliation for the arrest of a number of ethnic Greek activists in Albania. Although the deportees were not part of Greece's own indigenous Muslim minority, the potential linkages in such developments (at the level of regional relations, Greek politics, and popular perceptions among majority as well as minority), highlight the problematic questions surrounding the position of the Muslim community in Greece.

Notes

1   C. Rozakis, 'Ena Synafes Zitima: H. Mousoulmaniki Meionotita tis Dytikis
     Thrakis' [A Relative Issue: The Muslim Minority of Western Thrace] in
     Sychroni Elliniki Exoteriki Politiki [Modern Greek Foreign Policy] (Athens:
     Sakoulas, 1989), p. 63.

2   Concerning the identity of the Pomaks, Turkish sources claim the
     Pomaks are probably the descendants of the Cumans, a Turkic-speaking
     group that settled in the area in the 11th and 12th centuries and later
     adopted the Slavic language (Pomaks throughout the Balkans are usually
     labelled as speaking Bulgarian). Moreover, the same sources claim that
     the Pomaks consider themselves Turks. See K. Karpat, 'Bulgaria's Methods
     of Nation Building: The Annihilation of Minorities', *International Journal
     of Turkish Studies*, Vol. 4, No. 2, Fall/Winter 1989, p. 7.

3   A. Alexandris, 'Oi Mousoulmanoi tis Dytikis Thrakis' [The Muslims of
     western Thrace] in *Oi Ellinotourkikes Sxeseis, 1923–1987* [Greek–Turkish
     Relations, 1923–1987] (Athens: Greek Institution of Foreign and
     Defense Policy, Gnosy, 1988), p. 524.

4   *Kathimerini*, 14 March 1993.

5   According to research by Y. Frangopoulos, 'The Muslim Minority of
     Pomacs in Greece', paper presented at the Conference on *Islam in
     Europe: Generation to Generation*, Oxford University, 5–7 April 1993.

6   F. Shaikh (ed.), *Islam and Islamic Groups: A World-Wide Reference Guide*
     (London: Longman, 1992), p. 85.

7   *Ibid.*, p. 86.

8   The ten weekly newspapers are: *Akin* (started publication in 1957), *Ileri*
     (1975), *Gertsek* (1977), *Balkan* (1992), *Ortam* (November 1992),
     Trakianin Sesi (1982), *Gorus* (1991), *Tunel* (1989), *Aile Birlik* (1989),
     Dialogo (end 1992). All, apart from *Trakianin Sesi* which is published
     in Xanthi, are published in Komotini. Some of the editors are: Hasan
     Hatipoglou, a former MP (*Akin*); Salih Halil (*Ileri*); Ismail Mola
     Rodoplou, another former MP (*Gertsek*); Ahmet Sadik, MP (*Balkan*);
     Nazim Refica, a former teacher (*Aile Birlik*); Aidin Omeroglou (*Dialogo*).
     The publishing company Tanpinar is responsible for *Ortam*. *Gorus* is
     the official newspaper of the Mufti of Komotini, and is edited by his
     secretary, Abdouhalim Dede. The five monthly magazines are: *Yuvamiz*,
     published since 1987, with Hafouz Mustafa as its editor; *Yani Haka Davet*,
     published since 1983, edited by Ahmet Hatziosman; two children's
     magazines, *Arcadas Cocuk* and *Pinar Cocuk*; and a literature magazine
     Safak (*Kathimerini*, 4 April 1993).

9   Alexandris, *op. cit.*, p. 533; also Poulton, *op. cit.*, p. 33.

10   A. Wilson, *The Aegean Dispute*, Adelphi Papers, No. 151, Winter 1979/80
     (London: The International Institute for Strategic Studies, 1979). Oran
     raises the percentage of minority ownership of land in the area to 84 per
     cent at the time of the Lausanne Treaty of 1923; B. Oran, *Turk-Yunan
     Iliskilerinde Bati Trakya Sorunu* [The western Thrace Question in
     Greek–Turkish Relations] (Ankara: Mulkiyeliler Birligi Vakfi Yayinlari,

1986), p. 120, cited in T. Bahcheli, *Greek–Turkish Relations Since 1955* (Boulder/London: Westview Press, 1990), p. 178.

11   *Ibid.*, p. 179.

12   H. Poulton, *Minorities in the Balkans*, The Minority Rights Group Report, No. 82 (London: Minority Rights Group, October 1989), p. 33. Bahcheli argues that 'in accordance with a 1952 law, land holdings that exceeded the legally allowable 500 dunums were expropriated for subsequent distribution to landless peasants. Virtually no landless Turks have benefited from such re-distribution.' (*ibid.*)

13   *Ibid.*

14   Poulton, *op. cit.*, p. 33.

15   Bahcheli, *op. cit.*, p. 33.

16   *Kathimerini*, 28 February 1993.

17   Alexandris, *op. cit.*, p. 531.

18   Poulton, *op. cit.*, p. 33.

19   Alexandris, *op. cit.*, p. 531. According to Poulton, p. 33, Cemali resigned immediately, as a result of protests by the minority. He was replaced six months later by another appointee.

20   Bahcheli, *op. cit.*, p. 181.

21   In 1925 the Turkish authorities forbade the operation of the Greek Literature Association of Istanbul. The same fate befell both the Association of Greek Doctors and the Association of Greek Lawyers in Istanbul. When in 1933 the Turkish authorities permitted the establishment of the Greek Association of Istanbul, the registration of members was limited only to those that had a Greek citizenship and forbidden to those members of the minority that had Turkish citizenship. (Alexandris, *op. cit.*, p. 530.)

22   Bahcheli, *op. cit.*, p. 182.

23   *Kathimerini*, 28 February 1993.

24   Bahcheli, *op. cit.*, p. 180.

25   *Ibid.*

26   Poulton, *op. cit.*, p, 33.

27   Alexandris, *op. cit.*, pp. 532–3.

28   *Ibid.*

29   Poulton, *op. cit.*, p. 33; and Bahcheli, *op. cit.*, pp. 180–1.

30   *Kathimerini*, 28 February 1993.

31   *Ibid.*

32   Oran, *op. cit.*, cited in Bahcheli, *op. cit.*, p. 181.

33   Poulton, *op. cit.*, p. 32.

34   Bahcheli, *op. cit.*, p. 177.

35   Oran, *op. cit.*, p. 8, cited in Bahcheli, *op. cit.*, p. 178.

36   See for instance Bahcheli, *op. cit.*, p. 178.

37   A. Wilson, *The Aegean Dispute*, Adelphi Papers, No. 151, Winter 1979/80 (London: The International Institute for Strategic Studies, 1979), p. 17.

38   Poulton, *op. cit.*, p. 33.

39   H. Poulton, *The Balkans:, Minorities and States in Conflict* (London: Minority Rights Publications, 1993), p. 187.

40   *Amnesty International Report 1991*, p. 99.
41   In 1985 Greece ratified Article 25 of the Convention of Rome for the Protection of Human Rights and Fundamental Freedoms. Under this Article, each individual has the right to seek recourse to the European Commission of Human Rights in order to protect himself from state activities. (Rozakis, *op. cit.*, p. 64.)
42   *Ibid.*
43   Alexandris, *op. cit.*, p. 515.
44   Bahcheli, *op. cit.*, p. 176.
45   Greek sources claim that the Mufti of Xanthi, Mustafa Hilmi, who died in February 1990, and his son Aga Mehmet, have been spreading politically provocative messages challenging the authority of the Greek administration in the area. Aga Mehmet, in particular, has been accused of organising various activities aiming at strengthening the influence of nationalistic elements in the minority. See Alexandris, *op. cit.*, pp. 527–9.
46   *Ibid.*, p. 535.
47   Bahcheli, *op. cit.*, pp. 182–3.

PART III
WESTERN EUROPE

9

MUSLIMS, THE STATE, AND THE PUBLIC SPHERE IN BRITAIN

Steven Vertovec

1. Introduction

Although substantial numbers of Muslims have been present in Britain for well over a century, particularly in the form of foreign sailors who settled in port cities, it has only been since the Second World War that significant communities immigrated, settled and impacted in a variety of ways upon the British public sphere. In the immediate postwar years, the changing economic structure and the expansion of industry resulted in a need for cheap labour for undesirable jobs. Ex-colonies provided a ready source of such labour, particularly the South Asian subcontinent where active labour recruitment campaigns were undertaken by British employers. Chain migration patterns emerged among the young men who informed each other of work possibilities in Britain. They came with the intent of working, accumulating a given sum to support family members and to invest in resources back home, and of eventually returning to the subcontinent. By the 1960s the British government legislated various acts to stem the flow of migrants from abroad, although women and dependent children were generally allowed to join the men. The latter gradually came to replace their original livelihood strategies with ones based on longer-term, and eventually permanent, settlement in Britain. Subsequently, in the early 1970s, an influx of South Asian refugees from East Africa again added considerably to the number of Muslims living in Britain.

In the early 1950s, when labour migration from the South Asian subcontinent was in its early phases, the Muslim population of Britain was around 23,000. By 1961, Peach estimates there were about

82,000 Muslims in the country, rising to about 369,000 by 1971, some 553,000 by 1981, and about one million by 1991.[1] Although the Muslim population of Britain comprises large numbers of Arabs, Malaysians, Iranians, Turks and Turkish Cypriots, Nigerians and others, some 80 per cent of Muslims in Britain trace their origins to Pakistan, Bangladesh and India (albeit, for many of the latter, by way of East Africa). Not surprisingly, it is among this group that developments affecting the public sphere have had their greatest impact.

2. Muslims and the British 'public sphere'

Over the past ten years, Muslims have increasingly become conspicuous in the British 'public sphere' (defined for our purposes as that generalised sociological space of collective, 'dominant' discourses promulgated by news and entertainment media, material produced by a variety of social movements, discussions among and between political parties, studies and debates among academics, and policies and undertakings among government and social service agencies). This perceived increase is primarily due to the discrete – though in the public sphere, not wholly unconnected – processes surrounding (a) the emergence of effective organisation and political articulation among British Muslims, and (b) among non-Muslims, the construction of 'Islamic fundamentalism' as a global threat to democratic values and social systems.

British Muslims first prominently engaged the national public sphere in the early 1980s with regard to matters surrounding the provision of *halal* (Islamically permitted) food in schools and other public institutions such as prisons and hospitals. Muslim organisations engaged local government and educational authorities with calls for such provision, and this relatively new strength of Muslim purpose was given increasing attention in newspapers and public meetings. One of the key issues at stake was not the provision itself, but the fact that Islamic ritual slaughter (*dhabh*) was abhorred by many non-Muslims, since it is often interpreted as prescribing that the animal remain conscious when its throat is slit. The most vocal opponents to Muslim calls for *halal* food provision consequently emerged as the rather strange bedfellows of animal rights activists,

who were against the method of slaughter, and right-wing nationalists who were against accommodating seemingly alien customs of
minorities.[2] The right to engage in ritual slaughter was maintained,
largely through the political lobbying of Jewish rather than Muslim
groups, and provision of *halal* food soon became standard practice
in public institutions of many kinds, schools not least.

With the *halal* campaign behind them, with new British-reared
young Muslims entering into the picture, and with Muslim organisations becoming ever more effective in engaging the public
domain, by the mid-1980s Muslims increasingly voiced their concerns more strongly with regard to educational provisions in state
schools. This coincided with a period in which 'multiculturalism'
gained a central place in educational philosophy throughout Britain.
Muslim concerns and non-Muslim debates over multicultural education converged and gained widespread notoriety in 'the Honeyford
Affair'.[3] The conservative and confrontational statements surrounding the accommodation of (mainly Asian) minorities in British state
schools, made in a right-wing journal by Bradford head teacher Ray
Honeyford, stimulated much public debate over the place of minorities in British society, strategies of assimilation or cultural pluralism,
and whether an apparently racist head teacher should be in charge
of a largely Asian school. Throughout the debate, Bradford Muslims
held demonstrations calling for his removal. Honeyford was eventually convinced by his local educational authority to take early
retirement; nonetheless, education had become firmly established as
a key sphere of concern and public engagement for Muslims and
the wider society.

The attention reaped by the Honeyford Affair was soon sur-
passed by 'the Rushdie Affair'.[4] Though it was some time after the
book was actually published, the 'Affair' rapidly broadened and
eventually concretised (in a negative fashion) Muslims' place in
the public sphere. The nature of media coverage surrounding the
Rushdie Affair transformed the dominant view toward Muslims in
Britain.[5] The book-burning in Bradford on 14 January 1989 (orches-
trated by Muslim groups as a media event, yet without much fore-
thought as to its 1930s Nazi allusion) was seized upon by the press as
evidence of an 'uncivilised' and 'intolerant' Muslim nature. The
Ayatollah Khomeini's *fatwa* of 14 February 1989, calling for the death
of Salman Rushdie, was taken as further evidence of this, portrayed
as a worldwide Muslim threat which had infested the body Britain.

Little attention was ever given to the Muslims' own perceptions and feelings of offence and hurt laying underneath the public demonstrations. Media treatment of the Rushdie Affair (which, it must be said, included some irresponsible and inflammatory statements by alleged 'Muslim leaders') created or bolstered an image of a Muslim population, homogeneous in anti-modern values and dangerous in its passions, which posed a challenge both to nationalist ideologies of 'Britishness'[6] and to liberal notions surrounding freedom and human rights.[7] Thus by 1990, albeit in a largely undesirable manner, Muslims had gained a firm place on the national political agenda.

Not long after the Rushdie Affair had been quelled, during the Gulf War public attention was again cast upon the British Muslim population. Because they were portrayed generally as somehow linked to a worldwide anti-West, Islamic fundamentalist movement, the loyalty of British Muslims to the allied cause against Iraq was questioned.[8]

Since then, newspapers have given considerable attention to a great variety of Muslim-related matters, including education (especially the battle for a recently turned-down request for government funding of the Islamia school in Brent), mosque disputes, and almost anything to do with the so-called Muslim Parliament or any utterance by its leader Kalim Siddiqui. Further, in March 1993 the BBC's flagship news programme *Panorama* was controversially devoted to 'lifting the veil' of the alleged Muslim 'underclass' in Britain, whose evidence of low educational attainment, high unemployment and ghetto isolation was spuriously linked with a supposed drift toward family violence, prostitution and drug-linked crime. In addition to these national examples, Muslim citizens and Muslim issues have increasingly engaged local public spheres as well.[9]

The establishment of the Muslim position in the public sphere has co-evolved with ideologies of multiculturalism and 'the politics of difference' which implicitly tend to fix and 'essentialise' or stereotype cultural and communal identities. Hence '*the* Muslim community' is often evoked in this sphere. The late 1980s and early 1990s have also been characterised by public concerns, on an international scale, with an undefined global movement called 'Islamic fundamentalism' characterised by terrorist methods, anti-Western rhetoric, and anti-modern, anti-liberal sentiments.[10] Essentialist notions of 'culture' – by which all persons of a particular descent are considered to have the same social relationships, behaviours and values – promulgate an understanding by which there is such a thing as '*the* Muslim community' which, further, must in essence be of the same nature as 'those fundamentalists' seen in North Africa or the Middle East. Muslim Fundamentalists make political demands; they are a threat to Western established social and philosophical order; British Muslims increasingly make political demands; therefore, the 'commonsense' logic runs, British Muslims must pose a parallel, if not identical, fundamentalist threat. Yet when one examines the kinds of demands made by British Muslim organisations and spokesmen, it is apparent they are for the most part only asking for an exercise of liberal rights according to wholly British procedures and standards. But because these are made by Muslims – tarred with the same brush as Middle East extremists – the demands are usually not perceived as such.

A brief review of structural considerations, facets of discrimination and accommodation, and potential ways forward may help to put British Muslim demands in perspective.

3. Some structural-political considerations

3.1. *Citizenship and voting rights*

Until 1962, British colonial subjects held identical citizenship with persons born in Britain. Hence immigration into Britain posed no serious legal problems, as overseas subjects were given right of free access. In that year, legislation was enacted which restricted entry to foreign subjects; a series of subsequent legal Acts (1968, 1969, 1971) have done so further, effectively cutting off primary immigration and making extremely difficult secondary immigration (that is, of spouses and dependants).[11] The 1962 Commonwealth Immigrants Act cut off the right of access of British citizens of Commonwealth countries; the 1971 Immigration Act created classes of persons based on degree of 'Britishness'. In 1981, the British Nationality Act removed the right to automatic citizenship of those born in Britain to immigrant parents (this must now be applied for). Nevertheless, in contrast with immigrant-descent minorities in most European countries, Blacks and Asians in Britain today are citizens, having entered as immigrants with citizenship rights or having gained citizenship after being born here.

Along with citizenship, they have full voting rights in local and national elections (again, in contrast with other European states). The size and impact of 'the Muslim vote', especially in local elections, is not insubstantial, but it is often exaggerated.[12] Muslims in Britain tend overwhelmingly to support the Labour Party (on the one hand, there is considerable Muslim support since Tories are branded as racist and since some Labour politicians were sympathetic to Muslim sentiments during the Rushdie Affair and in calls for Islam-friendly educational provisions; yet on the other hand, some Muslims think Labour has deeply failed Muslims on these and other issues).[13] In 1991 the Islamic Party of Great Britain contested its first seat; then, and since, it never received much support, however. The Islamic Party now has reconciled itself to being more of a local lobbying movement than a political party *per se.*

3.2. *National representative bodies*

The Muslim Parliament is an organisation with high aspirations of speaking on behalf of all British Muslims; up to now it is unrepresentative (members are selected from local sources) and largely only self-serving. Its forerunner, the Muslim Institute, published *The Muslim Manifesto* which was to be a comprehensive set of 'general guidelines for the life of the Muslim individual in Britain'. While faithfully conveying the feelings of many British Muslims, it also propounded a number of less common views.[14] The vociferous leader of the Parliament and Institute, Dr Kalim Siddiqui, is loved by the non-Muslim media for his willing ability to say controversial things of an extreme and separatist nature (foremost were his statements in support of the Ayatollah Khomeini's *fatwa* against Salman Rushdie and, at the opening of the Muslim Parliament in January 1992, his suggestion that British Muslims be willing to engage in acts of civil disobedience with regard to aspects of British law and society considered unIslamic). Many other Muslim leaders throughout the country disdain his statements and media coverage. Other national Muslim bodies, particularly the Union of Muslim Organisations of the UK and Eire (UMO) and the United Kingdom Action Committee for Islamic Affairs (UKACIA), are prominent lobbying groups with greater credibility in the eyes of Muslims and non-Muslims alike. On the whole, however, British Muslims are without a common, authoritative or representative voice in the public sphere.

3.3. *Local representative bodies*

One recent survey (conducted by the Religious Resources Centre, University of Derby and the Inter-Faith Network for the UK) suggests there are some 950 Muslim organisations in Britain. By far the bulk of these are very localised, serving specific regional/linguistic or even family/caste-based groups in one part of a city or neighbourhood. Such organisations are generally not lobbying groups, tending instead to keep themselves to themselves in order to organise specific functions. Credit must be given to them and their leaders, particularly for their role in the early days (1960s) when the local British public sphere was new to them and they to it. Notwithstanding their own unfamiliarity with British local government structures and British ignorance of Islamic values, they managed to gain a number of significant concessions and accommodations including planning permission for mosques, permission to perform religious slaughter, and sites for Muslim burial.[15] Times have changed considerably. Now, not only are such matters permitted routinely, Muslim organisations are regularly included in local government consultations regarding community relations matters. In some cities, they have effectively linked to provide a common front in dealing with local and county authorities (the Bradford Council of Mosques and Leicester's Federation of Muslim Organisations being two successful examples). It has been on this local level that Muslim political engagement has emerged most strongly. Nielsen makes the following observation:

> The decade until 1988 had witnessed a major change in the way in which Muslim organisations took part in public life. They had previously been marginal and often timid; they had tended to implicitly present themselves as ethnic minorities as they sought to fit in through the community and race relations structures. By the end of the decade many had laid claim to participation in the public space; they had effectively integrated into the organisational politics of the local scene functioning like most other special interest groups, standing out only by the express Muslim identity.[16]

One reason for this shift is doubtless Muslims' greater familiarity with, and confidence in engaging with, formal structures such as government agencies. Part of this familiarity and confidence came through the emergence of a younger, largely Britain-raised generation of Muslim community activists and organisers. Another reason for the shift is probably linked to the changes in the late 1970s and early 1980s surrounding local government funding of minority groups.

3.4. *Public resources*

In Great Britain, religious institutions receive no direct support from the state, as in for instance Belgium, although they can qualify as charities for tax advantages.[17] Matters relating to public aid for immigrant religious groups have long come under the scope of ethnic minority funding. During the 1960s and 1970s local authorities throughout Britain, regardless of political orientation, were reluctant to accede much by way of minority resourcing:

> Indeed at that time any pandering to racial minority demand leading to separate provision was seen on the political Right as an attack on the doctrine of assimilation and as a concession to 'communalism' – the enemy within, while on the Left it was feared as a manifestation 'of the colour bar' and as a concession to racism and fascism.[18]

With the rise of multiculturalist discourses, the 1980s ushered in a 'new political drive towards pluralistic welfare provision'.[19] Subsequently many local authorities began to make funding more available as part of wider moves toward empowering (some critics would say co-opting) minority groups. These moves often resulted in 'the politicisation of ethnicity, a process where the state elicits certain claims from social categories which could previously be loosely described as cultural or religious enclaves'.[20] Many local government authorities long maintained formal policies precluding the extension of funding toward any kind of religious activities, institutions or centres. At times, some authorities bent their own policies, with the collusion of ethnic-religious organisations, by way of calling certain groups, activities or centres 'cultural' rather than 'religious'. Other authorities specifically rolled back their preclusions and offered funds to religious communities deemed ethnically different. With regard to Muslims in particular, this often had negative consequences. For example, Ellis describes how Coventry City Council's policy on resourcing and view of '*the* Muslim community' fostered competition for Council funding among rival Islamic organisations and Muslim leaders which, in turn, deeply divided the bulk of the local Muslim population.[21]

4. Facets of discrimination and accommodation

In recent years the rise of specifically anti-Muslim forms of racism has lead to calls for new or extended legislation. It was doubtless the 'Rushdie Affair' which fuelled these forms and propelled into the public sphere numerous examples, issues and questions surrounding Muslims, anti-Muslims, and the facets of law.[22]

At present, Muslims *qua* Muslims are not protected from discrimination by law in Britain. An important ruling by the House of Lords in 1983 (*Mandla v. Dowell-Lee*, following a head teacher's refusal to allow a Sikh boy to wear a turban in school) established that Sikhs, and by extension, Jews, are considered an 'ethnic group' and are thus protected by the 1976 Race Relations Act. However, a case in 1988 (*Nyazi v. Rymans Ltd.*, concerning an employer's refusal to allow an employee time off to celebrate *Eid al-Fitr*) ruled that Muslims do not constitute such a group, and, therefore, are not protected by the Act, since their regional and linguistic origins are more diverse. The implications of this ruling were evident in a 1991 case (*Commission for Racial Equality v. Precision Engineering Ltd.*) after an employer blatantly stated that he refused to employ Muslims because he considered them 'extremist': he was found guilty only of 'indirect discrimination' against Asians (since most British Muslims are of such descent), while his anti-Muslim sentiments were unassailed. More recently, Muslim workers in Yorkshire mills have alleged that Muslims are treated worse than other employees with respect to tasks, pay, and holiday benefits.[23]

With the support of Muslim organisations and Muslim newspapers, the Commission for Racial Equality (CRE) has advocated measures to redress the situation.[24] This includes a call for legislators to consider enacting special laws (as there is in Northern Ireland) on religious discrimination and on incitement to religious hatred, similar to existing laws with regard to racial discrimination and incitement to racial hatred. It also sees the need for change in the law concerning blasphemy: at present, only Christianity is protected under such law (a feature historically linked to the legal 'establishment' of the Church of England as official national religion.[25] Critics say that by its nature, 'establishment' reduces all other denominations and faiths to a kind of second-class status.[26] One telling example of the Church of England's dominance is the presence of twenty-six Anglican bishops in the House of Lords). The CRE and others believe that the blasphemy law should either be extended to other faiths, or be abolished altogether. Many Muslims prefer the former option, since this, they say, would therefore remove *The Satanic Verses* from British bookshops. A law protecting ethnic minorities by way of group libel or defamation has also been mooted,[27] an option which would, in fact, bring Britain into line with its international law obligations (including the International Covenant on Civil and Political Rights, and the UN Declaration on the Elimination of All Forms of Intolerance and Discrimination based on Religion or Belief).[28]

Education represents another key area of public debate engaging British Muslims and questions of discrimination and accommodation.[29] Here, Muslim organisations, Muslim educationalists and other Muslim spokesmen have become increasingly articulate and effective in voicing concerns, and gaining, in many cases, concessions from local state authorities.[30] With regard to Muslim pupils in state schools, among such concerns are:

- the provision of *halal* food in cafeterias,

- allowing time off school for attendance of Friday prayers at mosques,

- designating space as prayer facilities for Muslims students and staff in the school,

- recognition of Islamic religious holidays,

- preservation of female modesty by way of school uniforms (allowing *shalwar-kameez*, traditional forms of South Asian dress) and in Physical Education and swimming classes (allowing track suits instead of shorts for girls in the former, providing single-sex sessions and separate shower stalls for the former and latter),

- ample presence of Muslim staff and governors,

- a place for Islamic religious education in schools (distinct from – some would argue, opposed to – the 'comparative religion' approach used in most state school religious education classes), and

- sympathetic treatment of Muslim values, society and history in the curriculum of a variety of subjects.

There has also been much concern voiced over maintaining all-girl state schools, where many Muslims prefer to send their daughters. Additionally, Muslims have continued to campaign – to date, unsuccessfully – for 'voluntary aided status' for selected Muslim schools (whereby state funds would be available for non-state schools, such as already provided for most Catholic and Jewish schools). The government's August 1993 decision against granting voluntary aided status to Islamia school in Brent, on the grounds that there were too many surplus places in other schools in the area (although the 180-pupil Islamia school itself has a waiting list of over 1,000), struck a profound blow to Muslim educational efforts. In so doing, it exacerbated Muslim feelings of discrimination in the educational sphere.

There are several aspects of what is usually referred to as family law in Britain which currently have a bearing on Muslims. Legal specialists have been examining this field for some years now, and while few legal adjustments have actually been made in the system, in the legal profession there has been a growing call for greater sensitivity toward rulings involving traditional South Asian and Islamic values and precedents concerning marriage, polygamy and divorce, inheritance, burial, and religious slaughter.[31]

Finally, there are many areas of discrimination generally concerning government and social service provision. In a consultative paper submitted to the Commission for Racial Equality, British Muslim journalists highlighted a number of these, including:

> same-race adoption and fostering policies which place black Muslims with black Christians, and Asian Muslims with Hindus and Sikhs; social work based on Asian needs which can lead to a

Muslim being given a Hindu home-help who does not know about Muslim sensitivities or whose own inhibitions (about meat for example) prevent her from fulfilling her duties; the recent decision by the Housing Corporation to reverse its policy of registering housing associations catering for religious communities in favour of race; recruitment monitoring and targeting in terms of 'Black' or 'Asian' statistics which obscure the level of Muslim disadvantage and under-representation and fail to measure whether the equal opportunity policies are making any difference to the Muslim position; arts funding for anti-Muslim but not Islamic artists; racial harassment figures which fail to register that the majority of victims are Muslims and that there is a specific anti-Muslim harassment which even white Muslims suffer.[32]

There is considerable need and scope, therefore, for accommodating Muslim concerns and safeguarding Muslim equality. 'It ought not to be necessary,' Modood concludes,

for Muslims in Britain (who form at least a third, and increasingly more, of all non-whites, are more cohesive than the remainder, and are now repeatedly coming into political conflict with British society) to have to go off on their own with their own agenda and in search of their own allies and points of political leverage. For not only would such a development weaken the racial equality consistency, but it is clear that there can be no British race relations settlement without the Muslim communities.[33]

5. Progressive frameworks for British Muslims?

Beyond everyday anti-Muslim sentiments developing in Britain, a variety of structural disadvantages, outlined above, mitigate against fair and positive Muslim incorporation. Dutch social scientists have observed that 'Muslims in Great Britain appear to face more difficulties in achieving forms of recognition . . . Political commitment to the institutionalisation of Islam appears to be entirely lacking, and the government in Britain is scarcely interested in developing initiatives of its own.'[34] New structural frameworks are needed for engaging Muslims in public life – on both local and national levels –

toward goals involving equality, opportunity, political representation, freedom of expression and freedom from discrimination.

One important arena in which to build such frameworks, as described above, is the legal one. In July 1993, the UK Action Committee on Islamic Affairs (UKACIA) launched a memorandum entitled 'Muslims and the Law in Multi-Faith Britain: Need for Reform' to be submitted to the Secretary of State at the Home Office.[35] The document calls for legislation in three areas affecting Muslims: there is pressing need, it says, for laws concerning (a) vilification of religious beliefs and practices as well as group defamation, (b) incitement to religious hatred, and (c) discrimination on religious grounds. Such legal frameworks would likely do much toward safeguarding Muslims from certain emergent forms of 'anti-Islamic racism', although their effect on local, everyday spheres of social, economic and political life would probably be minimal.

New frameworks for Muslim social and political incorporation are called for. On the national level, one such new framework for potential progress is the Inner Cities Religious Council, established by the Department of the Environment in 1992 as part of its 'Action for Cities' initiative. Currently consisting of eleven representatives of different faiths (including two Muslims, from UKACIA and the Islamic Cultural Centre), the Council is to function as a consultative body considering policy issues affecting religious communities. The Council has so far conducted three regional conferences as well, promoting dialogue among religious communities within given regions, and between regional groups and central government. For the most part, the Council's activities are still very much on a kind of trial basis.

In national politics, Muslims are without conspicuous representation. One point of entry may result from the Labour Party's decision, at its 1993 party conference, to have compulsory adoption of women-only candidate shortlists for most of its winnable seats (in addition to the party's promise to include more ethnic minority candidates contesting safe seats). Najma Hafeez, chair of a Social Services Department, has been selected to be one such candidate, making her likely to become Britain's first Muslim Member of Parliament.

On the local level, I would suggest developments in Leicester represent a positive social and political framework for greater Muslim incorporation. In 1991, Leicester's population of 270,493 included no less than 23 per cent Asians (22 per cent Indians, from both the subcontinent and East Africa, 1 per cent Pakistanis and 0.3 per cent Bangladeshis). This substantial Asian population is predominantly Hindu: it has been estimated that Leicester's highly plural religious makeup comprises 14 per cent Hindus, 4.3 per cent Muslims and 3.8 per cent Sikhs.[36] Although Muslims thus form a minority-within-a-minority, their linguistic, regional, and 'sectarian' backgrounds are complex.

The bulk of Leicester Muslims are Gujarati-speaking Deobandis (although from various parts of Gujarat and East Africa). Muslim complexity is evident by way of the presence of over fifty separate Muslim organisations, catering to groups based around family or caste groups, neighbourhoods, regional-linguistic groups, or sects: examples are the Dawoodi Bohra Jamaat, Ahmadiyya Muslim Association, Gujarati Muslim Association, Ismaili Jamaat, Rawal Community Association, Surati Muslim Khalifa Society, King Faisal Jam-e Mosque (a Gujarati group) and the Islamic Centre (the main Pakistani group). These organisations have been formed by distinct groups to cater to specific needs. They raise their own funding, manage their own premises, elect their own leaders, and interact independently with the City and County authorities for various reasons, usually to do with planning. This broad 'horizontal spread' of Muslim institutions ensures very localised participation in Islamic activity sanctioned by local government approval.

Almost all of these fifty-some organisations belong to Leicester's Federation of Muslim Organisations, which was formed entirely by and for Muslims themselves in 1984. This is in contrast to the well-known Bradford Council of Mosques, which was created by the city authorities in the early 1980s. The 'grassroots' formation of the Federation is a source of much pride and cohesion in Leicester, as opposed to the Bradford case where:

The Metropolitan Council wanted a tame Bradford Council of Mosques to control the discontented youth and for this purpose arranged for funding through the Manpower Services Commission. The result was to unify and institutionalise the religious leadership and increase their influence over the Muslim community at the expense of their secular opponents. However, the rivalry between the secular and religious elements undermined their ability to extract the maximum concessions from the council.[37]

The Leicester Federation of Muslim Organisations, which includes elected officers and various sub-committees, has continued to function effectively as a single Muslim voice engaged with City and County authorities. Representatives of these authorities, including the chief executives, regularly consult with the Federation on matters affecting Muslims and other minorities. It was through the Federation, for instance, that Muslims received favourable decisions regarding the provision of *halal* meat in public institutions and the accommodation of several Muslim concerns in state schools.

Finally, within Leicester there is an abundance of 'high profile' Muslims (many of whom belong to the Federation of Muslim Organisations) who represent actual as well as symbolic aspects of direct incorporation. These include the Chief Executive of the City, two County Councillors and five City Councillors, the Chairman and several members of the County Council's Race Relations Committee, a Police Superintendent, two Head Teachers and several Schools' Governors, as well as prominent professionals and business people throughout the area. Though small in overall numbers, and as a population largely resident in the poorest area of Leicester, Muslims are well represented in the public sphere in profile and activity. Despite the fact that there has been an evident rise in anti-Muslim sentiments and incidents (especially during and following the Gulf War) as elsewhere in the country, Leicester Muslims have been sufficiently well placed (in terms of influential personnel) and well organised in neighbourhoods and area-wide, to face it on a strong footing.

6. Conclusion

Since the early 1980s, British Muslims have doubtless gained greater prominence in public space, both local and national. Yet the kind of essentialised (and usually negative) images of Muslims in this space have had serious repercussions by way of structural and day-to-day treatment of Muslims by others. Unfortunately, the kind of 'multi-culturalism' often espoused in the public sphere usually exacerbates separatist and isolationist views among Muslims and non-Muslims alike. Yet as Parekh wisely points out,

Multiculturalism doesn't simply mean numerical plurality of different cultures, but rather a community which is creating, guaranteeing, encouraging spaces within which different communities are able to grow at their own pace. At the same time it means creating a public space in which these communities are able to interact, enrich the existing culture and create a new consensual culture in which they recognise reflections of their own identity . . . I think that multiculturalism is possible, but only if communities feel confident enough to engage in a dialogue and when there is enough public space for them to interact with the dominant culture.[38]

Rather than institutions of increased isolation – seemingly the cause of both anti-Muslim British nationalists and British Muslim extremists like the Muslim Parliament – a pattern of localised institutions, effective and truly representative umbrella organisations, and strategically placed and symbolically powerful individuals, as found in Leicester, may well amount to one of the kind of new frameworks needed for creating the kind of public space Parekh advocates, enabling the greater Muslim freedom, equality and participation called for by many Muslims and non-Muslims alike.

Acknowledgement

Research toward this article was carried out under the auspices of a grant (No. F697) from the Leverhulme Trust.

Notes

1   C. Peach, 'The Muslim population of Great Britain' in *Ethnic and Racial Studies*, Vol. 13 (1990), pp. 414–19; C. Peach and G. Glebe, 'Muslim Minorities in Western Europe' in *Ethnic and Racial Studies*, Vol. 18 (1995), pp. 26–45. Also see J. Nielsen, *Muslims in Western Europe* (Edinburgh: Edinburgh University Press, 1992).

2   R. Charlton and R. Kaye, 'The politics of religious slaughter: an ethno-religious case study', *New Community*, No. 12, pp. 455–80.

3   M. Halstead, *Education, Justice and Cultural Diversity: An Examination of the Honeyford Affair 1984–1985* (London: Falmer Press, 1988).

4   For general material see L. Appignanesi and S. Maitland, *The Rushdie File* (London: Fourth Estate, 1989); and M. Ruthven, *A Satanic Affair: Salman Rushdie and the Wrath of Islam* (London: Hogarth Press, 1990).

5   B. Parekh, 'The Rushdie Affair and the British Press: Some salutary lessons' in *Free Speech – Report of a Seminar* (London: CRE and the Policy Studies Institute, 1990), *Discussion Papers*, 2, pp. 59–78.

6   T. Asad, 'Multiculturalism and British identity in the wake of the Rushdie Affair', *Politics and Society*, 18 (1990), pp. 455–80.

7   T. Modood, 'British Asian Muslims and the Rushdie Affair', *The Political Quarterly*, 61 (1990), pp. 143–60.

8   S. Khanum, 'War talk', *New Statesman & Society*, 1 February 1991, pp. 12–13.

9   J. Ellis, *Meeting Community Needs: A Study of Muslim Communities in Coventry* (Coventry: Centre for Research in Ethnic Relations, University of Warwick, Monographs in Ethnic Relations No. 2, 1991); S. Vertovec, 'Local contexts and the development of Muslim communities in Britain: Observations in Keighley, West Yorkshire' (Coventry: Centre for Research in Ethnic Relations, University of Warwick, *Research Papers in Ethnic Relations*, 1994); P. Lewis, 'Being Muslim and being British: The dynamics of Islamic reconstruction in Bradford' in R. Ballard (ed.), *Desh Pardesh: The South Asian Presence in Britain* (London: Hurst, forthcoming).

10 J. Esposito, *The Islamic Threat: Myth or Reality?* (New York: Oxford University Press, 1992).

11 C. Peach, V. Robinson, J. Maxted, and J. Chance, 'Immigration and ethnicity' in A. Halsey (ed.), *British Social Trends since 1900* (London: Macmillan, pp. 561–615).

12 M. J. Le Lohe, 'Political issues', *New Community*, 16 (1990), pp. 447–54.

13 —, 'Political issues', *New Community*, 17 (1991), pp. 427–42.

14 'A Muslim agenda for Britain: Some reflections', *New Community*, 17 (1991), pp. 467–75.

15 J. Nielsen, 'Muslims in Britain and local authority responses' in T. Gerholm and Y. G. Lithman (eds.), *The New Islamic Presence in Western Europe* (London: Mansell, 1988), pp. 53–77.

16 J. Nielsen, 'Islam, Muslims and British local and central government' (Birmingham: Centre for the Study of Islam and Christian–Muslim Relations, Selly Oak Colleges, *CSIC Papers: Europe* No. 6, 1992), p. 16.

17   J. Rath, K. Groenendijk and R. Penninx, 'The recognition and insti-
       tutionalization of Islam in Belgium, Great Britain and the Netherlands',
       New Community, 18 (1991), pp. 101–14.
18   F. Reeves, *Race and Borough Politics* (Aldershot: Avebury, 1989), p. 183.
19   *Ibid.*
20   I. Kalka, 'Striking a bargain: Political radicalism in a middle-class London
       borough' in P. Werbner and M. Anwar (eds.), *Black and Ethnic Leaderships
       in Britain* (London: Routledge, 1991), pp. 203–25, 220.
21   Ellis, *op. cit.*
22   See Commission for Racial Equality, *Law, Blasphemy and the Multi-Faith
       Society – Report of a Seminar* (London: CRE and the Inter-Faith Network
       for the UK, Discussion Papers 1, 1989); *Free Speech – Report of a Seminar*
       (London: CRE and the Policy Studies Institute, Discussion Papers 2,
       1990); *Britain: A Plural Society* (London: CRE and the Runnymede Trust,
       Discussion Papers 2, 1990); and J. Horton (ed.), *Liberalism, Multicultural-
       ism and Toleration* (London: Macmillan, 1993).
23   *The Guardian*, 15 February 1993; *Q-News*, 2–9 May 1993.
24   *Second Review of the Race Relations Act 1976* (London: CRE, 1992); T.
       Modood, 'Muslim views on religious identity and racial equality', *New
       Community*, 19 (1993), pp. 513–19.
25   Rath, Groenendijk and Penninx, *op. cit.*
26   T. Modood, 'Establishment, multiculturalism, and British citizenship',
       Political Quarterly, Vol. 64 (1994).
27   —, 'Muslims, incitement to hatred and the law' in J. Horton (ed.), *op. cit.*,
       pp. 139–56.
28   S. Lee, 'Religion and the Law: Ways forward' in D. G. Bowen (ed.), *The
       Satanic Verses: Bradford Responds* (Bradford: Bradford and Ilkley College,
       1992), pp. 73–8.
29   J. Nielsen, 'Muslims in Britain and local authority responses', *op. cit.*,
       and M. Parker-Jenkins, 'Muslim matters: The educational needs of the
       Muslim child', *New Community*, 17 (1991), pp. 569–82.
30   Vertovec, *op. cit.*
31   See D. Pearl, 'South Asian communities and English family law', *New
       Community*, 14 (1987), pp. 161–9; J. Nielsen, 'Islamic Law and its signific-
       ance for the sitation of Muslim minorities in Europe' (Birmingham:
       Centre for the Study of Islam and Christian–Muslim Relations, Selly Oak
       Colleges, *Research Papers: Muslims in Europe*, No. 35, 1987); and S. Poulter,
       Asian Traditions and English Law: A Handbook (Stoke-on-Trent:
       Runnymede Trust with Trentham Books, 1989).
32   T. Modood, 'Muslim views on religious identity and racial equality', *op.
       cit.*, pp. 516–17.
33   *Ibid.*, p. 519.
34   Rath, Groenendijk and Penninx, *op. cit.*, p. 114.
35   *The Muslim News*, 20 August 1993.
36   Leicester City Council/Leicester County Council, *Survey of Leicester 1983*.
37   Y. Samad, 'Book burning and race relations: Political mobilisation of
       Bradford Muslims', *New Community*, 18 (1992), pp. 507–19, 512.
38   In B. Parekh and H. Bhabha, 'Identities on parade', *Marxism Today*, June
       1989, pp. 24–9, 27.

10

ISLAM IN BELGIUM AND THE NETHERLANDS: TOWARDS A TYPOLOGY OF 'TRANSPLANTED' ISLAM

Felice Dassetto and Gerd Nonneman

1. Introduction

A combined analysis of the Muslim presence in Belgium and the Netherlands is not often undertaken but, in addition to the two countries' contiguity and historical links, there are other good grounds for doing so.

Firstly, the composition of the Muslim population of both countries is similar, with Turks and Moroccans accounting for the majority. This derives from the fact that these two countries are at the crossroads of Germanic Europe – where the Muslim population is predominantly Turkish – and Atlantic Europe, where the Muslim population is predominantly Maghrebi.

Secondly, in both countries, the main wave of immigrants from Muslim countries began in the early 1960s when migration agreements were signed with the Maghreb states and Turkey. These new migration accords came at a time when emigration from Italy and southern Europe on the one hand, and from East Europe on the other (following the construction of the Berlin wall in August 1962) had ended.

As regards relations with the Muslim world during the colonial period, Belgium had no such experience, while the Netherlands had some contact through its Indonesian colonies and, to a more limited extent, in the Antilles. However, compared with the number of Algerians in France or of Asians in the United Kingdom, the numbers of Moluccans or Surinamese in the Netherlands is relatively small.

Finally, a further important point in common between the two countries is the relationship between the state, the public sphere, and the religious bodies or spiritual expressions in general. In both countries, the pattern is one in which the state stipulates its neutrality in religious affairs (in contrast with French-style secularism or the upholding of a state religion as in the Nordic countries) and establishes an agreement with the religious and spiritual authorities for the management of many aspects of collective life. In other words, the religious or para-religious authorities have full legitimacy and play an integral role in the operation of the welfare state (in schools, hospitals, the health service, trade unions etc.), through the channels of corresponding political parties. In Dutch-language political parlance (mainly in the Netherlands and Flanders, but increasingly also among French-speaking commentators) this is known as *verzuiling* (the organisation of society and polity on the basis of various confessional 'pillars').[1] As a result, the question in both countries is whether, in the process of inserting itself into the existing institutional arrangement, the Muslim population will, in the medium-term, become a new such pillar.

2. Population of Muslim origin

It is difficult to estimate the population of Muslim origin. The criterion of nationality habitually used is becoming less and less relevant as Muslims, with their children and grandchildren, progressively acquire Belgian or Dutch nationality.

Also, as we shall see, the definition of Muslim identity has many nuances. There is therefore little scientific justification for the oft-used device of categorising as Muslim all people originating from Turkey and Morocco. We therefore prefer to speak of 'people originating from Muslim countries'.

Table 10.1

Population Originating from Muslim Countries in Belgium and the Netherlands, by Nationality (1989)

	Belgium	percentage	Netherlands	percentage
Turkey	79,460	33.7	186,700	46.0
Morocco	135,464	57.4	155,700	38.4
Algeria	10,647	4.5	–	–
Tunisia	6,244	2.6	3,700	0.9
Pakistan	1,591	0.7	9,100	2.2
Indonesia	671	0.3	6,800	1.7
Suriname	–	–	25,000	6.1
Others	2,000	0.8	19,300	4.8
Total	**236,077**	**100.0**	**405,900**	**100.0**
Total of Muslim origin (estimate)	**260,000**		450,000	
Total population	**9,927,612**		**14,300,000**	
Population of Muslim origin as % of total population		**2.6**		**3.1**

Source: National Statistical Institutes

The overall data for the size of the Muslim populations give a relatively poor indication of the impact of their presence which is particularly heavily concentrated in the towns, and within these in certain localities. Table 10.2 shows the proportion of Muslims in Belgian and Dutch towns. In many, Islam is highly visible – to the extent that some localities are being labelled 'Muslim' by the non-Muslim population. This is a wholly new experience for these towns and their inhabitants.

Table 10.2

Percentage of Population of Muslim Origin in Selected Belgian and Dutch Towns (1989)

	Total population (000)	Muslims as % of total population
Belgium		
Brussels	1,331	7.9
Antwerp	668	7.6
Liège	484	2.7
Ghent	250	4.0
Hasselt-Genk	127	6.4
Netherlands		
Amsterdam	700	8.6
Rotterdam	580	8.2
The Hague	444	6.3
Utrecht	230	9.6
Nijmegen	145	3.4
Arnhem	130	4.6
Breda	124	3.2
Venlo	64	4.6

Source: National Statistical Institutes

In addition, the proportion of young people in the total population of Muslim origin, compared especially with the Belgian population, makes the Muslim presence appear particularly substantial. For example, in Brussels 23 per cent of the population under the age of 20 is of Muslim origin.

3. The Muslim cycle: stages of development in Belgium and the Netherlands

Islam has grown increasingly visible since the early 1960s. This can be explained partly by factors internal to the growth structure of the immigrant population, partly in the context of the crisis which began in the mid-1970s, and partly by developments in the Muslim world itself.

Several main stages can be observed in the cycle of Islam's European development: The first is from the early 1960s to the mid-1970s. During this period the Muslim population consisted mostly of primary immigrants, mostly men and usually without their families. Islam's requirements were relatively small and its visible aspects were limited to a simple prayer-room in workers' centres or to the establishment of associations for the repatriation of the deceased.[2] During this period, Muslims' self-image and their concerns with regard to the indigenous inhabitants of the two countries were primarily cultural.

Changes in migration patterns occurred at the beginning of the 1970s: a huge and relatively uncontrolled flow of immigrants took place between 1969 and 1974. This period also saw the beginning of family reunion, which is still taking place today and which is modifying the demographic profile of the first immigration wave. Next came the 1974 crisis and the cessation of immigration flows. Migratory intentions consequently changed irrevocably and the illusion of return gave way to hopes of settlement within the European space.

Meanwhile, the dynamics of the Arab Islamic world also changed: after the Six-Day War, Nasserist Arab nationalism was gradually superseded by, on the one hand, the Saudi strategy of hegemony over the Arab–Muslim world (with the financial backing, after 1974, of accumulated oil revenues) and, on the other, the growth of both rhetoric and action of Islamic movements in Egypt and Libya as well as Morocco and Tunisia.

This laid the ground for the second stage which lasted from the mid-1970s to the mid-1980s. During this period, Islam's presence became increasingly visible both spatially and institutionally. The number of mosques in all European countries with immigrant Muslim populations grew at a spectacular rate. Thus, while in the early 1970s there was barely a handful of mosques in the two countries, by the mid-1980s, there were 200 in the Netherlands and more than 100 in Belgium.[3]

Several factors combined to inspire this enthusiasm for mosque-building. Among the most important were the need to transmit religious practice to children; the mosque's role as a symbol of identity and support at a time of crisis; and the recovery of the father's status.

This development was made possible by Islam's flexible 'organisational structure': there is no clear hierarchy comparable to that of the Catholic Church, for instance, and the believer's relationship with Allah is first and foremost a direct one, without the need for clerical intercession (although Shiism, the minority form of Islam embracing some 10 per cent of all Muslims, diverges from this pattern). This enables and legitimates the spontaneous and autonomous establishment of religious structures even in the absence of leaders.

In this period, Muslim men (there was relatively little involvement by women) became actively engaged in promoting mosque-building projects. The financial resources to pay for this were obtained mostly from the faithful. Contrary to popular belief, governments and Islamic organisations contributed comparatively little to the financing.

The increasing visibility of the Muslim space through the medium of architecture, bringing Muslim architectural codes into the heart of European towns, took place in different ways in different countries. In most cases, with few exceptions, mosques were constructed by converting existing buildings located in old districts inhabited by immigrants, such as old warehouses or factories, shops or cinemas, many of which were bought up and refitted.

In addition, Muslims also began to make other inroads into towns and to develop institutions there, such as butcher's shops, Islamic bookshops and travel agencies specialising in pilgrimages to Mecca.

This increase in visibility took place in a particularly difficult and hostile environment. Unemployment was hitting the population in general but the immigrant population in particular; the latter tended to be the target of growing hostility from other sections of the population. In addition, Khomeini's rise to power, Qadhafi's actions and the increasing tension in the Middle East raised the spectre of 'Islamic fundamentalism' and the threat it was thought to pose to Europe's future. Islam was thus developing and becoming more visible at a time of crisis and hostility towards it. Often, Muslims who strengthen their connections with Islam find themselves and their actions endowed by others with a significance which far exceeds their intentions. In fact, they generally simply want to incorporate Islam (often a popular and conservative version) into their daily lives and to convey it to their children. Instead, they find themselves caught up in a geopolitical game which has little to do with their own reality.

At the institutional level there were increasing efforts to create Islamic associations or federations, to spread the teaching of Islam in state schools and, in some cases, to set up Islamic schools. In these early years when Islam became more manifest several important power plays can already be seen at work; thus, for instance, the everyday requirements of immigrant Muslim populations were (and are) often anticipated and encouraged by the offer of services. The latter come from specialist and para-state organisations, such as the Muslim World League – Islam's major propaganda organisation controlled by Saudi Arabia, or Turkey's Directorate of Religious Affairs (*Diyanet*) – the official state organ for the control of religious affairs which, through its nationalist and modernist form of Islam, has some hold over a large proportion of Turkey's Sunni population. Such services are also provided, to a lesser extent, by organisations under the jurisdiction of the Moroccan government (such as Moroccan workers' associations – *Amicales des travailleurs marocains*).

Sometimes, this demand for services is also conveyed by European government authorities which intervene to create order and to make organised Islam (whose operational logic they find difficult to comprehend) more transparent. Their need to do so has increased as the image of Islam became coloured with Qadhafi- or Khomeini-style policies and actions, and associated – often mistakenly – with terrorist attacks emanating from the Middle East against European countries.

In Belgium, a law passed in 1974 gave Islamic worship the same status as that accorded to religions historically established in Belgium: Catholicism, Protestantism and Judaism. Since then, Orthodox Christianity has been given the same status also. This law had two important effects. In the first place, it entailed the introduction of the teaching of Islam in state schools on the same basis as other religions. At present, there are about 700 teachers of Islam in both primary and secondary schools. Secondly, the law allowed for financial provision to be made for Imams and places of worship. So far, this provision has not been put into effect because to become effective it requires the identification of a Muslim authority, an issue which is as yet unresolved.

In the Netherlands, the state has intervened in two capacities. In 1976, it made arrangements for the financing of prayer-halls and in 1983, in a different context, it recognised the right of minority cultures to organise themselves and for state aid to be provided for this purpose. Since then, fear of Islam has led the Dutch government to exercise extreme caution and even to take some steps backward. Thus it has introduced school courses on 'religions' – as cultural facts – in order to avoid the introduction of specifically Islamic courses. It has also put a brake on the appointment of Imams from overseas.

Immigrants' requirements were also conveyed by a variety of Islamic 'movements'. These could be traditional brotherhoods (*tariqa*, plural *turuq*), which sometimes found a new lease of life in Europe's climate of freedom; or contemporary devotional movements, such as *Jama'at at-Tabligh* (Association for the Message), which was founded in India but has since spread throughout the Islamic world and Europe; or movements with political overtones, derived from or inspired by the Muslim Brotherhood or by their anti-Kemalist Turkish equivalents such as the *Milli Görüs*[4] in particular.

In the mid-1980s, a new dimension was added to the process of Islam becoming more 'visible', marking the start of the third stage. This was the use of mosques as a consolidated base from which various actors – Muslim leaders, fathers and brothers – attempted to reconstruct local societies based on Islamic practices and to set up small sections of Islamic civil society which overflowed into urban space.

4. Who is Muslim? The question of affiliation

4.1. *General observations*

The lack of in-depth empirical research on affiliation to Islam in Western Europe means that usually no distinction is made by public and political opinion, and even by social scientists, between different kinds of 'affiliations' (ways in which people wish to define and put into practice their Muslim identity). However, in the context of transplanted Islam where, after migration, a rift occurred between individual identities and collective affiliation, the question of Muslim identity and its reformulation has become central to an understanding of the evolution of these people in their new environment.

In the absence of quantified data, it is only possible to formulate hypotheses about a possible typology.

In transplanted Islam, the range of forms of affiliation is governed by two inverse kinds of logic. On the one hand, the direct confrontation with the West and the weakening of the influence of traditional political, religious and social regulatory authorities has led to considerable diversity and reformulation. In Europe new centres for the reformulation of Islam and its propagation can be set up more easily than in Muslim countries. But on the other hand, immersion in a setting which is both different and potentially or actually hostile, can lead to affiliations becoming more rigid, or to a quest for formal orthodoxy. In addition, the reconstitution of the social structures of Islam, which have not been transplanted 'naturally' along with the migratory flows, together with efforts to set up new regulatory mechanisms, can lead to uncertainties, and to fluidity of meanings and behaviour; more than two decades of such 'transplantation' have not been able to resolve this.

In this overall dynamic context, which links the migratory, Islamic and global cycles, some types of affiliation may be transitory and conjunctural, forming part of a general cultural change.

To construct a typology implies a classification. To this end, the relevant criteria and indicators must be defined. These are of two types. First, one set of indicators belongs to the realm of speech and ideas. Far from being homogeneous and fixed, belief in Islam, as in all religions, can be founded on one element or another drawn from the vast resources of the scriptures and holy deeds. Without going into detail, suffice it to say that the elements which seem to be most

indicative of differences in attitude are the following: (1) the pro-
clamation of the faith (*shahada*); (2) the reference to the body of the
faithful (*umma*); (3) Muslim society expressed in different ways (*dar
al-'adl, dawla, dunya*); the Muslim community (*jama'a*).

The second set of indicators relates to Islamic conduct and practices – both the major, orthodox ones (the 'pillars' of Islam) and the
smaller but nonetheless also important ones such as dietary restrictions and rules of dress.

More specifically, these affiliations can be viewed from two vant-
age points: one concerning the person, the individual and his/her
subjectivity, and the other regarding specific organised forms. Transplanted Islam is the combination of personally motivated attitudes,
opinions and practices, and the actions of specific organisations. The
former will be explored in the present section; the latter in section 5
below.

From the point of view of the individual, several types of affiliation (several ways of being and experiencing the reality of what
it means to be Muslim) can be observed today.

4.2. *Declared or silent agnosticism or indifference*

4.2.1. One type of affiliation is 'negative', expressed in a *refusal to proclaim the faith* and would thus indicate unbelief or apostasy. However,
such refusal does not offer the same social possibilities in the Muslim
context as it does in the Western liberal one. In transplanted Islam,
this type of affiliation is less common today than 15 or 20 years ago
when declarations of agnosticism were more frequently observed. In
this sense, the dynamic of Islamisation has borne fruit. This declared
agnosticism has been replaced today by two other types of affiliation.

4.2.2. The first is what could be called *silent agnosticism or indifference*
– such silence being understood as conformity in the sense of recognising the need to maintain the cohesion of 'Muslim society' even if
only in appearance. This type of affiliation can obviously coexist with
the rites of passage (such as circumcision, marriage, death and so
on). As far as dietary restrictions are concerned, it can result in a
double standard of behaviour among such social actors: in keeping
with the 'negative' conformity, these restrictions and obligations are
respected in the Muslim social context but ignored outside it. This

'hollow' affiliation can be pushed to define itself at times of tension or when unity is questioned, either because of positions taken by Muslim leaders (for example, Khomeini's *fatwa* condemning Salman Rushdie to death), or by the hostility of non-Muslims.

4.2.3. The second type of affiliation can be termed *culturalist* and is widespread among westernised elites and among parts of the second generation. The main characteristic of this affiliation is an interpretation of the Koran and of tradition in terms of culture. It concerns mainly people of Arab origin, because of the close links between the Koranic text and the Arabic language and culture. The culture concerned, then, is the 'Arab-Islamic' culture.

This attitude may coexist with respect to the rites of passage which may be reformulated or whose significance may be modernised with the help of social science and history. It suspends or by-passes the enunciation of the *shahada*. Today this is a fluid form of affiliation, open to the influence of re-Islamising missionary action which emphasises the importance of the link between culture and Islam. Such missionary activity tends to advance (1) through intellectual approaches; (2) by reviving the broad Muslim community (the *umma*); or (3) through the local community (the *jama'a*): in other words through the re-Islamisation of people's world view or social behaviour.

In this vein, the work of the Moroccan historian Abdallah Laroui, *Islam et modernité* (1987) (which, he says in the Introduction, should have been entitled *Arab Islam and its problems*), and even more so that of Fatima Mernissi in *Le Harem politique* (1987), shows how authors who in earlier works developed their thought on the basis of a culturalising hypothesis, have, in their recent works, made a 'detour' via Islam.[5] These are writers of note in the 'culturalist' domain and key examples of the process at work.

One example of re-Islamisation through the social sphere can be observed among groups of young people motivated to organise schools for young children, and who define themselves as 'Islamic' groups; another example in recent years are cultural associations which solemnise the observance of Ramadan and turn it into a group activity.

The above, however, are arguably not the 'central' types of Islamic 'belonging'. The latter can, for the sake of convenience, be divided into (1) types that stay at a distance from organised forms; (2) those types where Islam is experienced and lived at least in part through membership, or making use, of organised forms; (3) organised and active missionary and militant types; as well as a number of 'fringe' affiliations.

4.3. Types of 'affiliation' to Islam which retain a distance from organised forms

4.3.1. The first of these is *home-bound devotionalism*, common among fathers and the first generation of immigrants. This type of affiliation expresses itself in a spiritual understanding of the *umma* and an individualised interpretation of 'effort' (*jihad*). It expresses itself in personal piety and devotion, with an ethical dimension founded on a strong profession of faith and rigorous adherence to religious obligations and dietary restrictions. This conduct takes place mainly at home, however, with only very irregular, 'instrumental' visits to the mosque. A living experience rather than a theoretical formulation, it constitutes an expression of private Islam, situated particularly at the level of personal faith. It might be understood as fulfilling within the family the statutory function of a refuge, and perhaps of affirmation. In this sense, one might speak of a *pater-familial* devotionalism. It is a relatively 'distant' type of affiliation, which is potentially critical of all concrete expressions of the *umma* or the *jama'a*, as given shape in the mosques or other groupings.

Nevertheless, such groupings do aim to capture this element of the Muslim population. They try to attract it, mobilise it, or speak in its name. After all, however distant from officialdom, this group of individuals does provide, even if only in appearance, an increase in the active Muslim population base. Thus it is conceivable that this type of actor contributed to some extent to the success of the electoral registration organised by the Preparatory Committee for the elections to the Muslim Council in Belgium which took place on 12 and 13 January 1991; this would account for the discrepancy between the number of regular mosque-goers from whom registration cards were collected, and the final total.

4.3.2. The second of these non-institutionalised kinds of 'being Muslim', is one where a *reinterpretation of some of the founding principles of Islam* is taking place. This is only just starting to work out its ideas.

With a few exceptions, these are still poorly formulated, reveal divergent opinions and are often a patchwork of elements of Islamic and Western culture. In general, this involves a reinterpretation of the *dawla* in terms of individual rather than social ethics and the spiritualisation of *jihad*. However, this trend still remains somewhat uncertain about going as far as the total privatisation of religion and a secularisation similar to that practised in Europe.[6]

This type of affiliation might, at the purely formal level, be considered merely as a more explicit form of the previous type. But in practice, its distancing also applies to Islamic ritual and prohibitions. The question remains open, as to what extent a reformulation of Islam which affirms itself only as *din* (faith) and dissociates itself from all the other components (*umma, dawla, jama'a*) can survive.

4.4. *Affiliation via organised forms of membership.*

4.4.1. One type of affiliation via established organised forms may be called '*ritualist conformist orthopraxis*'. This consists of a moderate profession of faith, belief in the Koran and Islamic traditions, together with more or less formal and fairly frequent observation of obligations and rituals. Apart from this conformist ritualism, this type of affiliation is characterised also by the acceptance of, but utilitarian attitude towards, the established forms of religious organisation and authority. This can in fact effectively mean a *distancing* from institutions and authority. Conformist orthopraxis can be seen, then, as expressing a 'privatisation', in the Western sense of the term. Fairly typical of this type of affiliation is the attitude of a section of the Turkish population towards the religious authority which the Turkish state has, de facto, imposed: the *Diyanet* (which in many ways functions as the state's religious arm). A similar attitude can be observed among some members of the Muslim population in Belgium towards local mosques and particularly towards the *Cinquantenaire* mosque in Brussels, the seat of authority and official institutions.

4.4.2. All of the types listed so far dissociate affiliation to Islam from the particular location: where there is a local reference, it is secondary. In contrast, there are others for whom the firm local establishment of the Muslim reality becomes an important factor in their affiliation to Islam. This is the *localist form of affiliation*, which has played a definite role in the development of mosques since the mid-1970s. At the same time, the aim has been to set up, or to try to set up, systems of social control inspired by Islam. A variety of meanings are built round this local Muslim reality. For some, the local presence has a primarily practical significance – this may be the case, for instance, for shop owners who appreciate the flow of people which a mosque brings with it. For others, the local Muslim presence means religious education for their children. For yet others its significance is devotional, while at the same time providing ritualisation of their urban environment and the simultaneous creation of an *umma* and a *jama'a*. Since the time when immigrants began to think of settling in the country to which they had emigrated, the mosque has become a place which delimits the territory, in time and space.

4.5. *Organised missionary and militant affiliations*

There are a number of other forms of affiliation which, although also articulated at the local level, are more far-reaching in scope. In these, the categories in which the individual's Islamic identity is formulated flow not only from his/her everyday life as a Muslim, but also from a conscious and explicit reformulation and conceptualisation. This takes us into the domain of those organised forms of Islam which target, and aim to function throughout, the whole of the Muslim community. These organisations encompass three types of affiliation.

4.5.1. One might be called *organised missionary Islamism*. This kind of affiliation entails both Islamic affirmation and propagation aimed at the Muslims themselves. Its central aim, indeed, is one of re-Islamisation. This type of affiliation is well developed in countries of the Muslim heartland, but also much in evidence in countries of emigration because of the relaxation of traditional affiliations there.

4.5.2. A second type which has attracted attention in recent years is that related to forms of collective protest in the name of Islam. Bruno Étienne[7] has called this 'radical Islam', and it has usually – and confusingly – been described as *intégrisme* in current continental European vocabulary, and as 'fundamentalism' in English usage. As to the latter, it should be stressed that, in making reference to the 'fundamental' elements of Islam, this category of Muslims are actually interpreting them within a fairly fixed interpretative schema. It is a social protest, inspired by the idea of a return to the roots, but is divided over what is the precise model to be found in those roots. For some, it is a question of returning to the text of the Koran exclusively. For others, the majority, the model is the society of Medina, as led by the Prophet. For yet others it is the Caliphate, or Ottoman society. In all cases, the social and political aims are inextricable from the religious one. Their political model oscillates between authoritarian, *dirigiste* and populist forms. For the most part, however, they profess a kind of pan-Islamism which is translated into active international solidarity. Hence in mosques associated with these movements, it became not unusual to see collections and other acts of solidarity being made for groups involved with the Afghan guerrillas, the Palestinian *intifada*, or the Bosnian Muslims. (This same Islamic universalism has led to some Islamic movements in Turkey attracting Kurdish adherents.)

The question of the community's temporal leadership, the *dawla*, is crucial, whether it is seen as a utopia or as a reality. In Muslim countries this has led to conflict with the established authorities and the *ulama* who support them, whereas in the European public sphere it explains the cases of vehement agitation over Islamic issues (such as in the Rushdie affair, or in defence of Muslim law and Islamic schools). In these groups, hostility to the West – read the US and Europe – is widespread. It includes hostility to economic and political domination, to Western support for existing governments in Muslim countries, and to Western lifestyles. This hostility is manifested by particular external signs, such as the growing of beards, or the wearing of the *jellaba* by men and of the Islamic *hijab* (headscarf) by women.

Usually, these Muslims' interpretation of the scriptures remains close to classical schemas although it may be expressed in seemingly new language. This results in part from the limited Islamic education of these movements' leaders, who tend rather to have scientific or social science backgrounds. Their *jihad* has, of course, an element of missionary zeal; however, it is aimed not only at giving renewed vigour and purpose to Islam but also at purifying Islam from layers of tradition added to it by various cultures. Radical Islamists, therefore, tend to be hostile to the traditional celebrations of popular Islam.

4.5.3. Closely related to the above type of affiliation, although in a continual position of hostility to it, are a number of *bureaucratised state-led types of affiliation*. These derive from the 'newness' of the contemporary Islamic world – in the sense that Muslim countries for the most part became independent (or developed their modern state structures) only recently. These new states, with modern structures and recognised on the contemporary world scene, in a number of cases declared themselves to be 'Islamic', but even if secularly organised, they have tended to propagate a pro-Islamic image, in an attempt both to increase their own legitimacy and to extend their influence over Muslims elsewhere (often in competition with other sources of Islamic mobilisation). Such states tend, therefore, to encourage affiliation to their own version of 'state' Islam. Saudi Arabia is a typical example, and Turkey is a particularly interesting and complex one (as shown in the activities of the *Diyanet*). Such efforts have met with varying levels of success and reaction among Muslims in Western Europe, including in Belgium and the Netherlands.[8]

4.6. *'Fringe' affiliations*

To the above affiliations which derive from orthodox Islam, two other special forms should be added, which in part intertwine with those already mentioned.

4.6.1. First there is affiliation to a religious *brotherhood*, based on faithfulness to a spiritual master who has established a particular path (*tariqa*), imbued with mysticism. Such forms of affiliation have existed from the first centuries of Islam and have, since the nineteenth century, been subject to revivalist moves. Membership of a brotherhood 'mediates' membership of Muslim society. For this reason, it is true but imprecise to describe the brotherhoods as specific types of affiliation to Islam. It is true in the sense that the brotherhoods create specific social structures which regulate knowledge and social conduct. On the other hand, however, the brotherhoods cannot, in their orthodox forms, be dissociated from Muslim society's overall structure of meaning and its general conduct. Thus, some brotherhoods emphasise personal and collective devotional practices, while others, like the old brotherhood of the *Naqshbandi*, attach more importance to the advent of the *dawla* (Islamic state) and could therefore be related to, and act as, a specific sub-section of radical Islam.

4.6.2. Finally, on the margins of orthodox Islam there are several types of affiliation through the *magico-religious universe*. Here also, apart from a few extreme cases, it is inaccurate to speak of specific forms of affiliation. In fact, the belief in *jinn* (genies) (which are in any case mentioned in the Koran), healers, *marabouts* and evil spirits, spans the spectrum of popular forms of Islamic affiliation. Its roots go back to pre-Islamic times and to elements introduced in the founding discourse of Islam, and subsequently given extra importance by popular reinterpretation.

4.7. Conclusion

Sections 4.2–4.6 above have described the various forms of belonging to Islam which can be observed today; in other words, the different ways which social actors adopt to give their belief active shape and translate it into practice. Any such form is an evolving reality which continues to be reconstructed today, in part because of its immersion in a new environment.

The dynamic and evolving character of these types of affiliation also results from the fact that within Islam itself the leadership is in the process of being reconstituted. This will be expanded on below. In particular, the first 'second generations' of Muslims have appeared on the scene of transplanted Islam. These will, in the years to come, add new dimensions to the types and methods of affiliation.

Attempting to quantify these various affiliations would be a perilous exercise: it would fix an essentially evolving reality in figures, falsely suggesting a certain stability. It would require a considerable research effort and funding which is unlikely to be forthcoming. The only indication one can give, based on previous observation, is that the affiliations that we have classed as 'via organised forms of membership' (4.4), 'organised missionary or militant' (4.5), together with the brotherhoods (4.6) – in other words, all of those who regularly attend mosques – represent *less than one-third of the adult male population*. There thus remains a large floating population of *pater-familial devotionalists*, but also a significant group of silent agnostics.

5. The organised presence of Islam in Belgium and the Netherlands

To describe Islam's organised presence, it is helpful to distinguish three levels of analysis. The first is the level of 'basic Islam', that of mosques and prayer-halls which occur throughout the two countries, act as gathering points and poles of identity and help to make Islam visible in Belgian and Dutch towns. The second level is that of the many associations which pervade local Islam, stimulating and animating Muslim life. And the third is that of the organisations which try to construct a framework for Islam at the national level.[9]

5.1. 'Basic Islam'

Belgium and the Netherlands had some 500 mosques and prayer-halls as of the early 1990s, of which about 200 in the former and 300 in the latter. No more than 20 of these are new, purpose-built mosques. The others are existing premises and buildings which have been converted. Usually these premises are owned by local mosque committees and mostly have been bought with funds collected from the faithful, or to a lesser extent with money from Muslim countries (particularly from the Muslim World League) and from public funds – the latter especially in the Netherlands. Most of these mosques are characterised very strongly by the socio-national connections of their members. Their distribution in the two countries is laid out in Table 10.3.

Table 10.3

Number of Mosques in Belgium and the Netherlands, by National Affiliation (1990)

	Belgium	Netherlands
Turkish	72	134
Maghrebi	127	104
Surinamese	–	21
Pakistani	–	6
Others	10	27
Total	**209**	**292**

Sources: for Belgium: UCL/GREM; for the Netherlands: N. Landman, *Van Mat tot Minaret* (see note 8), and W. Shahid and P. van Koningsveld, 'Institutionalisation and Integration of Islam in the Netherlands' in W. Shahid and P. van Koningsveld (eds.), *The Integration of Islam and Hinduism in Western Europe* (Kampen: Kok Pharos, 1991), pp. 89–121.

Table 10.4

Estimated Number of 'Muslim' People per Mosque

National origin	Belgium	Netherlands
Turkish	1,100	1,400
Moroccan	1,200	1,600

When the number of mosques is compared with the number of potential Muslims, a similar ratio is found in both Belgium and the Netherlands, namely about one mosque for every 1,400 to 1,500 people.

The mosque density is slightly higher in Belgium than in the Netherlands. Also the density of Turkish mosques is higher in both countries than that of Moroccan mosques.

It would seem worth inquiring also into the rate of visits to these mosques, the 'frequentation rate'. To the best of our knowledge, there has not been any research on the frequentation of mosques or observance of other practices in the Netherlands. In Belgium, a study carried out by Dassetto in 1983, gave a frequentation rate of 6.7 per cent for the Friday mosque (this is the main mosque, where the weekly Friday prayers are held). Analysis showed a 17 per cent frequentation rate for men. At the time, there was not much difference in frequentation rates between those aged under 25 and those who were older. At the time of writing, no further quantified data are available. However, the evidence which does exist clearly shows that frequentation rates have not dropped.

5.2. Movements and associations extending across transplanted Islam in Belgium and the Netherlands

Two movements are of major importance within the Muslim population: the *Jama'at at-Tabligh* among the Arab population and the *Milli Görüs* among the Turkish population.

5.2.1. The *Jama'at at-Tabligh*[10] is a type of religious grouping founded in the 1920s and 1930s in northern India. Its centre is currently in Delhi. The movement is oriented towards pietism and the re-Islamisation of daily life. Although it has modern organisational and operational features, the *Jama'at at-Tabligh* has other aspects derived from the Sufi tradition and strongly linked with the movement's founder, Mohammed Ilyas (1885–1944), a scion of a major Sufi family from Uttar Pradesh. Members of Mohammed Ilyas' family still lead the movement. After a period of apprenticeship with, among others, the *Deobandi*, and numerous pilgrimages to Mecca, Mohammed Ilyas committed himself to continuing an educational programme started by his father among the rural population of the Meos in the Mewat region to the south-west of Delhi. These people were impoverished, socially marginalised and superficially Islamicised. It was in this terrain that the organisational principles and the new technique of religious action characteristic of the *Tablighis* were worked out. This consists of sending out organised groups of itinerant preachers who in turn set up new preaching teams.

In the mid-1930s, the movement became very popular in the Mewat; hundreds of mosques and *madrasas* were built. Visible non-Muslim signs were eradicated from daily life. Preaching was also extended to the rich merchants of Delhi among whom Ilyas had considerable success, and who he asked to devote some of their time to missionary action and to purifying their commercial practices. The movement is currently widespread in northern India, Bangladesh and Pakistan. It is also well known in the Maghreb and in European countries of immigration, and also has a presence in the US and Canada.

Mohammed Ilyas' movement grew in the context of the indifference of official Islam, which was somewhat scornful of this popular Islam, an Islam conducted by simple and uneducated Muslims energetically engaged in propagating the faith. In 1944, he published a manifesto addressed to the Indian Muslim leaders, which summed up his missionary intentions.

The aim of *Tablighi* missionary activity is 'to touch the hearts' of the believers, rather than trying to attain power in order to impose Muslim practices on the people: no religious act, Ilyas felt, should be the result of coercion.

The activities of the *Tabligh* show several special features. For example, it addresses primarily Muslims and, among them, especially the least educated strata. The *Tablighis* criticise the elitism of other Islamic movements such as the Muslim Brotherhood. Born into the context of Indian Islam, they appear to conduct and think of themselves as a minority group in the religious and political terms. They have developed an autarchic kind of missionary activity, following a logic requiring limited means and an attitude of strict neutrality towards the government and politics. Through their political neutrality, the *Tablighis* avoid any confrontation, as this could destroy the movement.

They have positioned themselves at the heart of Islamic orthodoxy. They are thus obliged to develop their specific action in a way which avoids rupture or separation. Defenders of a practical form of Islam, the *Tablighis* base their activity on a few simple rules: faith in God, prayer, modest deportment, the acquisition of knowledge and its transmission, pursuit of the straight path, and the welcoming of all believers; in other words: the virtues of the pious Muslim together with the idea of transmission of knowledge and of invitation to believers.

Prayer plays a large part in regulating the lives of the movement's adherents. *Tablighi* mosques are among the most frequented in Europe and can be classed in the category of 'devotional' mosques referred to earlier.

Acquisition of knowledge and its transmission is another of their rules. To know Islam, in contrast with a merely repetitive and conformist practice of religion, is the *Tablighis'* response both to the misunderstanding of Islam among the masses and the excessive specialisation of religious scholarship. The obligation to proclaim to Muslims the correct path to follow – i.e. missionary action – is a result of this understanding. This is considered to be the duty of all believers in furtherance of the activities of the Prophet.

The *Tabligh* has an organisational structure which may appear traditional and outdated (the men have beards, wear the *jellaba* and have little technological equipment), but is in fact in other ways very modern. The Islam of the *Tabligh*, therefore, is far from 'fundamentalist'.

About a quarter of the Moroccan mosques in Belgium (the *Tabligh* does not exist among the populations of Turkish origin) can be considered as more or less within the orbit of the *Tabligh* movement. Members of the movement visit them regularly. The *Tabligh* developed considerably from the 1970s onwards by centring its activity on the mosques and local Islamic affairs. In Belgium, it attempted for a short time to divert the general development of Islam and its relationship with the State, but this was subsequently abandoned as contrary to the spirit of the *Tabligh*.

Adherence to the *Tabligh* seems to be motivated above all by the fact that it allows fathers – whose authority within the family has been thrown into crisis by unemployment, by sons growing up in a European context in which they are more at ease than their fathers, by daughters who no longer fully accept the traditional roles that the men would have them play – to recover status as members of the mosque, which gives them the symbolic strength and motivation to transfer this status to the family context. Over and above the Islamic missionary activity, this has the aim of maintaining family structures and power relationships within the family in the face of pressures towards changes in family life and the breakdown of paternal authority.

What of the *Tabligh*'s future? In Belgium and the Netherlands today, it appears to be composed mainly of fathers (and grand-fathers), the unemployed, the handicapped and pensioners, rather than by shopkeepers, taxi drivers, labourers and so on. However, the younger generation of fathers is also represented. The present dynamic might continue for about a decade. But early in the next millennium, the question of the succession between the first and second generations of fathers would arise. Will the latter turn to the *Tabligh* with the same motivations as their own fathers did? Or will they find new reasons for doing so? Will the *Tabligh* by then have come to fulfill new roles? Might it, for instance, fulfil an ethical func-tion, acting as a 'conducting wire' for restructuring the personality? (It should be noted in this context, that some of today's younger adherents are delinquents who have served or are serving prison sentences. The *Tabligh* representatives, like those of other Muslim groups, pay regular visits to these prisons). Finally, there is the factor of the *Tabligh*'s international links. Some missionaries have arrived recently from Morocco, the United Kingdom (Pakistanis and Bangladeshis with British passports), Pakistan and Bangladesh. It remains to be seen how the transfusion of missionary energies will take place.

5.2.2. The *Milli Görüs* ('National View') is a religious movement with a strong political connotation among the Turkish population. It has its origins in opposition to the reforms of Mustafa Kemal, the creator of modern secularist Turkey. The *Milli Görüs* can be considered the cultural/religious wing of the former Party of National Salvation (MSP), which after the 1980 coup became the Party of Well-Being (*Refah Partisi*, RP) (sometimes translated as Welfare Party). The party, led since its foundation by Necmettin Erbakan, does not enjoy wide overall representation in Turkey, but by the early 1990s held power in some 80 municipalities, including Istanbul and three other major towns. The MSP and RP grew out of efforts to merge three com-ponents: reference to Islam as a project of society; reference to the affirmation of Turco-Ottoman identity; and reference to technical and scientific modernity. While the RP may be considered as the 'engineers' party' it is just as much the party of those who hark back with nostalgia to the greatness of the Ottoman era.

In Belgium and the Netherlands, there are about 30 mosques controlled by the *Milli Görüs*; the movement's centre is in Germany.

These mosques have often been set up by people who have left the 'official' Turkish mosques of the *Diyanet*. The most active members of these mosques are young fathers of the first 'second generation', who came to Belgium as adolescents and had some of their education in Belgium and so have experienced two types of socialisation. In this movement, there is a particular blend of political activism and mysticism, of traditionalism which gives the *Milli Görüs* the appearance of a form of traditional brotherhood, and of modernity.

The movement is well organised, and financed from its own resources, derived from the sale of goods through cooperatives. It has its own publications and a daily newspaper (*Milli Gazete*) which is distributed fairly widely. It has established well-structured youth organisations.

5.2.3. There are also a number of other movements represented in Belgium and the Netherlands, but they are less well implanted and organised.

In the Arab context, the oldest and most influential is that of the Muslim Brotherhood (*Ikhwan Muslimin*). Several big mosques and associations are inspired by the Brotherhood. Its ideas appear to attract particularly young people, both boys and girls, who have access to the texts of *Ikhwan* authors in numerous European languages. They find in these ideas elements which help them to understand their situation, and motivation for their social behaviour. This has, among other things, led to the creation of several Associations of Muslim Students.

Among the Turkish immigrant population, several additional movements are also active. Thus, for example, the movement of the *Suleymancilar*, which is similar to the *Milli Görüs*. Secondly, there is a missionary movement, the *Nurçu*, which has a greater intellectual component than the *Tabligh*. Like the *Tabligh* it believes that re-Islamisation of Muslim society is needed. But it seems to put emphasis on training leaders who can carry out this project. The *Nurçu* movement (founded in the tradition of the *Naqshbandi* school by Sayyid Nursi who died in 1960 and who opposed the secular reforms of Mustafa Kemal), calls for the opening of Koranic schools and Islamic training institutes which should be independent of the Turkish state. The *Nurçu* has centres in both Belgium and the Netherlands.[11]

There are several brotherhoods but none of them has any predominance. They include the *Derkawa*, the *Naqshbandi*, and the more successful *Alawiyya*. There are also the more distinctive *Alevites* (a Turkish–Kurdish group) and the *Ahmadiyya*.

5.2.4. *A typology of associations and movements.* It may be useful at this point to try to categorise these various groups and movements in order to get an overall view of their nature and ideological stance.

For the purposes of this chapter, a typology may be constructed by crossing several axes of classification. The first of these relates to the movements' religious orientation and discourse. Along this first axis, three classes are theoretically distinguishable: (1) that of a discourse which we will call 'traditionist', and which restores in a fairly rigid manner the classical interpretation of the fundamental 'facts'; (2) a 'modernising' class which reshapes this discourse in a new form but one drawing considerable inspiration from traditional attitudes; and (3) a 'remoulding' class, which is embarking on a new exercise but does not yet appear to have taken organised shape, being instead limited to the work of individual thinkers.

A second axis situates these organisations according to the orientation of their activities. These can be placed on a continuum, in terms of Western categories, from the public to the private. In other words, these movements can be classified according to the extent to which they tend overtly towards spiritualisation and individualisation of the religious or towards bringing the latter into the public domain.

A third axis allows these organisations to be differentiated according to the spatial orientation of their activity, i.e. according to whether they behave like satellites around the central Islamic lands or places of origin, and direct their activities primarily in relation to these centres; or whether, on the other hand, they target 'transplanted' Islam; or, indeed, whether they envelop or subjugate this local transplanted Islam to a pan-Islamist and 'transnational' vision.

On this basis an overall typology can be put together of Islamic movements currently active in transplanted Islam in Belgium and the Netherlands (and indeed further afield). This is laid out in Table 10.5.

Table 10.5

A Typology of Islamic Movements in Belgium and the Netherlands

	Satellite	Transnational	Local
Private	———————— Alawiyya ————————		
	———————— Nurçu ————————		
	———————— *Tabligh*		
Ethno-segmentary	———————— *Derkawa* ————————		
	— *Suleymancilar* ————————		
Public	———————————————— 'Amicales'		
	———————— *Naqshbandi* ————————		
	———————— Muslim Brotherhood ————————		
	———————— Associations of Muslims students		
	— *Milli Görüs* ————————		

Note: the traditionist interpretations are in italics. The modernist ones are in roman type.

A few remarks may be added. The *Tabligh* rightly appear in a localised area of the diagram, but reach beyond it through their missionary action. They are bearers of a 'traditionist' discourse, and their complex organisation allows skilful handling of both the local and transnational aspects. The two Turkish organisations, *Suleymancilar* and *Milli Görüs*, while implanted in immigrant communities, have not forgotten their own origin, which lay in opposition to the secularisation of the state by Mustafa Kemal. They continue their action for the re-establishment of a more Islamically oriented state in Turkey. Many of the leaders who brought the movements to Europe had had to leave Turkey and obtained refugee status in European countries, especially Germany. From their European refuge, they tried to pursue their original aim. Yet their activities have been modified over the years, becoming increasingly oriented towards transplanted Islam in Western Europe itself, rather than the future of Turkey.[12]

The *Derkawa* are typical of a brotherhood which continues to structure itself – as well as to manage and 'reactivate' its adherents' sense of belonging – on its traditional segmentary base, but in forms which are essentially private. The associations inspired by the Muslim Brotherhood and those which are close to Muslim students, on the other hand, are examples of associations oriented towards public action, with a strong element of protest and pan-Islamism. Implanted in local neighbourhoods which are intended to act as poles of support for their activities, these associations have an impact beyond the local context, becoming engaged in protest actions carried out in the name of Islam. Their fragmentation and their 'left-wing' tendency weakens them considerably on the terrain of action, although they have had some success with young people because of their ability to offer a modernising discourse and an international perspective (other than the anti-imperialist and anti-Western ones).

In conclusion, then, since the early 1970s Belgium and the Netherlands have seen a considerable development of Muslim associative dynamism. Today it encompasses a large section of the first generation adult male population, and is well-organised and well-focused. Muslim organisations and associations are now also being established and joined by young people, who are beginning to express themselves actively in the mosques, particularly the non-traditionist ones.

The importance of this development should not be overstated, though. While the strength of these movements certainly in part derives from their ability to mobilise people, from their dynamism and voluntary character, it also derives from the ideological crisis and running-out-of-steam of *non*-Muslim associative life. This crisis is due to the latter's increasing bureaucratisation, which has progressively immobilised it. It is also probably due to the intervention of the authorities, who have invested in cultural institutions which have contributed to the stifling of associative life.

By the same token, however, Muslim associative life must not be underestimated or devalued either. It must not be underestimated because it is the bearer of ideas which currently are proving able to mobilise people. Often, other social actors appear to believe that this movement might be countered on its own ground. This is illusory since no social force today in Belgium and the Netherlands is in a position to oppose organised Islam, nor should it. Some political and media commentators have implicitly or explicitly expressed a certain distrust of this Muslim associative movement. Judged by its activities and methods, however, it is no more or less 'trustworthy' than any other associative social expression. Specific expressions of this Muslim associative life may well be unpalatable, but it is quite untenable to define the whole trend as adversarial towards the majority society. This would imply that it can be 'generalised' and endowed with static qualities, whereas in fact the trend and its expressions – variegated at any point in time – are continually evolving in the context of the evolution of wider social dynamics.

5.3. Organisations aiming to put transplanted Islam in a national-territorial framework

In both countries organisations have been established to create a framework for, or to coordinate, action at the national-territorial level in each country. Many of these organisations are the expression at that level of the movements described in the previous section.

Such, for example, are the Turkish Islamic Federations which in both the Netherlands and Belgium coordinate the *Milli Görüs* mosques. Opposed to these are the Turkish Islamo-cultural Federations which are the voice of the Turkish state's official Islam and are coordinated by that country's Directorate of Religious Affairs. The Moroccan mosques are less organised: the *Tabligh* have some coordination and so do the Moroccan friendly associations (*Amicales*). In the Netherlands, there are also the Pakistani mosques affiliated to the World Islamic Mission.

In addition, the Muslims have made efforts to establish 'representative' structures which span the different forms of religious and ethno-national expression, to respond in particular to the governments' expectations and thus gain access to public finance. This process is far from simple. As early as 1974, the *Federatie van Moslim-organisaties in Nederland* (Federation of Organisations of Muslims in the Netherlands) had been set up in the Netherlands. It was dissolved in 1980 after a dispute but re-established for a short time in 1981 as the *Moslim Organisaties in Nederland*. More recently, this has been succeeded by the *Islamitisch Landelijk Comité* (Islamic National

Committee) which has not, however, yet been recognised by the government.

In Belgium, de facto representation was assumed by the *Centre Islamique et Culturel de Belgique* (Islamic and Cultural Centre of Belgium), an offshoot of the Muslim World League. This arrangement resulted from an agreement between the Belgian and Saudi governments, upon which the Belgian government gave a 99-year lease on a building in Brussels and more or less recognised this centre as representative of Belgian Islam. This provoked protest from both the Muslim and non-Muslim communities. At the end of the 1980s the Belgian government refused to continue treating the Islamic centre as representative. First it said it wanted a vote to be held among the Muslim community, but when this was set in motion, it retracted. At the time of writing, there are two structures in Belgium which claim to be representative: a Higher Council of Belgian Muslims, elected by a relatively orthodox electoral process but in which the Turkish *Diyanet* refused to participate (because of the participation of the *Milli Görüs*); and a 'Council of Wise Men', appointed by the state and based on the French model. The precise composition of this council has remained a contentious issue, as has the extent, or lack, of its influence.

6. Conclusions

In both countries, Islam now irrevocably forms part of society. This has changed the cultural scene considerably, and may conceivably in future modify the political scene. In any event, the on-going process of implantation and insertion leaves open several questions and issues.

The process of increasing autonomy is especially relevant. Until very recently, the experience of Belgian and Dutch Islam has been one of issues and problems imported from outside. Currently, however, issues and problems are emerging which are specific to the Muslims of these two countries.

The future of Islam in these two countries is linked to the evolution of its leadership. Until now this has consisted of men of the first generation of immigrants (fathers, and now grandfathers) or religious teachers and imams imported from Muslim countries. In general, they have been poorly educated and/or poorly equipped to deal with Western reality. In this respect, Muslim immigration in the Netherlands and Belgium differs from that in the United Kingdom. A major question, then, must be how the transition 'from the Islam of the fathers to the Islam of the sons' will take place, and where the future European Muslim leaders will be trained.

A related question is to what extent, and until when, Turkey and Morocco intend to retain control over their respective populations through the medium of Islam. While this influence sometimes re-assures politicians, since these two countries are considered to be friendly to the West, it is nevertheless contradictory to the process of integration.

Future relations between the Muslim and non-Muslim popula-tions will be an issue of particular concern. The 1980s witnessed a range of knee-jerk reactions from non-Muslims. Muslims, for their part, showed a relative inability to understand the questions (or even the basis of the questions) asked by the non-Muslims with respect to the future development of these communities and their place and role in the dominant society (for instance regarding the status of women, political *intégrisme*, family law, and so on). These questions need addressing urgently; yet very few on either side seem capable of doing so. The future will thus bring further such unthinking re-flexes and consequent tensions. It is imperative, therefore, to establish mechanisms which will allow such questions to be put on the table and dealt with constructively.

The institutionalisation of Islam as a new 'pillar' of these soci-eties (among the already existing 'pillars' referred to at the outset of this chapter) can be envisaged for the future. It is not, however, on the immediate agenda. Ethno-national fragmentation and the frag-mentation of religious persuasions and attitudes is hindering this process. The concrete experience of the *umma*'s diversity in the countries of emigration does not facilitate the translation of the ideal into organised reality.

Notes

1   Dutch *zuil* = pillar.

2   A special case in the Netherlands is the history of the Moluccans of Indonesia, former members of the colonial army, who emigrated to the Netherlands at independence in 1951 and some 1,000 of whom were Muslim. Among these, some members of the *Ahmadiyya* movement built a real mosque as early as 1956.

3   See F. Dassetto and A. Bastenier, *Europa nuova frontiera dell'islam* (Rome: EL, 1988).

4   G. Kepel, in his work *La Revanche de Dieu* (Paris: Seuil, 1991), translated as *The Revenge of God: The Resurgence of Islam, Christianity and Judaism in the Modern World* (Cambridge: Polity Press, 1994), makes a distinction between 'higher' and 'lower' Islamist movements. In reality this distinction is blurred and overvalues the speech and ideologies of these movements. Their Islamisation methods are in reality very similar and consist of measures to increase awareness of Islam in daily life.

5   Abdallah Laroui, *Islam et modernité* (Paris: la Découverte, 1987); Fatima Mernissi, *Le Harem politique* (Paris: Albin Michel, 1987). The earlier works referred to are Laroui, *La Crise des intellectuels arabes* (Paris: Maspero, 1974); and Mernissi, *Sexe, ideologie, islam* (Paris: Tierce, 1975).

6   M. Arkoun, a figure of considerable intellectual standing, can be placed in this group. It is also not difficult to see that Arkoun's stance was modified in the second half of the 1980s. While he previously questioned primarily Muslim thought, the 'Islamic reason', today he seems to want to question above all Western reason, and to be in search of a third way between the mythical thought of the Islamic tradition and Western rationalism. To do this, in a kind of neo-illuminist procedure, he seems to trust scientific analysis as applied to the 'religions of the book', as able to reach into the true core of these revelations.

7   B. Étienne, *L'Islamisme radical* (Paris: Hachette, 1987).

8   See also the chapter on Germany in this volume.

9   For more information on Belgium see: F. Dassetto and A. Bastenier, *L'Islam transplanté. Vie et organisation des minorités musulmanes de Belgique* (Bruxelles: EVO, 1984); A. Grignard, 'Profil des organisations islamistes' in R. Bristolfi and F. Zabbal (eds.), *Islams d'Europe. Intégration ou insertion communautaire?* (Paris: L'Aube, 1995), pp. 110–17. On the Netherlands, see W. Shahid and P. van Koningsveld (eds.), *Islam in Dutch Society: current developments and future prospects* (Kampen: Kok Pharos, 1992); N. Landman, *Van Mat tot Minaret. De institutionalisering van de Islam in Nederland* (Amsterdam: VU Uitgeverij, 1992).

10   On the *Tabligh*, see F. Dassetto, 'The Tabligh Organisation in Belgium' in T. Gerholm and Y. Lithman (eds.), *The New Islamic Presence in Western Europe*, 2nd edn (London: Mansell, 1990), pp. 159–73.

11   See also Chapter 12 on Germany.

12   A similar trend has been visible in Germany; see Chapter 12.

11

MUSLIM COMMUNITIES IN FRANCE

Jim House

This chapter intends to show how French political culture has, both at conceptual and practical levels, placed constraints on the acceptance of Muslims in France. These constraints and other patterns of long-term hostility have also delimited reactions to Muslims when they mobilise for religious equality.[1] Examples from institutional and non-institutional contexts will be taken to illustrate the complexity of the current situation.

1. Frameworks for analysis

An analysis of Muslim communities in France has to be based on a multiplicity of methodological approaches. There is no one 'Muslim community' as such, and the different definitions applied to 'Muslims' from the outside are likely to vary considerably from those used by the actors themselves.[2] Even the idea of Muslim communities (in the plural) tends to amalgamate groups which do not always see themselves as having the same areas of interest culturally, socio-economically, politically or linguistically. Indeed, part of the weakness of Islam in France is due to its internal divisions and the lack of a single, institutionally recognised authority through which to negotiate its place *vis-à-vis* state and civil society. This heterogeneity of interests has led to internal struggles for the representation of what are often fictionalised unities, and all generalisations and amalgamations must be approached with great caution.

The term 'community' is problematic within the context of French political culture, due to the predominance (but not exclusivity) of the individual assimilationist model which views communities

219

negatively as the supposed proof of a lack of commitment to assimilate. Thus even where communities can be said to exist, they are seldom recognised by the state. Expressing the dominant academic opinion on the subject, the sociologist Alain Touraine, giving evidence to the Nationality Commission in 1988, claimed that any form of multiculturalism (which would involve the recognition of 'communities') could 'lebanise' France.[3] Community-based action concerning religious demands is unlikely to attract much sympathy from politicians and, as will be shown, often has to be formulated in universalistic terms, such as the right to worship, when (for example) campaigning for planning permission for mosques.

Since 'assimilation' and 'integration' are terms which are often confused, it is necessary for analytical purposes to differentiate between them. Assimilation can be used to refer to socio-cultural aspects, often seen in terms of socio-cultural conformity.[4] Integration can more usefully be applied to socio-economic and civic and civil rights.[5] Both terms have ethnocentric connotations but are here used and defined to reduce their polysemous qualities often played on in political debates.

Studies of the 'Muslim communities' in France also need a broad historical framework, to examine how these 'communities' have negotiated their place in French society, as a part of French society, throughout this century, and their evolution from a position of socio-economic weakness to a capacity to formulate demands. Islam in France is largely the result of colonial-based immigration, and the power relations that continue to be embodied in a post-colonial era.[6]

The most important methodological question must be, however, to know just who constitutes a 'Muslim'. As with immigration, the fixation with statistics is often undertaken within an approach that exaggerates their numerical strength.[7] If the word immigrant (immigré(e)) in contemporary France has come to connote purely and simply North Africans (or those perceived as such), then it is equally true that the dominant logic is that every North African (including the children of primary immigrants) constitutes if not a 'Muslim', then at least a potential one. Thus the definition from outside, one that is imposed in the media and in political discourse, has significant weight. Following Wihtol de Wenden,[8] we will differentiate between, on the one hand, this imposed identity used to define 'imaginary Muslims' from the outside (and hence usually covering all following categories due to its indiscriminate nature) and, on the other, those who strictly speaking can be called Muslim since they regularly practise their faith. A third category would refer to those actors defining themselves as Muslims in terms of cultural belonging. The fourth and numerically largest category, especially amongst young people, concerns those adopting the label Muslim as regards socio-political identity. This is where Roy's typology of 'sociological Muslims' is helpful, describing those who are 'non-practising but who continue to use the term Muslim'.[9] The term 'sociological Muslim' can also be applied when speaking of older-generation primary immigrants who have either lost the practice of their religion since their settlement in France or, as is the case with many Algerians and Moroccans, whose passage to France came after a period of 'de-Islamisation' in the Maghreb due to rural–urban migration.[10]

Socio-political Muslim identity for young people (but not exclusively them) tends to surface at times of international conflict (for example the Gulf War). It is limited, however, and is more often once again to be seen in terms of an externally-imposed identity than a self-proclaimed one (i.e. Arab–Muslim solidarity etc.).[11] As Étienne has argued,[12] young people in France of Maghrebi, Sub-Saharan African or Turkish origin 'are not Muslims but are stigmatised as such', socialisation through religion simply not being operative in the French context. These factors help to explain why estimates concerning the number of 'Muslims' in France vary from 1.75 million to 4 million depending on one's definitions (or lack of them).

In the list of nationalities containing large numbers of Muslims in the widest sense of the term, the most sizeable group are the Algerians, Moroccans and Tunisians (in descending numerical order), followed by the Turks, West Africans (mostly Malinese, Senegalese and Mauritanians) and much smaller groups of Lebanese and Pakistanis. About 90 per cent are Sunni. A large minority of the Maghrebi group speak Berber, and organisation along ethnic lines is common for West African Muslims. The 'sociological Muslims' of French nationality are made up of some of the sons and daughters of these mainly primary immigrants, and also of the 'French Muslim' community ('harkis' – those having fought for France in the Algerian War of Independence, 'repatriated' to France after 1962 to avoid reprisals). A further category which would include French converts to Islam, is numerically impossible to determine. This should really apply to those who are 're-Islamised', especially young people (see below).

It is worth stressing the marginality of Islam for the (grand-) children of primary immigrants from North Africa, and emphasising the rarity of the decision to be a practising Muslim. Young people often use the term 'Muslim' to refer to their (grand)parents rather than to themselves.[13] Religious practice amongst the 'sociological Muslims' is often limited to varying levels of observance of Ramadhan as a sign of respect for and solidarity with their parents. The situation is further complicated by the fact that the terms 'Arab' and 'Muslim' have become largely synonymous in French political discourse. This gives some idea of the multiplicity of identities at play. The idea of a diaspora, taking into account transnational characteristics, is arguably the most relevant for these 'sociological Muslims'. All this highlights the difficulties of an overly rigid categorisation when applied to complex situations.

The socio-economic position of communities of recent immigrant origin is difficult to evaluate on ethnic or religious lines, since official statistics can legally only use French/foreigner criteria. Multigenerational approaches to socio-economic integration are thus made hard to establish. The colonial past is still very much present and has meant that, in particular for Algerians and their descendants, length of time spent in France has not proven to be a guarantee of socio-economic integration. Borkowski has shown how multi-generational socio-economic integration for sons and daughters of North African parents is often worse than for all other categories of recent immigration. The articulation of past and present hostility especially towards North Africans and their families is crucial in explaining perceptions of 'Muslims', whether real or imagined.[14]

2. Neo-racism and 'Muslims'

Since the presence of North Africans in France is nothing new, especially from the First World War onwards,[15] a periodisation of hostility would have to take into account certain specific long-term factors concerning French political culture which often see 'difference' in antagonistic terms (for example nationalism, franco-centric universalism, assimilationist logic, and secularism or *laïcité*). Conjunctural factors must also be considered.[16] Their influence on the political imaginary is often to reintroduce, in re-worked form, some of the long-term factors described earlier, particularly in times of economic crisis linked to a crisis in 'national identity'. The reinvention of the 'problem' of immigration can be seen as an example of this process. One of the keys to understanding continuing hostility comes from the fact that the colonial and 'religious' dimensions cut across both of these categories.[17]

Traditional French nationalism, which is inward-looking, and based very much on French Catholic 'identity', continues to be influential within the main vector of racism in France, the Front National.[18] There are close links between the catholic fundamentalists (*intégristes*) and Jean-Marie Le Pen, who hark back to Barrès and the Action française. Taguieff has argued that the result of 'differentialist' racism, formulated principally by the French New Right (Nouvelle Droite) from the early 1970s onwards and appropriating antiracist affirmations of the 'right to difference', was to stereotype a 'difference' presented increasingly in cultural and religious terms.[19] The racism of the Nouvelle Droite (especially that of the GRECE[20]), defines the base of French 'identity' on a European rather than a strictly national level. Centred round what appears to be a distortion of the work of Georges Dumézil, this ideology rejects 'non-Europeans' theoretically no matter what their religion (Christianity being targeted as the source of the egalitarianism detested by the differentialist elitism of the GRECE),[21] although some religions are presented by the Nouvelle Droite as being more different (and hence more 'dangerous') than others.

Current Front National discourse is very much an unsteady amalgamation of the two 'logics' of traditionalism and the Nouvelle Droite within the far right in France. Forced to go outside the purely nationalistic base as regards the construction of the European Community and the 'threat' posed by immigration, the protection of 'European identity' (never defined and hence posited in simply oppositional terms which is where the immense stock of historical hostility to Islam comes in) means that the conflation of 'ethnic' and 'religious' belonging is then made into a stereotype. North Africans (their families by definition being included in this stereotyping, or 'essentialising') are the particular targets of such racism where the religious 'coefficient' is arguably higher now than 25 years ago. Yonnet[22] is merely the most recent in a long line of writers who talk of the supposed threat that 'Muslims' present to the 'bio-ethno-religious homogeneity' of France. All North Africans (or those seen as such) according to this discourse are thus not simply 'potential Muslims' (a vision shared by the Islamists in their proselytising mission) but 'hereditary', always already 'Muslims'. One could say that the French far right has succeeded in 're-Islamising' North Africans in the political imaginary. This has spread across to more mainstream parties in terms of the idea of the 'non-loyalty' of North Africans as citizens due to their religious belonging.

Hostility to difference, as has already been suggested, has also existed due to the republicans' stress on assimilation, crossing Left/ Right divisions. For example, the idea that an 'ethnic vote' could exist would be anathema to dominant French conceptions of citizenship which demand that the individual shed his/her 'identity' in the civic sphere.[23] Whereas the extreme right argues that Muslims (however defined) be different but not equal, assimilationism states that they should be theoretically equal as regards political rights but not show any signs of 'difference'.[24] Linked to this is the a posteriori theorisation of the supposedly successful assimilation of Italian and Polish immigrants. This paints a picture of a complete 'national-isation' of the French population which the 'new' immigrant (i.e. North African) presence has allegedly destabilised due to its sup-posed 'inassimilability'.[25] Now that the vast majority of primary im-migrants from the Maghreb, Turkey and West Africa have decided to settle in France, this assertion of 'inassimilability' is arguably a way of making their presence seem definitively provisional on a socio-cultural level, whereas until the early 1970s it was presented more in economic terms. This is not to argue that the economic aspect of discriminatory discourse has disappeared (although there has been a shift within this discourse to focus on immigrants as rival consumers rather than rival producers and workers), but rather to suggest that it now has to compete with the more dominant socio-cultural argu-ment.

This change in emphasis towards the cultural can be observed through studies of the press, which have shown how the subjects con-cerning immigrants (or those perceived as such) changed during the early 1980s: from portraying them as suffering from disadvantages in employment, housing or working conditions, and as actors trying to fight this discrimination, to focusing more on the 'religious' aspects (mosques, 'fundamentalism', polygamy, terrorism and recent events in Algeria).[26] Bonnafous sees 1983 as being the turning-point in much of the written media, since when it has been the very presence of non-European immigrants which is portrayed as a problem, especially in relation to demands for 'religious equality' from Muslims, and how this change in emphasis tied in with the ascendant cultural differentialist racism (or neo-racism) of the Nouvelle Droite and also, in part, the Front National.[27]

3. Public responses to Muslims as social actors

The context of hostility described in the previous section is important to help understand the reaction by public authorities to what is seen as 'Islam-as-a-problem'. When Muslims put forward certain specific religious demands these negative attitudes are often reinforced. Sometimes authorities perceive religious demands even where they do not exist.

Many reasons have been put forward to explain the increased 'visibility' of Islam in France from the mid-1970s onwards, as regards demands by the actors themselves to affirm religious identity and equality concerning immigrant hostels, factory space for worship and planning permission for mosques. When analysing these issues, important differences must be taken into consideration concerning type of immigration, modes of worship and nationality. Many immigrants decided to stay and settle permanently in France after the 1974 decision to stop all primary immigration other than family regrouping. As long as the myth of an ultimate return to the country of origin was maintained, reference to life in France was mostly temporary and unlikely to give rise to demands for greater recognition of Islam. This realisation of the permanence of settlement took place from 1974 for the North and sub-Saharan Africans, and only around 1980 for Turkish immigrants.[28]

Demands for 'space' for Islam in the workplace came firstly from West Africans (1976) and then spread more widely. Companies were often willing to allow what they considered as 'pacifying measures' – worth much in terms of production for relatively little cost. Barou has argued that what was new about these events was not Islam in the factory *per se* but more the official acceptance of its visibility.[29] Managers recognised that it was more a question of adapting Islam to the factory situation than the reverse. These demands (centred around the creation of prayer rooms and the modification of shifts during Ramadhan and for imams) proved most successful in large companies with long histories of employing successive waves of immigrants (e.g. Renault), and where the numerical strength of Muslim workers in certain workshops was particularly high.[30] In the late 1970s, governments were likely to support this 'right to difference' obeying a logic of social peace that, at least for a time, toyed with vague notions of multiculturalism. The main unions, keen to be seen to be winning more worker rights in a climate of increasing deunionisation, eventually supported religious demands. These demands, along with those involving hostels and rent strikes, have been described as the 'passage to the political' by extra-political means, that is to say, means outside the traditional political parties since most workers concerned did not have the right to vote.[31]

Strikes in the car industry in the period 1980-3 tended to exacerbate existing tensions and misunderstandings between politicians, management and unions concerning Muslim workers.[32] The political class as a whole proved largely incapable of interpreting the essentially socio-economic demands of the strikers (i.e. whether Muslim or not), and was mesmerised by the post-1979 context of Islamic 'fundamentalism' whose Iranian model of militancy was then transposed directly onto the French national scene. Those on strike were not acting according to religious motivations, although that did not stop the then Prime Minister, Pierre Mauroy, declaring that the strikers at the Renault factory in 1983 were 'being stirred up by religious and political groups whose action is determined by criteria which have little to do with social reality in France', summarising a widely held view at the time.[33]

Demands for planning permission for the construction of mosques have brought into play the crucial role of mayors who have had greater influence over local decision-making since the decentralising legislation of 1981.[34] Mosques are usually organised along national lines, which often does not help the formulation of collective demands needed to influence local authorities. Gender, generational and spatial characteristics must here be taken into consideration, since after family regrouping, Muslim communities are more diversified within these three categories (amongst others). Opposition to the construction of mosques has provoked considerable problems for those town councils willing to grant planning permission. The Muslim associations have a variety of institutional agents to deal with at both local and national level.[35] The universalistic demands for the right to worship are theoretically difficult to reject since Islam is numerically the second religion in France.

The role of the Muslim associations in poor outer-city suburbs (*banlieues*) has been significant in a climate of reduced state/local intervention in the socio-cultural field.[36] Islam is thus often viewed with ambivalence at local level by decision-makers; in the political imaginary Islam is considered pejoratively by almost all actors, whilst 'on the ground' it is viewed as a useful barrier to further social exclusion, in particular for many children of North African parents.[37] It is thus wrong to say that at local level there has been no institutional recognition of Islam, although this recognition remains admittedly limited.

Efforts at '(re-)Islamisation' of immigrants should be seen in a variety of contexts, depending as they often do on the amount of control that countries of origin can exert over their (former) nationals. Pietist movements such as the *jama'at at-Tabligh*, devoid of any political message, had a certain success amongst some North African immigrants, since they offered poor, single male workers what Kepel has called 'immediate resocialisation'.[38] Kepel sees this form of proselytising as answering the need for a defence mechanism against social exclusion. Étienne talks of this process as one of 'retraditionalisation through too much modernity'.[39]

Whilst this apolitical stance can sometimes disgruntle younger people enough to encourage them to go elsewhere for a more political message, some children of North African parents have also been attracted by its very apoliticism, after their initial politicisation through campaigning or associational action (for example previous participation in the antiracist movements of 1980–7).[40] The longer-term aims of the Muslim Brotherhood tend to attract young, well-educated Muslims due to the vaguely utopian promise that modernity will be Islamised.

The terminology used in the debate, however, is very often imprecise. Firstly, the term 're-Islamisation', when applied to primary immigrants resident in France, would suggest that this process ends in the same forms of religious practice as those 'lost' in the course of migration. In fact, the modalities of re-Islamisation will have been transformed by the migratory experience; a simple 'reproduction' of previous forms of worship and linked sociability is unlikely. The maraboutism (the following of holy men or hermits) prevalent in the Maghreb has often been stigmatised by Islamists in France, for example. Secondly, and more importantly, it is difficult to see how the term re-Islamisation can be applied to many young people with Muslim parents: the experience of Islam provided by, for example, the Muslim Brotherhood, will almost certainly be the first containing a coherent set of religious values which these young people have been offered. Again the risk is present of stereotypically categorising these young people as always already Muslims; there is scant empirical evidence to prove any large-scale conversion to Islam amongst these categories of the population. The 'return' to religion amongst young people is not simply an 'Islamic' phenomenon. On the one hand, it extends to others faiths.[41] On the other, there is a *socio-economic* dynamic involved in conversion to Islam amongst young working-class people, which is evidence of a distrust of 'salvation' through politics.[42] As Burgat has argued, a degree of distance from purely national issues is needed on behalf of the analyst to be able to take into account transnational aspects, but also sufficient proximity to national issues to be able to undertake the deconstruction of stereotypes.[43]

The importance of generational aspects can also be seen in the appointment and training of imams who, when brought from the Maghreb or Egypt, have little chance of attracting the adhesion of young people born and raised in France who are suspicious of external (e.g. Algerian) government interference in France. Not the least of the paradoxes in former Interior Minister Charles Pasqua's policy of encouraging closer institutional control of Islam in France, was that those imams trained with very much a French context in mind could ultimately have more success than before amongst young people, whereas the driving idea behind his policy was arguably to contain and channel Islam.[44]

Inter-associational and inter-elite rivalries at local level, and inter-federation rivalries for representativeness at national level have meant that, with the transnational aspect also to be taken into account, the prospects for a single institutional body representing Islam in France remain distant.[45] Étienne has shown how the anti-'fundamentalist' position of the French authorities is often used to de-legitimise the moderate reading of Islam promoted by the lobbyists working for the community-level integration of Islam within the secular state (the majority position amongst practising Muslims).[46] Secularism, however, has proven to be remarkably intolerant of Islam within the French context.

4. French secularism

The 'Headscarf Affair' of 1989, in which three young Muslim women were excluded from attending school classes on account of their Islamic headscarves (*hijab*), revealed the place currently assigned to Islam within France.[47] The debate provided more insight into the conceptual blindness of much of French political culture and its discourse than about the majority of practising Muslims, who confine their religion to the private sphere, in spite of general assumptions to the contrary.

The debate should, however, be seen in its historical context. The French state school system, theoretically secular since the 1880s, constitutes, according to the interpretation usually given to the term by republicans, a supposedly neutral space. In this specifically educational context, the idea of secularism is that all pupils can come together devoid of their religious or any other form of belonging, to study in a world hermetically sealed from the rest of society, thus sparing them from possible proselytising. Only in 1905 was the separation between Church and State made official. Secularism (*laïcité*) should be seen in terms of the victory of the Third Republic over the opponents of the revolution of 1789, and indeed in the late 19th century the political debate was structured around a mutual vilification: republicans (atheists or otherwise) against 'obscurantists', 'Progress' and 'Reason' against the 'forces of reaction'. Although many of these terms seldom recur in political debate nowadays (the 'Headscarf Affair' showing that they have yet to disappear), the consolidation of the Republic is no longer the central factor: culturally speaking, it is now more a question of how open or closed French society should be concerning public manifestations of religious 'differences'. However, the binary categories so characteristic of the political discourse of modernity were given a brushing down for public display in the months following the start of the 'Affair', which occupied an exceptional amount of attention in the French media in late 1989 and early 1990.

The French revolution, while having started a process of desacralising religion to some extent, in turn made sacred the politico-religious settlement of secularism, which became the 'state religion' – as Third Republic state school publications called it.[48] The neutrality of this secularism has been contested. Indeed, the State is traversed by Catholicism, since political culture has been imbued with religion.

As Étienne puts it: 'The secular state most often includes the ethos and practices of the majority religious group.'[49] For example, the school calendar in France is very much based around that of the Roman Catholic Church. A truly neutral secularism would postulate all religions as equally different. As it is, the Catholic church in France is very much first amongst 'equals' as regards state and civil society.

Historically, the role of the secular school system was to reduce cultural difference from the centralising, uniformising norm. Weber has highlighted the importance of the role of the education system in the 'nationalisation' of the French population from the late 19th century onwards.[50] The transformation of the child through schooling was based on the antagonistic relationship between school and household (in terms of language, religion and culture). Thus any continuity of religious practice (above all in what is considered a highly 'different' religion) between parents and children was and still is likely to arouse intense hostility from those secularists in a position to define the normalising standards at a given period. The insistence by the parents of the three young women on a 'right to difference' for Islam is thus considered doubly dangerous by the secularist hardliners. In some ways, of course, the justification on the basis of 'tradition' for wearing the Islamic headscarf is somewhat tenuous, as it obeys a logic quite different to that of tradition; the 'tradition' ostensibly in evidence is hardly devoid of contact with modernity: it is 'activated' precisely as a reaction against what are seen as modernity's most dangerous aspects. However, in the 'Affair', the terms of reference were largely binary and therefore (at least superficially) mutually exclusive – tradition vs. modernity, good vs. bad, depending on the position of the actors.

Williame has pointed out how the secularism of 1905 has itself been mostly secularised, in that the state no longer wants to mould individuals as a counter-religion to the Catholic Church.[51] That this former concept is not entirely dead, however, was shown by the 'Affair', when the socio-economically disadvantaged religion that is Islam in France was portrayed as a serious threat to the continued existence of the Republic. The separation between public and private spheres, an important reference point for the Conseil d'État (State Council), called upon by the then Education Minister Lionel Jospin (Parti Socialiste) to give its interpretation on the existing legislation concerning the matter,[52] should not obscure the fact that Catholicism is present in the public sphere.

In analysing the distortions in representations of Islam in France which took place during the 'Affair', a double centre-periphery relationship can be sketched. Firstly, in much of political and media discourse, Islamic 'fundamentalism' is placed at the centre of Islam in France, whereas it is of purely marginal concern not simply to the 'sociological Muslims', but also to the various schools of worship as regards regular religious practice. Secondly, Islam is then made ex-centric and marginalised as far as general perceptions of tolerance are concerned, the first schema being used in media and political debates to reinforce the quasi-permanence of the second. This often results in the non-extension of tolerance in the public imaginary to Islam in general and to all those defined abusively from the outside as 'Muslims'.

Tolerance of 'difference' on much of the French Left has often been transient, since it is presumed that all 'differences' in socio-cultural terms in an educational context are to be abandoned at the school gate and all signs of religious belonging cast off at the classroom door – very much as the Conseil d'État interpreted the existing legislation. The criteria for defining intolerance, although presented in pseudo-universalistic terms, remain resolutely franco-centric. Equality is to be accorded only since 'candidates' (illustrating the idea of examination and the proof of worthiness) are viewed as having decided to conform socio-culturally to a standard presented as neutral. This 'discriminating cognitive egalitarianism', as Gellner calls it, supposes that 'men and minds are considered equal, but *not* all cultures and systems of meaning'.[53] Although the Socialist Education Minister Jospin stressed the need for dialogue, he was unequivocal about his opposition to the Islamic headscarf being worn. He declared in an interview, after having expressed his rejection of both 'differentialism' and 'assimilationism', that: 'I'm [also] against the headscarf being worn at school. My only problem is the ways by which we can get to that point.'[54] His position was almost a caricature of implicit assumptions concerning non-European immigration: 'The Polish, Italian, Spanish or Portuguese immigrants were Europeans and Catholics. We now have to deal with non-European immigrants whose integration (and this is a fact) meets with more difficulties.'[55]

The sensitivity of the hardline republicans to the question of Islam in schools has no doubt been heightened due to debates in the media over the 'crisis' of the traditional state and non-state institutions concerning their assimilatory mission. These institutions have been seen increasingly as losing their pertinence and ability to impose a model of 'frenchness' (*francité*) on the population, due to the combined factors of decentralisation, internationalisation and post-industrialisation.[56] The school system has always played an important functional and symbolic role in this 'nationalising' mission. The creation and visibility of 'Islam-as-a-problem' can thus be understood from the perspective of debates internal to French political culture, its changes and permanence, as well as the internal development of Islam in France, which should perhaps be re-named French Islam. The inability of consensual Islam to impose its own definition of the situation, being excluded from the main sources of information, may be the main conclusion to be drawn from the 'Affair'. A debate in binary terms calls for 'either-or' solutions, where in fact the complex and heterogeneous identities of those taking part in the debate cannot but be distorted by having to situate themselves around the central pole of 'national-republicanism' (Wieviorka) – whether that of the Right *or* of the Left. This superficial reduction of identities[57] makes it almost impossible to negotiate equal space for the multiple identities and practices of French Islam. Instead, a logic of considering categories of 'both . . . and . . .' would have the advantage of including rather than excluding, understanding rather than condemning, given that we are talking of a 'problem' created mainly by the non-existence of conceptual frameworks capable of including 'differences'.

5. France, French Islam, and the Algerian question

The political, historical and socio-economic factors that explain the position of Muslims in France can be analysed in relation to national, international and transnational aspects. Each typology has to be applied differently whether we are talking about Muslims in the strictest sense of the word, the various identity-based uses applied by the actors themselves, or the dominant stereotypes applied from the outside. The generational aspects mentioned earlier are extremely important, as the modalities for French Islam in the future will be defined by people born and raised in France. French political culture remains ill-suited to community-based demands, in spite of partial and ephemeral conversions to the ideas of the 'right to difference' espoused in the 1980s and now out of favour on the French left. Mainstream republican political culture tends to invent communities of interest among groups of immigrant origin and yet ignore community demands where they can be said to exist. The resurgence of differentialist racism, highlighting and stereotyping ('essentialising') cultural and 'religious' identities, has succeeded in imposing a framework of interpretation which the French media is often only too happy to reproduce. Such a climate is unlikely to result in sympathy for the demands for religious equality currently being put forward by Muslims. The position of socio-economic disadvantage in which many Muslims find themselves further weakens their ability to mobilise political support and impose their own definition of the situation.

French Islam's identity is complex, and Muslims in France are out to show that the idea of a French Islam should not be seen as the contradiction in terms that it is often portrayed to be. Yet this is not made any easier by the radical political reassertion of Islam in the southern Mediterranean, especially Algeria, and the effects both real and imaginary which this has had or may have.

Many of the problems facing French Islam, indeed, are illustrated by the events of August 1994, which saw the arrest, detention and then deportation of 19 Algerian and one Moroccan alleged supporters or members of the Front Islamique du Salut (FIS) in an operation by the Interior Minister Charles Pasqua which attracted widespread media attention. The clampdown on those supporting the FIS in France came as a consequence of the killing by Islamist extremists in Algiers on 3 August of five French nationals – three gendarmes and two French consular officials. In order to establish the context for these events in France, the precedents for such action should be mentioned: Pasqua, as Interior Minister in the 1986–8 Chirac government had already dealt with threats of terrorism in France in September 1986. This period had consecrated the link made in the social imaginary of many in France between Islam and terrorism. Since the arrival of the right-wing Balladur government in the Spring of 1993, Pasqua had introduced wide-ranging legislation limiting the right to political asylum, making the obtention of French nationality no longer automatic at birth for many children of foreign parents, increasing the restrictions on the right to stay in France for certain foreigners, and introducing new legislation extending police powers to check identity papers and search vehicles. These measures had been seen as a direct attack by many of North African immigrant origin.[58] The number of Algerians seeking asylum (or simply a temporary home) in France had grown (although the government has strictly limited the number of successful applications), and support groups to help secularist Algerian intellectuals were created.[59] The possible return of all French nationals from Algeria (demanded by the most militant of Algeria's Islamist opposition) was also under discussion.[60]

In the long and confused history of French–Algerian relations, the overt support by the Balladur government for the Algerian military regime in its campaign against the Islamists – as opposed to calls for cross-party dialogue from other Western governments – made it a target for hostility from the most radical Islamists.[61] The first murders of French nationals in Algeria in October 1993 had led to the arrest, on 9 November, of 88 Algerians suspected of support for the FIS in France.[62] This had, at the time, provoked anxiety amongst Muslims in France, afraid that the homogenising discourse on Muslim terrorists would tar also the most moderate amongst them with the same brush.[63]

When, in August 1994, those suspected of being favourable to the FIS were detained and 20 of them eventually deported to Burkina Faso on the last day of that month, without any criminal charges having been brought against them, the same fears were voiced over the French authorities' amalgamation between those in favour of terrorism and more moderate Islamists. Dalil Boubekeur, rector of the Paris mosque, and close to the regime in Algeria, spoke out over his fears that 'France would see a potential terrorist in every Muslim', and that there was the possibility of 'a return to the climate of the Algerian war [of independence]'.[64] These fears had been present also during the Gulf War of 1990–1, when the 'loyalty' of Arab Muslims had been questioned by some politicians and the media.[65]

The lack of differentiation by majority public opinion between moderate and extremist Islamists was at the heart of the policies pursued by Charles Pasqua, who strayed into pronouncements on foreign policy – outside his portfolio – taking advantage of the Summer recess.[66] The detention of Larbi Kechat, imam of the important Paris Al-Dawa mosque in the Rue de Tanger, and noted for his moderate opinions, aroused protests across religious denominations (he was not, in the end, deported).[67] Antiracist and human rights groups protested over the dubious legality of the detentions, and also over the massive police presence in Paris, subsequently extended throughout all major provincial cities. In ten days, 26,000 people in Paris had their identities checked specifically as a result of this police action – termed 'ensuring security' – undertaken in the main Arab immigrant districts.[68]

These events must be seen, as suggested above, within the context of a difficult period for Algerians living in France. Although the media talked unhesitatingly of 'the Muslim community', it was precisely the absence of any single, united Muslim voice that emerged from the debates over the role of French Islam. There was little attempt to give voice to the vast majority of moderate Muslims in France. Particular attention was paid in the media to the possible influence of the FIS in the *banlieues* (poor outer suburbs) and the north of France. This theme had developed since the first action against the FIS in France in November 1993, notwithstanding Bruno Étienne's evidence at the time that the FIS in France was in fact quite marginalised.[69] Most politicians hesitated between support in theory for measures to prevent terrorism and concern about the way such measures were being implemented.[70]

The results of the operation were arguably that a debate on the attitude which France should take towards the political complexity of developments in Algeria, became a priority, and that the necessary clarification about the diversity of French Muslim attitudes to such events was not forthcoming.

Notes

1   See E. Balibar, *Les Frontières de la Démocratie* (Paris: La Découverte, 1991).

2   J. Leca, 'L'Islam, l'État et la société en France. De la difficulté de con-
    struire un objet de recherche et d'argumentation' in B. Étienne (sous
    la direction de), *L'Islam en France* (Paris: Éditions du CNRS, 1990),
    pp. 41–72, p. 47.

3   Touraine's comment was to criticise a 'purely multicultural France' in
    'Être Français aujourd'hui et demain', Rapport de la Commission de
    la Nationalité (1988), Vol. 1, p. 408.

4   M. Silverman, *Deconstructing the Nation: Immigration, Racism and Citizenship
    in Modern France* (London: Routledge, 1992), p. 33.

5   See V. De Rudder, 'Assimilation' in *Vocabulaire historique et critique des
    relations inter-ethniques*, Pluriel Recherches, Cahier No. 1 (Paris: L'Harm-
    attan, 1993), pp. 22–7.

6   See E. Balibar and I. Wallerstein, *Race Nation Classe: Les identités ambigues*
    (Paris: La Découverte, 1988).

7   Typical of this widely held notion is the report in the weekly centre/
    centre-right magazine *Le Point* (No. 1093, 28 August 1993), whose cover
    headline, over a photograph of the back of a man in a jellaba in front
    of a mosque, reads: 'Islam: 4 million Muslims in France'. On page 45
    these 4 million Muslims have become merely 'potential followers', and
    we learn that of these 4 million 'it is very difficult to say how many are
    actually practising Muslims'. The highest numerical estimation is here
    topicalised with little regard for the more guarded comments in the ac-
    tual report.

8   C. Wihtol de Wenden, 'Discours sur l'Islam', *Projet*, No. 231, Autumn
    1992, pp. 7–17, p. 12.

9   O. Roy, 'Le Néo-fondamentalisme: Des Frères Musulmans aux FIS
    Algérien', *Esprit*, March–April 1992, Nos. 3–4, pp. 78–90.

10 P. Bourdieu and A. Sayad, *Le Déracinement: La crise de l'agriculture
    traditionelle en Algérie* (Paris: Éditions de Minuit, 1964).

11 C. Benayoun, 'Identité et citoyenneté: Juifs, arabes et pieds-noirs face
    aux événements du Golfe', *Revue française de Science Politique*, Vol. 43, No.
    2, April 1993, pp. 209–28; and D. Schnapper, 'La Citoyenneté à
    l'épreuve: Les musulmans pendant la guerre du Golfe', *Revue française de
    Science Politique*, Vol. 43, No. 2, April 1993, pp. 187–208.

12 B. Étienne, *La France et l'islam* (Paris: Hachette, 1989), p. 260.

13 Y. Gonzalez-Quijano, 'Les "nouvelles" générations issues de l'immigra-
    tion maghrébine et la question de l'islam', *Revue française de Science
    Politique*, Vol. 37, December 1987, pp. 820–32; and C. Lacoste-Dujardin,
    *Yasmina et les autres, de Nanterre et d'ailleurs: Filles de parents maghrébins en
    France* (Paris: Seuil, 1992).

14 J. Borkowski, 'L'insertion sociale des immigrés et de leurs enfants' in *Les
    Données Sociales 1990* (Paris: INSEE, 1990), pp. 310–14.

15 Étienne, *La France et l'islam*, p. 102.

16 For the First World War, see T. Stovall, 'Colour-blind France? Colonial

workers during the First World War', *Race and Class*, Vol. 35, No. 2 (1993), pp. 35–55; for the 1920s, N. MacMaster, 'The Rue Fondary murders of 1923 and the origins of anti-Arab racism', paper given to the *Annual Conference for the Study of Modern and Contemporary France*, Sheffield, September 1993; for the 1930s, R. Schor, *L'Opinion française et les étrangers en France 1919–1939* (Paris: Publications de la Sorbonne, 1985); for the 1950s, A. Girard, *Français et immigrés: Nouveaux documents sur l'adaptation: Algériens, Italiens, Polonais*, INED Cahiers et Documents No. 20 (Paris: INED/Presses Universitaires de France, 1954); and for the early 1970s, A. Girard *et al.*, 'Attitudes des Français à l'égard de l'immigration étrangère: Nouvelle enquête d'opinion', *Population*, Vol. 29, No. 5 (1974), pp. 1015–67; and F. Giudice, *Arabicides: Une chronique française 1970–1991* (Paris: La Découverte 'Enquêtes', 1992).

17   J. Henry has shown how in colonial Algeria essentialisation of the administrative category 'Muslim' in legal texts was commonplace: 'La norme et l'imaginaire: La construction de l'altérité en droit colonial algérien', *Procès: Cahiers d'analyse politique et juridique*, years 1987–8, pp. 13–28. See also G. Périès, 'L'Arabe, le musulman, l'ennemi dans le discours militaire de la "guerre révolutionnaire" pendant la guerre d'Algérie', *Mots*, No. 30, March 1992, pp. 53–71, for the Algerian War of Independence.

18   See M. Wieviorka, 'L'Expansion du racisme populaire' in P. Taguieff (sous la direction de) *Face au racisme*, Vol. 1: *Les moyens d'agir*, Vol. 1 (2 Vols., Paris: La Découverte, 1991), pp. 73–82.

19   P. Taguieff, *La Force du préjugé: Essai sur le racisme et ses doubles* (Paris: La Découverte, 1987).

20   *Groupement de Recherche et d'Études pour la Civilisation Européenne* (founded in 1968).

21   P. Taguieff, 'Origines et métamorphoses de la Nouvelle Droite' (interview), *Vingtième siècle*, No. 40, October–December 1993, pp. 3–21.

22   P. Yonnet, *Voyage au centre du malaise français. L'antiracisme et le roman national* (Paris: Gallimard Essais, 1993), p. 80.

23   See J. Leca, 'Individualisme et citoyenneté' in P. Birnbaum and J. Leca (eds.), *Sur l'individualisme: Théories et méthodes* (Paris: Presses de la Fondation Nationale des Sciences Politiques (FNSP), 1991), pp. 159–212. For a critique of the supposed openness of French citizenship see G. Noiriel, *Population, immigration et identité nationale en France: XIX–XXe siècle* (Paris: Hachette, 1993).

24   J. Rex, 'Stratégies antiracistes en Europe' in M. Wieviorka (ed.), *Racisme et modernité* (Paris: La Découverte, 1993), pp. 327–44, p. 334.

25   G. Mauco, *Les Étrangers en France* (Paris: A. Colin, 1932), used a similar typology to try to differentiate between East European and Belgian/Italian immigration in the 1930s (where those in the former category were considered 'unassimilable' compared to the latter).

26   C. Hamès, 'La Construction de l'Islam en France: Du côté de la presse', *Archives de Sciences Sociales de Religions*, 34th year, Vol. 68, No. 1, July–September 1989, pp. 79–92.

27   S. Bonnafous, *L'Immigration prise aux mots* (Paris: Kimé, 1991).

28 Wihtol de Wenden, 'Discours sur l'Islam'.

29 J. Barou, 'L'islam, facteur de régulation sociale', *Esprit*, No. 102, June 1985, pp. 207–15. See also B. Stora, *Nationalistes Algériens et révolutionnaires français au temps du Front Populaire* (Paris: L'Harmattan, 1987).

30 Interview with C. Wihtol de Wenden, Paris, 24 November 1993. See also Wihtol de Wenden, 'Trade Unions, Islam and Immigration', *Economic and Industrial Democracy*, Vol. 9, No. 1, February 1988, pp. 65–82.

31 C. Wihtol de Wenden, *Les Immigrés et la Politique* (Paris: Presses de la FNSP, 1988).

32 See F. Benoît, *Citroën, le printemps et la dignité* (Paris: Messidor/Éditions Sociales, 1982).

33 Cf. *Le Monde*, 11 February 1983.

34 M. Bekouchi, *Du bled à la ZUP et/ou la couleur de l'avenir* (Paris: CIEM/L'Harmattan, 1984). Openness to Islam by mayors is more complicated than a simple Left/Right split. For example, many Parti Socialiste mayors are imbued with secularist convictions and hence unlikely to embrace Islam with open arms. See also A. Jazouli, *Les Années banlieue* (Paris: Seuil, 1992).

35 R. Leveau, 'Les associations musulmanes', *Projet*, No. 231, Autumn 1992, pp. 78–80. After 1981 certain restrictions were lifted concerning cultural associations with non-French presidents and majority members under the 1901 law. This has greatly facilitated associative life across a wide scale. The favourable conditions for religious associations (*associations culturelles*) defined by the 1905 law are not applicable to islamic associations, since these do not limit their action to the strictly religious. Islamic associations are often then refused registration by mayors under the claims that they also do not conform to the statute of the cultural associations under the 1901 law (S. Pierré-Caps, 'Les "Nouveaux Cultes" et le droit public', *Revue du Droit Public et de la Science Politique en France et à l'Étranger*, Vol. 4, July–August 1990, pp. 1073–119). See also Étienne, *La France et l'islam*, p. 62.

36 See G. Kepel, *Les Banlieues de l'Islam: Naissance d'une réligion en France* (Paris: Seuil, 1987), and C. Wihtol de Wenden, 'L'Islam en France', *Regards sur L'Actualité*, No. 158, February 1990, pp. 23–36.

37 See Kepel, *Les Banlieues de l'Islam*.

38 *Ibid.*

39 B. Étienne, 'L'Islam à Marseille', *Les Temps Modernes*, Nos. 452–4, March–April 1984, pp. 1616–36.

40 Wihtol de Wenden, 'L'Islam en France', p. 28.

41 See G. Kepel, *La Revanche de Dieu: Chrétiens, juifs et musulmans à la reconquête du monde* (Paris: Seuil, 1990).

42 See F. Dubet, *La Galère: jeunes en survie* (Paris: Seuil, 1987).

43 F. Burgat, *L'islamisme au Maghreb: La voix du Sud* (Paris: Karthala, 1988), p. 6.

44 See M. Reeber, 'A study of Islamic preaching in France', *Islam and Christian–Muslim Relations*, Vol. 2, No. 2 (December 1991); and *Le Monde* 3–4 October 1993 and 23 November 1993.

45 The CORIF (Council for the Reflection on Islam in France) was set up in 1990 by the then Interior Minister Pierre Joxe to promote greater civil equality for Islam (for example in the provision of halal meat in

hospitals and canteens, etc.). This was the first example of state recognition of Islam. Its efficacy has been hampered by various internecine disputes concerning who should have the right to sit on the Council. The then Interior Minister, Charles Pasqua, had not recalled the Council by the end of 1993.

46 B. Étienne, *L'Islamisme radical* (Paris: Hachette, 1987), pp. 304–5.
47 P. Siblot ('Ah! Qu'en termes voilés ces-choses-là sont mises', *Mots*, No. 30, March 1992, pp. 5–17) has shown how the various terms used to designate the 'headscarf' during the 'Affair' were often chosen to stress the 'difference' of the practice.
48 J. Williame, 'Le Religieux dans l'espace publique', *Projet*, No. 225, Spring 1991, pp. 71–9, p. 72.
49 Étienne, *L'Islamisme radical*, pp. 314–15.
50 E. Weber, *Peasants into Frenchmen* (Stanford: Stanford University Press, 1975).
51 Williame, *op. cit.*, p. 74.
52 The definition of 'public' space outlined in the decision of the State Council was not so much the entire school premises but rather the classroom. This subtle differentiation enables headteachers to exclude pupils from classes whilst letting them study in the school library. The text of the decision is reproduced in J. Williame, 'Le Conseil d'État et la laïcité. Propos sur l'avis du 27 novembre 1989', *Revue française de Science Politique*, Vol. 41, No. 1, February 1991, pp. 128–58.
53 E. Gellner, *Postmodernism, Reason and Religion* (London: Routledge, 1992), p. 37.
54 L. Jospin, 'Le moment ou jamais' (interview), *Le Débat*, No. 58, January 1990, pp. 3–19, p. 16.
55 *Ibid.*, p. 17.
56 See Silverman, *Deconstructing the Nation*.
57 See J. Derrida, 'La déconstruction de l'actualité' (interview), *Passages*, No. 57, September 1993, pp. 60–75.
58 S. Naïr, *Lettre à Charles Pasqua de la part de ceux qui ne sont pas bien nés* (Paris: Seuil, 1994).
59 See *Le Monde*, 23 and 30 July 1994.
60 See *Libération*, 23 August 1994.
61 See Vidal-Naquet in *Libération*, 4 August 1994.
62 *Le Monde*, 29 October, 10–13 November 1993; *Libération*, 10–13 November 1993.
63 See Tincq in *Le Monde*, 12 November 1993.
64 *Le Monde*, 10 August 1994.
65 A. Battegay and A. Boubaker, *Les Images publiques de l'immigration* (Paris: CIEMI L'Harmattan, 1993).
66 See Millet in *Libération*, 19 August 1994, and *Le Monde*, 19 August 1994.
67 See Delorme in *Le Monde*, 20 August 1994, and Kechat in *Le Monde*, 2 September 1994.
68 *Libération*, 10–13 August 1994; *Le Monde*, 18 August 1994.
69 In *Libération*, 10 November 1993.
70 See *Libération*, 15 August 1994.

12

MUSLIMS IN GERMANY,
WITH SPECIAL REFERENCE TO THE
TURKISH-ISLAMIC COMMUNITY[1]

Yasemin Karakaşoğlu and Gerd Nonneman

1. Introduction

From small beginnings in the early 1960s, Islam has become the third-largest faith in Germany, after the two Christian denominations. It has also become increasingly the subject of fears and resentment in the host society. Although the total number of Muslims by the mid-1990s had grown to up to 2.5 million, the wider population still remained surprisingly ignorant about them and their religion.

Even though about 100,000 Germans (about half of them of foreign origin) profess Islam, the presence of Islam as a major visible phenomenon goes back only to the immigration of Muslims from Turkey, North Africa and the Balkans. This began with the First Employment Agreement with Turkey in 1961. A similar agreement was concluded with Morocco in 1969, and subsequently also with Tunisia. These agreements foresaw a temporary influx of workers, on the basis of rotation, in order to avoid a more permanent type of immigration. Even though this principle was abandoned fairly soon, as it was considered inefficient to keep replacing trained workers with untrained ones, the idea nevertheless persisted that the people who were thus brought to Germany should be considered *Gastarbeiter* (guest workers), and therefore 'foreigners' rather than 'migrants'.

Islam in Germany is for the most part a Turkish phenomenon: some 1.9 million people of Turkish origin (including Turkish Kurds), or over three-quarters of Muslims in Germany, now make up the largest migrant population in the country.[2] These are mainly of

Sunni Muslim background. The remainder is made up of Moroccan and Tunisian workers and their families, Iranians (usually middle class), Pakistanis and people from former Yugoslavia. The latter have grown significantly in number since the start of the war in Bosnia-Hercegovina, and now include mainly Bosnian Muslims. Islam is an important element in the identity of all these groups.

The term 'Muslim' is taken here to be in the first place a cultural description, not equivalent to actual religiosity. In this sense, the label 'Muslim' covers, for individual people, a great variety of ways of relating to their religion, just as is the case for Christians. Thus it may express a conscious, explicit piety, ranging from weekly participation in Friday prayers and/or fasting during the month of Ramadhan, to specific dress codes for men and women. Equally, some Muslims do not observe religious rules but nonetheless feel they are Muslims. In the Turkish community there is also a fairly small group who are extremely Kemalist/secularist in their attitudes, and have moved well away from practising Islam, while some Turks even would classify themselves as atheists. For most, though, Islam has played a significant role, not least in their education.

The important role of the Islamic religion in the cultural self-perception of the Muslim migrant population has been highlighted in numerous studies. These all stress that any consideration of this minority in Germany always must take into account the religious factor. This is true in the context of Turkish self-organisations,[3] where the Islamic organisations have built up the best organisational network across Europe. It also emerges from an analysis of the Turkish press in Germany,[4] which shows that although newspapers of this politico-religious tendency do not yet have a large print run, the number of buyers is nevertheless rising strongly. In the video market, Turkish-Islamic organisations are represented in part with religious–fundamentalist videos. A study on this subject also found that watching religious videos has for many Turks living in Germany become an integral part of their leisure-time occupation, although there has recently been a partial reduction in this, due to Turkish religious broadcasts now being available via satellite. Just how much importance must be attached to the religious factor in the quest for integration, is demonstrated by the results of a study on health consciousness among migrants in Nordrhein-Westfalen.[5] This showed that federal and Länder-level AIDS campaigns do not adequately reach the Turkish population, and that Islam plays an important role in attitudes towards this question. Islam, then, is clearly increasingly important. Why this should be so will be explored in section 2 of this chapter.

As long as the ambition of returning home remained preponderant among the migrant population itself, the latter on the whole accommodated themselves to a self-image of a Muslim minority temporarily residing among a Christian-secularised majority. Hence there were hardly any mosques in Germany during the early stages of inward labour migration; the establishment of places of worship was not part of the Employment Agreements.[6]

All surveys since the 1980s indicate that the majority of the Muslims in Germany intend to stay long-term; a recent survey by the Zentrum für Türkeistudien showed that 83 per cent of Turks living in Germany have decided to stay. Questions about the possibility of Muslims and Christians living together, therefore, can no longer be avoided. The new phenomenon of Muslim pensioners in Germany, for instance, which will shortly become an issue, is the subject of a number of recent studies.[7] These show that the federal social security system, which thus far worked under the assumption that migrants would re-emigrate in old age, is not prepared for those Muslims who are pensioners or in need of care and who have decided to stay in Germany.

In debates about Muslims in Germany, the religion is often viewed as an obstacle to integration. This would appear to be based on a definition of integration that equates it with 'assimilation' (adopting the characteristics and habits of the dominant group), rather than one that sees it as 'ein schrittweises Einleben in unsere Lebensverhältnisse und ein friedliches Zusammenleben von Menschen unterschiedlicher Herkunft im gegenseitigen Respekt vor dem nationalen, kulturellen und religiösen Selbstverständnis der jeweils anderen', as phrased by Liselotte Funke, the federal government's officer for the integration of foreign workers and their families, 1981–90. The latter view conceives of integration as a gradual easing into prevalent social and human relations, with 'peaceful coexistence of people of different origins, with mutual respect for the national, cultural and religious identities of the other'. In this sense, then, a concern with the integration of Islam should not take the form of a pursuit of 'sameness'. The search for rules of religious equal treatment and religious pluralism must, of course, be conducted in the framework of a society-wide consensus on the free democratic principles underpinning the German state.

Yet questions of German attitudes to, and the integration of, Muslims, are not just cultural. The country's attitude to migration policy is of central importance: even though so-called 'foreigners' make up 8 per cent of the population, Germany still does not see itself as a country of settler immigration. This is in part linked with the German concept of nationality: 'Germanness' is essentially seen as depending on ethnicity, not place of birth. Several restrictions apply for immigrants wishing to acquire citizenship (the rejection of dual citizenship being only one),[8] although a law passed in early 1991 has begun to change this somewhat. As a result of such restrictions, only few actually applied for citizenship until the beginning of the 1990s: the total number of Turks acquiring German citizenship in the period 1985–9 was only some 1,700.

Under the new law, dual citizenship remains unacceptable, but otherwise naturalisation has been made somewhat easier. Applicants still need to be able to speak German, and to have lived in Germany for 15 years or more or, in the case of those under 23, to have been in the German school system for at least 6 years (previously 8). The key change, however, is that, as soon as these conditions are fulfilled, they have the automatic right to become German citizens, whereas previously the decision depended on a bureaucratic assessment by officials. The effect of the law is clear from the figures: in 1991, the number of people of Turkish origin acquiring German citizenship jumped to 3,529, rising further to reach 12,915 in 1993. In 1995, an additional law was under discussion, which would reduce the residence requirement from 15 to 10 years.

The proliferation of Islamic organisations and groups who claim to be official representatives of Islam in Germany is a further cause for the somewhat problematic way in which Germans and Germany have related to Islam. These organisations will be discussed, therefore, in section 4 of this chapter. Before that, the changing nature of Islam in Germany will be laid out and explained in section 2 below, followed by an examination of one specific issue – religious education – that illustrates both the difficulties a Muslim diaspora may face living in a secularised Christian environment, and the demands of the Muslim community's representatives. Finally, the prospects for a 'European Islam', open to dialogue rather than inward-looking and/or extremist, will be considered in the concluding part of the chapter.

2. The transformation of Islam in Germany: demographic and social change, and international linkages

The development of Islam in Germany has been determined by a number of factors. The most important among these are (1) the trend in the migrant community from supposedly transitory migration to permanent settlement; (2) the associated trend from a homogenous male community of workers to a heterogeneous population whose members can be found in all walks of life; (3) socio-economic developments both in the host society and in the migrant community; and (4) political developments in Turkey, links between the two states, and international events. In combination, all this resulted in a higher level of practising Islam among migrants at the private level, and the creation of mainly Turkish-Islamic organisations, partly with a political background which in the case of some groups may be labelled 'Islamist'.

In the early days of labour migration to Germany, there were almost no Mosques in the country with the exception of some buildings, for instance in Hamburg and Munich, erected by Islamic states from the Middle East (Saudi Arabia, Iran), and of the mosques built in Frankfurt and Hamburg by the Ahmediyya movement (popular with German converts).[9] The first attempts by Muslims to practise their faith consisted of seeking to obtain prayer-rooms in the workers' hostels or in the factories. In this early period, the 'Imams' (who would lead prayers) were workers without any special religious qualification. The type of Islam in evidence in this period could be seen as a continuation of the popular Islam brought from Turkey: an Islam based on somewhat 'naive' popular beliefs mixed with some Sufi elements, and not always wholly in tune with the orthodox theological canons of Islam, even if usually classified as 'Sunni'. In this early community, mainly consisting of workers, strongly religious individuals were the exception rather than the rule.

Political activities with regard to Germany focused on the workplace; those with regard to Turkey, on the representation of Turkish parties that had established themselves as organisations in exile following the political developments in Turkey. These organisations ranged from extreme left to extreme right. Contrary to the left-liberal organisations, the conservative to extreme right end of the spectrum very early on recognised the potential of incorporating Islamic elements into their ideological package. Parties that cooperated as the 'National Front' in Turkish governments during the 1970s (Alparslan Türkes's Nationalist People's Party (MHP) and Necmettin Erbakan's National Salvation Party (MSP), were at the same time also represented in Germany in the form of associations and Islamic cultural centres. But on the whole it is clear that during the 1970s, politically motivated organisations were considerably more important than religious ones.

2.1. *Demographic change and the shift to permanent settlement*

It was only when migrant life 'migrated' from the hostels to houses, especially with the family reunification which began from 1974 onwards (after the employment stop in 1973), that a stronger interest in religion began to emerge, along with the search for properly dedicated buildings that could serve as mosques.

Until recently, Turkish mosques were situated without exception in the industrial areas of the large cities, or attached to housing complexes. This was in part because these communities had very limited financial resources to erect new buildings of their own. More important, though, were the reservations of the host society against buildings that looked recognisably 'Islamic'. In the case of the few 'real' mosques (with domes and minarets which for Turkish Muslims are very much part of the image of a real mosque) that were being built, this came almost always only after so-called *Moscheebaustreits* (mosque-building struggles). This is one example of migrant Muslims' pursuit of their constitutionally guaranteed cultural and religious rights coming up against various kinds of resistance. The arguments brought to bear by the host society included (1) the fear that the mosque would become a magnet, which could turn the neighbourhood into a ghetto; (2) the parking problem; (3) the argument that the architecture of a mosque would not fit in the overall cityscape; and (4) the argument that a mosque could foster the spread of Islamic fundamentalism.

The increasing importance of Islam was closely related to the changing demographic composition of the Turkish migrant community. The influx of wives and children strengthened social control among Turkish Muslims. As of 1994, 46 per cent of their community was female. The turn to Islam was in large measure fostered also by the move away from gender-segregated collective living areas, into residential areas of the towns, which had become necessary by the trend of family reunification. In the former they had been isolated from the majority society, but at the same time also been 'safe-guarded' against insecurities imposed by that society. In the midst of a society which rests on different norms and values, it becomes important especially for the first generation of migrants to safeguard (and indeed strengthen) their own cultural value orientation. From now on, it was no longer merely questions relating to the world of work which mattered: concepts such as the honour of the family, esteem as head of the family, and respect, became more important for mutual acceptance within the migrant community.

Especially the young among the Turkish community are subject to serious 'identity pressure' in Germany, because they are torn between two partly contradictory ways of thinking: that of the Turkish parental home, and that of the German environment. Girls are even more so afflicted than boys, as it is girls' 'proper behaviour' that represents the 'honour' of the family. In order to protect the family in the context of what they see as a very liberal environment, parents demand strongly conformist behaviour from their daughters. Boys, though, can on the one hand outwardly exhibit their traditional attitude and also demand this of their sisters, while, on the other, being able to live their own life more freely, as the Turkish environment sets less store by watching over their every step.[10]

The tension between the differing expectations thus imposed on them by the outside world, can lead young Turkish people either towards an 'overadaptation' to the value system of the majority, or, on the contrary, towards a withdrawal from the German environment. Many among the Turkish youth of Germany feel accepted neither in Turkey nor in Germany. Thus Turkish young men are sometimes heard to complain that they are called *Alemancı* ('German') when on holiday in Turkey, while in Germany their Turkish nationality is constantly pointed out. Nevertheless, a large part of those who have grown up in Germany have been able to function effectively in both cultures, and to fulfill the role of go-betweens between Germans and Turks. In doing this, many have developed a 'German Turk' identity, that corresponds fully neither with their parents' culture, nor with that of the German majority population. For some of these, part of this new identity has been a new way of finding access to Islam via German texts, or the attempt to learn Arabic in order to be able to read the Koran in the original.

A further important factor in the turn to Islamic associations, was the general recognition (especially when the 1983–4 Turkish law to encourage the return of Turks living in Germany, proved ineffective), that for Turkish families in Germany the country was indeed their permanent abode. Two-thirds of the Turkish minority now belong to the second generation or dependants. With respect to schools and even kindergartens, this inevitably led to a desire on the part of the Muslim minority to establish, in the otherwise Christian environment, new infrastructures in accordance with their own rules. Problems emerged in the confessional kindergartens (which make up 80 per cent of the total), and other difficulties arose in the schools. This meant that in areas where migrants were concentrated, educators, social workers and teachers had to take account of the cultural specificity of their clients and hence with Islam.

In addition, there is the problem of the lack of recognition of the second generation as belonging to German society. Even those born in Germany are treated as 'foreigners': as mentioned earlier, the notion of German nationality is in the first place concerned with ethnic Germans, and a range of restrictions are placed on those seeking naturalisation. This includes the refusal of dual citizenship: renunciation of Turkish citizenship would mean, for one thing, that family property (land) which might still be owned in Turkey cannot be held on to. For these locally born and bred people of Turkish (or other non-German) origin, the stigma attached to their supposed 'foreignness' still causes difficulties in access to the labour market, in public life, and in political participation. Disillusion with this lack of recognition in the host society fosters a return to contemplating 'own' values, which are found coherently expressed in Islam and its precepts.

Since the beginning of the 1990s a new socio-political challenge has been added by the group of Muslim (again mainly Turkish) pensioners who will not now return to their country of origin. Given the widespread conception (among Muslims as among Christian believers) of a 'reckoning' at the end of one's life, the increased turn to religion which can be observed among older Muslims in Germany is not surprising. The less of life remains, the less time is left to 'make up' for past transgressions.

2.2. The socio-economic situation and xenophobia

In addition to the above kinds of dynamics, rooted in the first two factors listed at the outset of this section (the shift to permanent settlement, and the changing demography), two further categories of factors need mentioning.

The first is the socio-economic situation, and its effect on the Muslim community. With the economic recessions of 1973, of the early 1980s, and of the early 1990s following German reunification, unemployment and insecurity about existing employment grew. In this situation an important role accrued to the Islamic organisations, which developed their own system of social support. In this context of increasing anxieties about life, Islam offered psychological support, as well as reassurance for a credible and secure safeguarding of one's own values.

Religion, then, is acquiring an increasingly important place not only for its own sake but also as reaction to social problems: unemployment and housing scarcity, but also inadequate integration of the children in school, these children being over-represented in the less academic schools (*Hauptschulen* and special education), and under-represented in the schools for academic 'achievers' (the *Realschulen* and the *Gymnasien*, the latter being the gateway to university). In addition, there has been a growing fear of xenophobic attacks, which have increased along with the host society's own economic problems, the 'different' migrant population being an easily identifiable scapegoat. Ironically, this tends to drive those groups which are targeted further into that very 'difference' – Islam. This is reinforced by the particular concern which the Islamic organisations display about such xenophobia: they present themselves as the spokespeople for the targeted population against the majority. This could be seen, for instance, in the dialogue between representatives of the two groups after the attack on a Turkish hostel in Solingen in May 1993.

2.3. Turkish politics and other international linkages

The final main category of determinants for the changes in the nature and organisation of Islam in Germany, among the Turkish population in particular, must be sought at the international level.

Changes in Turkish politics are one facet of this; the nature of the relationship between Germany and Turkey another; and international events relating to the Islamic world or to Turkey in particular are a third.

With the de-politicisation of society in Turkey, following the 1980 military coup by the strongly Kemalist General Evren – which brought to an end years of escalating political violence – the appeal of extreme political organisations also diminished among Turks in Germany. The idea of the 'Turkish-Islamic Synthesis' (*Türk-Islam Sentezi*), introduced by the Turkish military government and then propagated by the Özal government as an alternative to extreme nationalism and socialism, was supported in Turkey by the 'Club of Intellectuals' (set up by leading politicians, scientists and journalists), and found a good degree of acceptance among large parts of the population. This was also reflected among the Turkish population in Germany. Yet this only came after an initial period following the coup when, as a result of the outlawing of political parties in Turkey by the secularist government, mainly Islamist parties increased their activities in Germany. To counter this, the 'Synthesis' was then propagated also in Germany (and in Europe in general) through the vehicle of the *Diyanet Isleri Türk-Islam Birligi* (DITIB), or 'Turkish-Islamic Association' or 'Union'. This was subordinate to the Turkish government's Directorate for Religious Affairs, and set out, successfully, to control more of the mosques and Islamic services and teaching than the other organisations were able to do. The Diyanet is now by far the largest Islamic umbrella organisation in Germany (see below) and continues to propagate the moderate Islam of the 'Synthesis'.

The second facet mentioned above has been summed up elsewhere as follows:

> Turkey's close relationship with Germany, aided by Turkish membership of the North Atlantic Treaty Organization (NATO), has helped ensure that the Turkish minority retains links with Turkey and thereby the continuous flow of remittances. These links have, however, inclined German Turks to regard themselves more as Turks abroad than as one of Germany's ethnic and religious minorities with corresponding rights.[11]

The latter part of the quote is of course applicable mainly to the first generation, and will undoubtedly become a diminishing trend.

Finally, there is the impact which international actors and events have had on the intensity of religious orientation among the Muslim population of Germany. Of course, states and institutions in Islamic countries exert some influence through the financial support of Islamic organisations in the building of an Islamic infrastructure (mosques, courses, etc.) and through the supply of materials and scholars. But there is often a more widespread impact when Turkey or other Islamic states are seen to be the victims of world politics (this is true as much for the Muslim minority in Germany as for Muslims elsewhere in Europe). Muslims in Europe often feel, and show, solidarity with these 'victims' against, usually, Western states who are seen as aggressors – even though they might live in precisely those states. Examples of such events were the rejection of Turkey's full membership application to the European Union, the Gulf War, and most recently the civil war in Bosnia-Hercegovina. Discussions with representatives of Islamic organisations indicate that such events have led, especially among the second-generation Muslims in Germany, to a strengthening of their awareness of their religious background. Thus, for instance, the organisation of aid deliveries to Bosnia has become an important part of the activities of Islamic associations in Germany.

3.   The issue of religious education

Difficulties in the life of the Islamic diaspora occur especially where normal daily life is organised around the religious and philosophical values of the majority, i.e. the Christian population in the case of Germany. Thus Muslims will often criticise the fact that Muslim needs in schools and at work are not sufficiently taken into account. On the other hand it must be admitted that, even when the German authorities are willing to concede Muslim demands, it is often wholly practical difficulties in such adaptations which hinder the realisation of more equal treatment.

The issue of Islamic religious education may, in addition to its own intrinsic interest, also serve as a good example of the above.

Currently Islamic religious education does not have equal treatment with its Christian counterpart in any of the German *Länder*. Hence the demand that

Muslims should be enabled to have qualified religious education for their youth on the same basis as the Christian community, as a normal subject. Islamic religious education must have the same space in public schools as Christian religious education. In Länder where instead comparative religion is taught to foster the understanding of the religious-cultural heritage, Islam should be given full consideration.[12]

The idea then is that such religious education could help make life easier for young Muslims in Germany, where the majority belong to a different religion and have different values and attitudes. This is in fact precisely the message of a document from the Secretariat of the Permanent Conference of Ministers of Culture in the German Länder, of 20 March 1984. This states that religious education in Islamic schools in Germany should 'contribute to the development of a Muslim self-understanding in a non-Muslim world. It should contribute in helping Muslim children and young people to understand and accept the values and norms of German society, and to reduce tensions between different values and norms.' It should be noted in this context that in the federal structure, it is at the Länder-level rather than at that of the central government, that responsibility lies for matters of culture and therefore also of religious education. A further peculiarity setting Germany apart from the rest of Europe, is that in all Länder religious education can only be conceived and implemented in collaboration with, and under the responsibility of, the Churches, as the state is obliged to remain neutral in philosophical/religious terms when it comes to its role in education. The Christian and Jewish communities, moreover, are funded on the basis of a 'church tax' which the members of the particular community voluntarily pay to a representative body. This is not available to the Muslim community. Since on the Muslim side a recognised partner equivalent to the Churches does not exist (in Islam, outside Shiism, there are no structures, nor a clergy, comparable to those of the churches), the Länder have developed their own concepts for bringing 'religious education' to Muslim children. Such concepts are already being developed with the help of renowned Islamic scholars, and are in part also already being implemented. Since 1986 there is, for instance, an educational concept developed by Nordrhein-Westfalen's Institute for Schools and Further Education, about 'religious education for schools of the Islamic faith'. This comprises 24 educational units for the primary school, which are bilingual (German–Turkish). It originated as part of the Land's curriculum development.[13] Since then a book on religious education has also been published.

There are currently two main models in Germany for familiarising Muslim schoolchildren with their religion. Let us briefly introduce them here.

Nordrhein-Westfalen, because of this curriculum development and measures taken so far, has a kind of pioneering role for the other *Länder* in this field. In its model, the 'religious teaching for schoolchildren of the Islamic faith' which is offered to Turkish children, takes place in the framework of the *Muttersprachlicher Ergänzungsunterricht* (complementary education in the mother tongue) (MEU). In 1991 this was experimentally expanded to the fifth and sixth school years (11–12-year-olds), and subsequently made the norm. In 1995/6 this should be further expanded to schoolchildren of the seventh to tenth years.

This education happens under the responsibility of the Land and is carried out with specially designed teaching materials of its Institute for Schools and Further Education. Hence the teachers are employees of the Land, rather than of the Turkish state. The teaching is meant to relate to the specific living environment of Muslim children in Germany. It is wholly voluntary, and is not on an equal footing with the Protestant and Catholic education which is part of the German education plan.[14]

The other model is referred to as 'religious education on Islamic principles for Muslim schoolchildren'. This takes place in the context of the MEU which is run by diplomatic representatives. This education is provided mainly by Turkey but also other Islamic countries, for the children of their own citizens, with their own teachers and according to their own educational plans. The German side provides schoolrooms and sometimes a contribution to the cost. This type of religious education is found in those *Länder* where the 'sender' states' consular representatives organise MEU (Baden-Württemberg, Berlin, Saarland and Schleswig-Holstein). Legally, this is 'free' or 'private' education in the sense of the laws on private schooling in these *Länder*. Taking part in MEU is voluntary. A precise division into 'general language education', 'geography', and 'religious education' is not normally applied. Depending on the individual teacher (who is appointed by the home state, mainly Turkey), the proportion of religious teaching will vary. Because, for the Turkish children making up the vast majority in this MEU, teaching is in Turkish, these children are not given the ability to enter into a religious dialogue with their non-Turkish schoolfriends. This type of MEU is totally outside the orbit of the German school authorities and institutions, and because the teaching materials are brought in from the home countries, it generally is not oriented towards the specific circumstances of these children in Germany.

The aspiration of the main Islamic representative organisations (*Zentralrat der Muslime in Deutschland*, and *Islamrat für die Bundesrepublik* – see below) is the development, in collaboration with the various Islamic umbrella organisations, of a type of education, in German, that would be on an equal footing with Christian religious education. Currently, this ambition runs up against a number of practical obstacles. For one thing, there is a dearth of Islamic scholars who could teach in German – and there are also no places to train such teachers. Moreover, there is no 'spokesman' or accepted representative institution on the Islamic side which would be equivalent to the relevant Christian and other German institutions.

Apart from the above kinds of religious education, there are also the Koran schools[15] of Islamic organisations, which pious Muslims prefer for their children, but which are continuously criticised for inadequate pedagogical methods and for their teaching's inappropriateness for the living circumstances of young Muslims in Germany. Depending on the sponsoring organisation, the children may also be taught various Islamist ideologies, hence the accusation from some sides that Koran courses are 'anti-integration'. These courses take place outside normal teaching hours and can therefore make major time demands of Muslim children.[16] A study by the senate of Hamburg showed that 'about 24 per cent of all Turkish children of school age – that is some 2000 children – attend Koran courses. Survey results indicate that far more parents would like for their children to have a religious education, but either cannot or do not want to send them to Koran schools.'[17]

4. Islamic organisations in Germany

Currently, Islam is the most strongly organised of any of Germany's

ethnic and religious minorities; it boasts more than 2,000 regional organisations, with 50,000–100,000 members, and over 500,000
practising Muslims who regularly use their services. The Islamic
organisations in Germany are mainly Turkish. There are others, too,
but they are numerically less important and usually not home-grown.
Thus, the Muslim Brotherhood (mainly Egyptian, but also active in
other Arab countries) is active among parts of the Arab Muslim
population in Germany, while 'Shia activists are known to be influential among Iranians and other Shia-related groups, such as the
Alawi.'[18] In addition, 'The heterodox Ahmadiyya movement, which
originated in the Indian sub-continent in the 1880s, is favoured by
German converts, many of whom have been drawn to the sect's evan-
gelical orientation. The movement played an important role in the
construction of mosques in Hamburg, Frankfurt and elsewhere in
West Germany in the 1950s.'[19]

There are also branches of the Muslim World League, which
is based in Jeddah, Saudi Arabia. Below, the array of umbrella organisations among the Turkish Islamic community will be laid out. At
this point it is worth mentioning that there is also a Saudi-oriented
umbrella organisation, Islamisches Konzil, based in Frankfurt. This
is, however, not thus far functioning as a self-organisation of migrants, and is therefore of rather marginal significance for the
purposes of this chapter.[20] Finally, the Islamische Gemeinschaft
deutschsprachiger Muslime (Islamic Association of German-speaking
Muslime) needs mentioning. This brings together both German
converts and others, and is led by a German Muslim.

When attempting to determine the number of Turkish-Islamic
organisations in Germany, one has to rely on the data provided by
the various associations themselves; these are difficult to test, and can
be no more than an indication. The umbrella organisations in which
most Islamic organisations have by now come together, are more
easily identifiable, because of their public activities. However, the
number of member organisations is much more difficult to get at.
Here one can only make guesstimates. One of the problems is the
confusion caused by the term for 'member' (üye) and the meaning
of 'community' (cemaat): no distinction is made between a registered
and fee-paying member of an organisation, on the one hand, and
users of a mosque institution on the other. The cemaat, for some,
means the family of the registered member. In this case one needs to
multiply the number of registered members by 4 or 5 (the average

MUSLIM COMMUNITIES

size of a Turkish family in Germany is 4.1), to arrive at the 'community size' of the organisation. *Cemaat* can, however, also be interpreted more widely. In this interpretation, one should count all Turkish Muslims who, even if not registered members of an organisation, make use of what the Turkish-Islamic associations offer: mosques for prayer, or tea houses for socialising.

As mentioned earlier, many of these organisations started off as offshoots from political parties and movements in Turkey, which could not freely organise there because of the political situation and religious policy in Turkey. Turkish political competition, both official and underground, became reflected among the Turkish diaspora, and specifically in Germany. The shift towards less politicised but gradually more religious activity – as a result of the post-1980 events in Turkey – has already been referred to. While competition between secularist and religious strands persisted, equally the Turkish establishment's own brand of Islam now began to compete with the more anti-Kemalist versions already established.

Most Turkish-Islamic associations nowadays very much distance themselves from the political preoccupations of around 1980. The stronger focus on the Islamic element, as opposed to the earlier nationalist overtones, is connected to this distancing. The organisations are mainly concerned with being accepted as religious rather than political groups. Nevertheless, connections with political strands in Turkey continue to exist and are indeed supported by Turkish politicians: this is illustrated by the continued participation of such politicians in the large manifestations of some federations: thus Alparslan Türkes for the Turkish Federation (see item 5 below), and Necmettin Erbakan for the *Milli Görüs* (see item 2 below).

Across all organisations there is now a tendency no longer to operate with a view to the eventual return of the migrants to Turkey, but to work on the assumption that Turks living in Germany have decided to make their life there. This is reflected in the turnover of the leadership of these organisations. More and more Turks of the second generation, or with at least ten years' living experience in Germany, are determining the orientation of the associations. More and more of the leading members of the associations have completed higher education in Germany, and their work can therefore be quite different in content and expression from that of the leadership of the early 1980s. The DITIB (Diyanet), mentioned earlier, is an exception because it draws its religious scholars and teachers exclusively from Turkey, rotating them on a five-year basis.

Turkish-Islamic organisations have clustered together in eight umbrella organisations.

1. DITIB (often referred to simply as the Diyanet). Grouping 740 associations, this is in effect a union of mosques coordinated by the Turkish state through the religious attaché of the Turkish embassy. It was established in order to counter the associations that were challenging the secularist underpinnings of the Turkish state (see above). The Diyanet benefits from having trained and paid imams sent from Turkey. This, combined with the fact that the majority of Turkish Muslims in Germany do actually favour an interpretation of Islam that is more easily compatible with the Western view of life, helps to explain the fact that the organisation has become the largest of the eight.

2. *Avrupa Milli Görüs Teskilatlari* (AMGT), or the 'Organisation of National Vision' (Nationale Sicht) – often referred to simply as the *Milli Görüs* – is the second-largest grouping, with 262 member-associations. This is quite explicitly Islamist in orientation. They stand for the ideal of an Islamic state, although this is not pursued with radical means. They have criticised the involvement of the Turkish state in religious education and services abroad (such as through the Diyanet), as this is viewed as a ploy to control Muslim expression. There were links between this organisation and the National Salvation Party in Turkey, which was banned in 1972 for advocating an Islamic state against the very principles which Kemalist Turkey was built on. Since the reconstitution, under Necmettin Erbakan, of this strand in Turkish politics as the Welfare Party in 1983 (now a legitimate player in Turkish electoral politics), such links have again been in evidence. Erbakan actively and openly associates with and supports the organisation. This latter phase would appear to have gone hand in hand with a less confrontational stance towards the Turkish state, possibly because Turgut Özal (who became Prime Minister and then President) was known to have been a member of the original National Salvation Party. The *Milli Görüs* now also has a special link with the Turkish self-employed in Germany: since 1992 it collaborates with the Islamically oriented Turkish employers' union MÜSIAD.

3. Verband der Islamischen Kulturzentern (VIKZ) – the Union of Islamic Cultural Centres, or Avrupa Kültur Merkezleri Birligi). This organisation, headquartered in Cologne, brings together 250 associations which follow the Islamist, anti-Kemalist line of the Süleymanci sect (it should be noted that they themselves reject the appelation Süleymanci). The sect, an offshoot of the Naqshbandi order, was founded by Süleyman Hilmi (d. 1959), a religious reformer opposed to the secular transformation of Turkey following Atatürk's take-over. Like the *Milli Görüs*, the ideal of the Süleymancis is the establishment of an Islamic state, but, again like the *Milli Görüs*, they also do not favour radical methods. Official manifestations of the sect remain banned in Turkey. In Germany, its activities concentrate on Koran classes.

4. ICCB (Föderation der islamischen Gemeinden und Gemeinschaften) split off from the *Milli Görüs* in 1984, under the inspiration of the now deceased militant islamist 'Khomeini of Cologne', Cemalettin Kaplan. It has some 50 member associations, and is run along strongly hierarchical centralist lines. Kaplan, who had political asylum in Germany (Nordrhein-Westfalen), declared himself 'caliph' – the title of the worldwide leader of Islam which had been abolished after the creation of the new Turkish state and the deposition of the last Sultan. Subsequently, he even declared an Islamic State of Turkey in exile. Since the death of its leader, this grouping became divided into several groups.

5. *Türk Federasyonu*, the 'Turkish Federation' of strongly nationalist Turkish Idealistenvereine, is also known by the name of Grauen Wölfe (the Grey Wolves). This has about 180 affiliated associations. The movement has now retreated somewhat from its earlier pan-Turkic ideals. Interestingly, an Islamic component is being developed in this group, aiming to expand their appeal.

6. The Union of Turkish-Islamic Cultural Associations in Europe (ATIB), is another movement which used to propagate pan-Turkic ideas – but appears also to have mellowed. It brings together 122 associations and is currently headed by M. S. Celebi, formerly the president of the nationalist association RDÜTDF.

7. The *Nurculuk* movement, which embraces 30 educational establishments, is not a grouping of mosques but an Islamic Order, founded by Sayyid Nursi (d. 1960). Intellectually oriented, it aims to reconcile

elements of modernity with Islam. Like the Süleymancis, it started as a clandestine movement opposed to the secular Turkish state. In Germany it is mainly engaged in educational activities.

8. *Aleviler Birligi*, the most recent grouping, is the umbrella organisation of the Alevi community, with 82 affiliated associations.[21]

Membership (number of persons) of the last six should not be estimated quite as high as is often done. The *Milli Görüs* in Germany has over 13,600 members, and the VIKZ about 12,000. The other four together have about 25,000 members. It should be noted that members of the *Nurculuk* movement can be found among members of the mosque groupings, but also among Muslims who are otherwise not organised.

Numerous other sects or orders are also active in Germany, but they are less prominent. For the purpose of this chapter, suffice it to mention but two of the more important ones, namely the *Naqshbandiyya* and the *Qadiriyya*.

There is thus far no all-encompassing umbrella organisation for all Turkish-Islamic associations and groupings. Yet there is an ever clearer momentum towards the creation of a central body that could represent the interests of Muslims in the majority society. In 1986, the Islamrat für die Bundesrepublik Deutschland (Islamic Council for Germany) was set up in Berlin. The Council sees itself as a 'common forum for discussion and a coordinating body for the Islamic work' of the members. It was thus able to bring together quite different groupings, such as the *Nurculuk* movement, the *Milli Görüs*, the Islam-Archiv-Soest (an institution established by German Muslims), but also the Union of Turkish-Islamic Cultural Associations in Europe (ATIB). However, when it came to the offer to establish the position of a *Sheikh-ul-Islam* as official interlocutor for matters between the Christian majority and the Muslim minority, those organisations not part of the Council reacted negatively. They rejected this claim to sole spokesmanship, and did not see any need for it. The position was nevertheless established by the Council, and on 15 February 1991, Ali Yüksel, the secretary-general of the *Milli Görüs*, was appointed as its first incumbent.[22]

The Islamische Arbeitskreis in Deutschland (Islamic Work Society in Germany) was established in 1991 by those organisations that did not identify with the aims of the Islamic Council. The new body's aim was to concern itself with Islamic matters regarding Muslims in Germany, and to offer a common and permanent forum for information and discussion for their public interests. The grouping again brought together a varied selection of Islamic orientations, such as the DITIB, the Islamisches Zentrum Aachen (Islamic Centre in Aachen), the Deutschsprachige Islamische Frauengemeinschaft (Society of German-speaking Muslim Women), as well as the Shiite organisation Islamisches Zentrum Hamburg (Islamic Centre Hamburg).

In December 1994, the organisation renamed itself the Zentralrat der Muslime in Deutschland (Central Council of Muslims in Germany), better to reflect its expanding tasks. All large Turkish-Islamic groupings are now represented in the Zentralrat except for the *Nurculuk* movement and the *Milli Görüs*. The Alevis steered clear of membership in either the Zentralrat or the Islamrat, because of their different understanding of Islam. One other exception is the extremist Islamic ICCB (the Kaplan followers), which has remained outside any umbrella grouping and which, just because of its extremism, is excluded by all of the other organisations. The Zentralrat aims (1) to function as a forum for discussion amongst its members; (2) to represent them and the Muslim community with the representative institutions and individuals of the majority society; and (3) to improve the legal and social position of the Muslims in Germany.

All these Turkish-Islamic groupings represent quite distinct religious and political orientations. At the same time, it is clear that their interests with respect to their demands from German society for the migrant community largely overlap, and that they are able to cooperate towards the achievement of these aims. It would therefore seem likely that, even if not in the short term, an organisational joining of forces could be in prospect.

It can be estimated that only about 20 per cent of the Muslim population of Germany is actually a member of any of these organisations. Yet the services and facilities which they offer are used by a much larger number. The faithful generally choose their mosque depending on the proximity to their place of residence or work. It then depends on whether there is a choice of mosques belonging to different umbrella organisations – as is the case only in larger cities – or whether, as in the countryside, the Islamic infrastructure is thin on the ground. It is important, therefore, to distinguish between 'followers/supporters' and 'members': the latter may also be people who do not support the political aims of the organisation whose mosque they frequent for the purpose of prayer. It is because of these sorts of confusion in the data, that one often hears the much exaggerated estimate that the organisations would have hundreds of thousands of members.

As already indicated, these organisations are now concentrating on the needs associated with Muslims' long-term or permanent residence in Germany, rather than with concerns about return and changing the situation in Turkey itself.[23]

They all offer religious services such as prayer rooms, Koran courses, assistance in the transportation of the dead to Turkey, and the organisation of pilgrimages. In addition, they now also offer courses and advice that had previously been the preserve of state and church welfare bodies. One can list here special courses in literacy, German and sowing for Turkish women and girls, as well as leisure activities and courses in Arabic and, recently, computer courses. Many mosques also offer social advice, advice on dealing with functionaries, and translation services.

5.   Prospects: dialogue or extremism?

Particularly among second-generation Turkish Muslims in Germany, it is possible to observe on the one hand a great interest in Islam as an identity-building element, and on the other an attempt to develop their own way into the religion – a way that is often quite different from the popular Islam of their parents. Young Turkish Muslims increasingly learn Arabic in order to be able to undertake their own study of the Koran. In any case, German has often become the first language instead of Turkish, and religious discussion among the second generation often takes place in German. This is where one can discern a trend towards a new synthesis between elements of German society and the Sunni Islam of Turkey. How far the influence of the society in Germany on Islamic thinking in Turkey has gone cannot yet be stated with any certainty. But it is striking that, while until the mid-1980s these organisations were largely funded by their ideologically related parties in Turkey or from sources in the Middle East, they now themselves financially support movements in Turkey. They are especially active in the field of religious foundations: in many cases the construction of new mosques and Koran schools in Turkey can be traced back to funds from the Turkish community in Germany. The Union of Islamic Cultural Centres (VIKZ), for its part, maintains numerous student homes and residential schools in Turkey, through its religious foundations.

On the other hand, one can still find a strong influence in intellectual trends among Turkish Muslims in Germany, from the Islamic intellectual scene in Turkey. Books on these themes which appear in Turkey, inspire especially the second generation.[24]

For young Turkish Muslims, an Islamic renewal of their own, and their joining of ethnic-religious communities, are a way to maintain their cultural identity (even if redefined) and to take up socially important functions. This is particularly important as they are faced with a society which demands full integration from them while still treating them as 'foreigners', politically, economically and culturally. The hierarchy of the organisations offers those who are competent in both cultures the chance of rapid progression to leading positions, from which they can, as representatives of their ethnic-religious constituencies, approach the majority society with a new confidence.

In so doing, they are using the arguments of the European Enlightenment, such as 'human rights', 'freedom of religion', etc., to pursue religious-political aims. This has been the case for instance with the release of Turkish girls from the obligation to participate in physical education classes, on the grounds that this is supposed to be incompatible with their sense of shame. The Oberverwaltungs-gericht (high administrative court) in Berlin decided in August 1993, in a case between a school and a Turkish Muslim girl, that the right to freedom of religion is more important than the girl's obligation to participate in the non-segregated physical education otherwise obligatory for all schoolchildren. While this may appear a 'conservative' phenomenon, the point to note is that it was pursued by, and won on the grounds of, European notions of rights. Similarly, another manifestation of this 'post-modern Islamism' in Western society are visual phenomena such as the adoption of the Islamic headscarf by second-generation Turkish girls who at the same time follow European youth culture in the importance it attaches to the wearing of certain *marques* of sports clothes: thus they will combine the headscarf with brand-name jeans and brand-name trainers.

All of this illustrates a conviction that certain elements of modernity, and especially technological development, can be reconciled with Islamic traditions and rules, and that such a reinterpreted Islam can serve as an alternative for political ideologies that are seen as having failed.[25]

Without question, Islamism should, in so far as it represents a form of political extremism, be watched closely also in Germany. It is reasonable to require that political or religious interest groups which establish themselves in Germany, should demonstrate their acceptance of the democratic constitutional principles of German society not only in words but also in deeds. They must therefore be conscious of the fact that both the statements of their representatives and their German and Turkish publications will be followed attent-ively. Yet it must be stressed that Islam in Germany does not equal fundamentalist extremism. For one thing, data from the Verfassungs-schutz (Internal Security) show that Islamists and those propagating extreme ideologies constitute only 1 per cent of all Muslims in Germany.[26] For another, the Islamic organisations, including those of an Islamist persuasion, fulfil an often useful role which is much wider than political Islamist concerns. These organisations have built up a socio-religious infrastructure and are thus providing an important need of the Muslim minority. The identification, by the majority society, of Islam with 'fundamentalism', for a long time led to such needs being ignored. This in turn prepared the field for organisations some of which were indeed radical-Islamist. This self-fulfilling prophecy element of the increased (though still small) appeal of such groups, has been added to by the increasing processes of social disintegration. The latter is manifested in the marginal position of Muslim youth in education and training, the limited pos-sibilities for political and social participation, the lack of freedom of movement in Europe, and, most importantly, the apparent failure on the part of state institutions to recognise and value Islam as equal to other world religions present in Europe – all this in the context of a growing xenophobic reflex aimed mainly at the Turkish population.

Purposeful and effective integration of the Turkish population can contribute to the establishment in Germany of a European Islam with Turkish foundations, which would be open to the world and prepared for dialogue. The same would, *mutatis mutandis*, on the whole be true for the non-Turkish elements of the Muslim minority. Indeed, close inspection of the forms which Turkish Islam, at least, has taken on in Germany, allows a number of observations that in-dicate that a pragmatic orientation is likely to prevail.

Firstly, there are indications that the various Islamic organisations are moving closer together over a 'lowest common denominator' consensus. Attempts to create overarching umbrella organisations are one sign of this; joint actions by the different organisations are another. In addition, there is the mutual consultation that has been taking place, as well as 'friendship visits' (for example at the 1995 Book Fair of the *Milli Görüs*, where a representative of the DITIB read out greetings from his organisation's president). In some cases organisations that are otherwise opposed to each other, such as, again, the DITIB and the *Milli Görüs*, even share a mosque, or there are rules whereby one organisation will supply the mosque and another the imam. This clearly demonstrates the priority of pragmatism over ideological persuasion. It is only the Kaplan movement which does not fit this pattern.

Secondly, after a two-decade-long history, the organisations have become increasingly adept at dealing with the German authorities. This can also be regarded as a learning process in the form of democratic cooperation. A study on Hessen by the Zentrum für Türkeistudien has demonstrated a new trend of Islamic associations becoming actively engaged in the communal Foreigners' Advice Councils. Here too the fact that quite different orientations are brought together on so-called 'Islamic lists' illustrates the search for a minimal consensus, referred to above. In so far as this is taking shape, it would appear to concentrate on the following specific religious demands: (1) the recognition of Islam as a legal entity in public law; (2) permission to slaughter animals according to Islamic rules (as has been obtained by the Jewish community); (3) the introduction of regular Islamic education in German schools; and (4) the support of state-level and local administrative bodies in the acquisition or construction of new mosques. In addition, all Turkish-Islamic organisations also aim at (5) a widening of the room for political activity by their constituency. Hence there is a general demand for the right to vote in local elections, as well as for dual citizenship.

The cooperation of the Turkish-Islamic lists in the elections for the Foreigners' Advice Councils has been viewed with concern by some observers. They fear an 'infiltration' of the Councils by 'Islam'. A more dispassionate and pragmatic perception is appropriate in this regard. Indeed, the experience of the Councils in Hessen has shown for all of the participating lists, including the Islamic ones, that they cannot be a forum for the propagation of the interests of any single group, and that the room for manoeuvre of these Councils is in fact very small. Yet they form a place where democracy, the acceptance of majority decisions, and pluralism can be practised. The organisations also find themselves obliged here to nail their colours to the mast in cases of doubt – something which can only serve to make them more transparent.

Notes

1   Some of the material and arguments on which this chapter is based, were
    published earlier in a chapter by Y. Karakaşoğlu, entitled 'Turkish
    Cultural Orientation in Germany and the role of Islam' in E. Kolinsky
    and D. Harrocks (eds.), *Turkish Culture in German Society Today: Between
    Acceptance and Exclusion* (Keele: Keele University Press, 1996), Chapter 8.
2   Ministerium für Arbeit, Gesundheit und Soziales des Landes Nordrhein-
    Westfalen, *Türkische Muslime in Nordrhein-Westfalen*, 2nd edn (Cologne:
    Super Service, June 1995), p. 1.
3   See Zentrum für Türkeistudien (ed.), *Turkei–Sozialkunde*, 2nd edn
    (Opladen: Verlag Leske und Budrich, 1994).
4   Zentrum für Türkeistudien (ed.), *Zum Integrationspotential der türkischen
    Tagespresse in der Bundesrepublik Deutschland* (Opladen: Verlag Leske und
    Budrich, 1991).
5   Zentrum für Türkeistudien (ed.), *Gesundheitsbewußtsein der Migranten aus
    der Türkei in Nordrhein-Westfalen* (unpublished study, Bonn, 1991).
6   Baymirza Hayit, a Muslim scientist, has criticised the sender country as
    follows: 'It was a mistake, on the part of the Turkish government, to send
    the Turks to Germany without first having made sure that the basic
    requirements for the pursuance of their Islamic religious life were
    catered for.' B. Hayit, 'The Turks in West Germany', *Journal Institute of
    Muslim Minority Affairs*, Vol. 3, No. 2 (Winter 1981), pp. 264–76, p. 271.
7   Zentrum für Türkeistudien, *Lebenssituation und spezifische Problemlage
    älterer ausländischer Einwohner in der Bundesrepublik Deutschland* (Bonn:
    Bundesministerium für Arbeit und Sozialordnung, 1993).
8   F. Shaikh (ed.), *Islam and Islamic Groups. A World-wide Reference Guide*
    (London: Longman, 1992), p. 82.
9   D. Khalid, 'Der Islam in der Diaspora: Europa und Amerika' in
    U. Steinbach and W. Ende (eds.), *Der Islam in der Gegenwart*, 3rd edn
    (Munich: Verlag C. B. Beck, 1991), pp. 440–69, p. 452.
10 H. Straube, *Türkisches Leben in der Bundesrepublik* (Frankfurt: Campus
    Verlag, 1987).
11 Shaikh, *op. cit.*, p. 82.
12 M. Abdullah, 'Der Islam will in Deutschland heimisch werden' in *Islam
    im Abendland*, Special Issue of the journal *Die Brücke* (Saarbrücken: Die
    Brücke e.V., 1992), pp. 30–48, p. 38.
13 Landesinstitut für Schule und Weiterbildung, *Religiöse Unterweisung für
    Schüler islamischen Glaubens* (Soest, 1986).
14 G. Mahler, 'Möglichkeiten religiöser Unterweisung muslimischer Kinder
    an öffentlichen Schulen in den Ländern der Bundesrepublik
    Deutschland entsprechend dem Beschluß der Kultusministerkonferenz'
    in Landesinstitut für Schule und Weiterbildung, *Rahmenbedingungen und
    Materialien zur religiösen Unterweisung für Schüler islamischen Glaubens*
    (Berlin: Expres Edition, 1987), pp. 141–50, p. 146.
15 The necessity of specially dedicated Koran teaching – whether in Koran
    schools or elsewhere – follows from the position and importance in

Islam of the Koran as the literal word of God. This word is believed to have been revealed in Arabic. Not only the Koran itself, but also prayers, are therefore in Arabic, and both need to be learned by heart by non-Arabic-speaking Muslim children. Many parents, moreover, do not feel able to teach their children the details of religious practice, and therefore entrust this task to better-equipped scholars of religion.

16   See also H. Thomä-Venske, 'Religiöse Erziehung und rechtsradikale Politik. Zur Problematik der türkischen Koran-Kurse in der Bundesrepublik' in H. Brandt and C. Haase, *Begegnungen mit Türken – Begegnungen mit dem Islam* (Rissen bei Hamburg: EB Verlag, 1981), pp. 1–11. Yet the content of the courses mentioned therein relate to the situation in the early 1980s.

17   P. Kappert and R. Niemeyer, 'Islamischer Religionsunterricht für muslimische türkische Schüler in Hamburger Schulen' in J. Lähnemann (ed.), *Erziehung zur Kulturbegegnung [Pädagogische Beiträge zur Kulturbegegnung, Vol. 3]* (Hamburg, 1986), pp. 71–1, p. 73.

18   Shaikh, *op. cit.*, p. 82.

19   *Ibid.*

20   See also Zentrum für Türkeistudien, *Islamische Organisationen der türkischen, marokkanischen, tunesischen und bosnischen Minderheiten in Hessen* (Study for the Office for Immigrants and Refugees in the Ministry for Environment, Energy, Youth, Family and Health of Hessen, May 1995).

21   Alevi Islam, a specifically Anatolian form of Shii Islam, stresses more the cultural than the socio-political side of Islam. In contrast to Shiism in Iran, Alevi Islam is strongly influenced by pre-Islamic elements. As a religious minority, whose identity as Muslims was persistently put in doubt by Sunni (orthodox) Muslims, they traditionally stood in opposition to the Sunni rulers. Today, the majority of the Alevis can be found in political movements that propagate a democratic and secular attitude.

22   In the Ottoman Empire, this title had denoted the highest religious scholarly authority (the Sultan being of course the overall leader of the Islamic community). It was abolished by Atatürk in 1924. In the present case, the intention is rather to provide a point of entry to the Muslim community in Germany for the various German official bodies, and to represent the Muslims with those bodies.

23   See also M. Abdullah, *Was will der Islam in Deutschland?* (Gütersloh: Gütersloher Verlagshaus Gerd Mohn, 1993), p. 37.

24   It is worth mentioning especially the leading Turkish Islamist intellectuals Ali Bulac and Abdurrahman Dilipak.

25   See R. Schultze, *Geschichte des islamischen Welt im 20 Jahrhundert* (Munich: Verlag H. C. Beck, 1994), p. 310.

26   Bundesamt für Verfassungsschutz, *Islamischer Extremismus und seine Auswirkungen auf die Bundesrepublik Deutschland*, 2nd edn (January 1995), p. 6.

13

THE STATUS OF MUSLIM COMMUNITIES
IN SWEDEN

Åke Sander

1. Introduction

The comments in this chapter on the situation of the Muslims now living in Sweden, are based to a large extent on fieldwork among them: extensive conversations with a range of individuals and groups in different components of this minority group. I should emphasise that what is presented here as the ideas and feelings of Muslims, are in fact my interpretations, reconstructions and reformulations of what they, often in very different words, have told me in conversation. Reassuringly, in most cases my informants subsequently accepted that my formulations fairly well capture what they had, in different words, been telling me.

The results of this exercise were both promising and alarming, depending on one's point of view. Swedish Muslims now for the first time, 20 years after the foundation of the first Muslim national federation in Sweden, can be said to have reached the size and the stage in their establishment, organisation and institutionalisation process that allows them to turn away from the most immediate, practical issues (and for an outsider often futile internal squabbles), and instead turn to the larger and more strategic issues and problems concerning their presence, role and future in Sweden. The issues they now appear to focus on can be described as political, in the broad sense of the term. They can roughly be summarised as follows: (1) what kind of (multicultural) Sweden do we, as Muslims, want to have in the future? (2) what kind of multicultural state do we think is necessary to safeguard the long-term survival of the Muslims as a cultural, ethnic and religious minority group in

Sweden? and (3) what can (ought) we as Muslims do to bring that about?

By beginning to address questions about multiculturalism, or, in other words, questions about a minority group's rights to recognition, respect and existence, they do, of course, step right into the centre of a politically as well as scientifically problematic and controversial field with many dimensions. While this is not the place to review these dimensions, it is worth pointing out an often-overlooked point, namely that the basic problem one is confronted with here is of an ethical rather than of a technical, legal or procedural nature. Debates about the rights of a minority group lead, like most other debates about rights, directly into the rough terrain of moral philosophy. Here, most questions are normative in the sense that they revolve around what we *ought* to think, what attitudes we *ought* to take, what we *ought* to do and how we *ought* to live our lives. Normative questions are harder to make intelligible and precise than factual questions. Intelligible normative questions are also harder to answer than intelligible factual questions. Often we do not even know what kind of evidence a respectable answer to a normative question requires. While it may be fairly easy to agree that certain facts support or undermine certain answers, it is much harder to reach agreement on *which* facts support or undermine them, and *in what way* they support or undermine them. As long as these questions are open, as seems to be the case in much of the debate about multiculturalism; as long as we do not know more exactly what conditions of an epistemological kind have to be satisfied before a respectable answer can be obtained; and as long as it has not been made probable that these conditions can be satisfied, it seems wiser, in the spirit of Socrates, to inquire, meditate and problematise, than to proclaim and preach.

Against this background, and in view of the fact that Sweden has a relatively short experience as a multicultural country and thereby a relative unfamiliarity with, and lack of practice in, dealing with these kinds of questions, the aim of this paper is not to try to give solutions to problems, but the more modest one of exploring and raising questions.

According to Francis Fukuyama's famous article 'The End of History', what we have witnessed during the late 1980s and the early 1990s is not only the final breakdown of socialism/communism but also the final triumph of liberalism and the liberal democratic tradition. Even though it seems undeniable that the capitalistic societies have won a knockout victory over the communist ones when it comes to production of material things, the second part of the statement should not in fact be so hastily accepted.

If we view the human beings that make up the societies in the world not only, as Fukuyama tends to do, in their universal identity as consumers of things, but in their separate national, cultural, ethnic, religious, and gender identities, it would in fact appear, somewhat surprisingly, that liberalism, rather than being victorious, has proven to be fairly weak as a unifying force in many nation-states today. All over the world, in recent years, one has witnessed a resurgence of cultural, ethnic and religious demands by minority populations who do not control the power of their states; the movements wielding such demands, moreover, have proven increasingly militant. As Stavenhagen puts it: 'From the Australian Aborigines to the Welsh, from the Armenians to the Tamils, from the Ainu to the Yanomami, ethnics around the world are mobilising and engaging in political action, sometimes in violent conflict and confrontation, to establish their identities, to defend their rights or privileges, to present their grievances, and to ensure their survival.'[1]

That an analogous process of ethno-religious mobilisation is under way to some extent even in Sweden, was clearly demonstrated by the fieldwork. An equally clear finding is that this ethno-religious mobilisation process among the Swedish Muslims should be understood essentially as a local defence strategy and not (as believed by many caught up in the present media stereotypes of 'the Islamic Peril' and the like) as part of a worldwide offensive move masterminded by some global Islamic fundamentalist movement. They do not mobilise in order to Islamise Sweden and the Swedes, they mobilise to achieve recognition, to establish their identity and to ensure their survival as a distinct ethno-religious group, something which in their experience the Swedish 'difference-blind' (or, as one Muslim expressed it, 'equality-fascistic') immigration policies are jeopardising. Yet this mobilisation process directly defies fundamental principles on which the Swedish nation-state has been built, and therefore presents a serious challenge to our policymakers as well as social scientists.

The research clearly indicates that *specific nature* has substituted *equality* as the catch phrase for many Muslims in their discussions on what kind of society, what kind of Sweden, they want to build in the future. This sentiment of wanting to be recognised as Swedish citizens of Muslim nationality, has of course in recent years had its equivalent among minority groups in many parts of the world. For the purposes of this chapter, however, I shall only try to describe and articulate the attitudes and developments within the Muslim community in Sweden and the reactions from the majority society towards this process. From the point of view of the latter, the change in attitude – from that of the French enlightenment and British liberalism which focus on universal, individual equal worth and rights, to demands that the state shall recognise ethnic and religious groups *qua* groups and accept that they have rights and worth *as groups* – is creating conceptual, theoretical and, not least, political consternation.

2. The Swedish background: culture, popular attitudes and legislation

2.1. *History*

With few exceptions the modern history of Sweden can be described as that of an unusually ethnically, culturally, religiously and socially isolated and homogeneous society. One of the reasons for this isolation is that until fairly recently, Sweden, largely owing to its relatively low level of 'academic', economic and industrial development, its geographical position and its climate, was not a very attractive target for emigration and therefore remained relatively untouched by Europe's various population movements. Moreover, Sweden has never been colonised or been a colonial power itself, even if it had its own regional empire in northern Europe.

On the whole, Sweden can be said consciously to have tried to protect itself from foreign influence since the end of the sixteenth century – and, in the minds of the legislators, thereby from the risk of domestic disruption and split – with the aid of a highly restrictive legislation, particularly on religion. The formula on which Sweden was to be built and governed was: 'One nation, One people, One religion.'[2]

The strongly nationalist, authoritarian, conservative and xenophobic state religion kept its position of power until the last decades of the nineteenth century. Dissidents from the 'True Faith' could, for example, be expelled from the country up to the end of the 19th century, and the Swedes were not formally granted a Freedom of Religion Act until 1951.

The notion of a common culture and religion, including common manners, norms and value system, as well as a common way of thinking in general, implemented by the state, in cooperation with the church, in a strong assimilation policy, has throughout history exercised a tremendous influence on the Swedes' pattern of thought and life. That this policy has been highly effective is illustrated by the fact that there are virtually no visible traces today of the cultures of the few previous immigrants in the country.

Regardless of what many Swedes like to think, these old ideas about religious homogeneity still exert influence today. Despite the modernisation of recent decades, and despite the fact that Swedes do not go to church in great numbers any more, Swedish culture and patterns of thought and life are still saturated by the traditional Swedish Protestant Christian thought patterns and attitudes. There is no doubt that these ideas of unity, assimilation and homogeneity, despite much official phraseology to the contrary, still are the ideals for most Swedes, including most politicians, bureaucrats and administrators, today. The idea that all problems should have solutions which are as uniform as possible for everyone – often promoted in the name of equality and justice – runs strongly through the country even today.

It is only since 1945, and particularly in the last two and a half decades, that the situation in terms of unity and homogeneity has changed in any significant way. This change is mainly due to the arrival in Sweden of a relatively large number of immigrants and refugees. As a result, the number of people with foreign backgrounds living in Sweden today is estimated at almost 1.5 million, that is almost 15 per cent of the total population. Generally speaking, it is probably reasonable to claim, as Jørgen Nielsen does,[3] that Sweden as a country since 1945 has undergone a greater transformation in its character as a result of immigration than any other European country.

2.2. Assumptions, attitudes and policy before the 1980s

Swedes generally believe that Sweden is a globally aware, free, open, secularised and unprejudiced society with progressive and generous immigration policies. This picture is also largely accepted outside Sweden. One reason for this belief is that Sweden, together with Canada and Australia, is one of the very few countries in the world that have proclaimed multiculturalism as an official goal or regulative ideal for itself. The policies that should achieve this goal of a future multicultural society were summarised in the mid-1970s by the words: *equality, freedom of choice* and *partnership*.[4] The spirit of these policies was at the time thought to be as follows: ethnic minorities with cultures different from the majority should be given the possibility of maintaining, and creating the institutions necessary for maintaining, central, important characteristics of their own cultures (language, basic norms and values, religion, food, dress, manners and customs, for example), at the same time as having equal opportunities to participate in Swedish political, economic, social, and other institutions and in Swedish society and social life in general and obtain equal return on this participation. The idea that culturally different groups are accepted by the majority population without being discriminated against, are allowed to practice, and be identifiable by, central traits from their culture of origin, is what is normally referred to as a policy of integration (as distinguished from assimilation).[5]

The precise meaning of the terms used to summarise the Swedish immigration policies – and thereby, in a sense, how 'multiculturalism' was to be defined – were, however, never explicitly made clear. This turned out to be particularly problematic when it came to the first two: equality and freedom of choice. As to equality, it was obvious that the writers of the legislation had only had a liberal, universalistic and individually focused society in mind. Equality meant equality between universal individuals regardless of culture, ethnicity, race, religion and gender. Equality should, so to speak, be difference-blind. The idea behind this was, of course, the modern liberal assumption that all human beings, beneath their cultural varnish, are basically the same, and thereby have the same value. That 'equality' could be interpreted in other ways, have other meanings, does not seem even to have been considered. It was the universal, or essential, isolated individual, stripped of cultural, religious, and other differences, who had the right to equality, as well as other (universal human) rights.[6] That an individual could claim special rights based on her/his religious, ethnic or cultural specifities, or that ethnic, cultural or religious groups could have rights *qua* groups, was never officially considered. Let us call this 'the individualistic, liberalistic bias or fallacy'. This is not to argue against the Western liberal conceptions of equality and human rights. My point is only that we should be aware of the fact that they are the result of a historic process, of a historically derived self-understanding which had its early strong explicit proponents in the Romantic era of the 18th century, and that most people today have a tendency to take the creed of that time for granted as an 'objective, universal and eternal truth'. I do argue, however, that to fail to see that they are social and historical products, that there are other conceptions, and that the problems involved in trying to legitimise or justify one of them as the true one are most likely insurmountable, implies a kind of ethnocentrism that has had, and still has, dangerous ethical implications.

Another background assumption behind the policies that the Muslims now are putting into question, is what can be termed a *theory of modernisation* in combination with a version of a *theory of cultural evolution*. The basic tenet of the first 'theory' can be roughly summarised as follows: in order to be able to achieve economic and social well-being, the 'backward' countries must change their traditional institutions, norms and values and conform to the modern, Western model of market economy, urbanisation, industrial production and political bureaucracy. They must also shift their loyalties from village, tribe, religious community and ethnic group, to the nation and the State and its attendant institutions. One assumption or hypothesis connected with this 'theory' is that ethnic and cultural difference, at least within the national state, will tend to lose importance and disappear over time. Mainly for economic reasons and through modernisation, increasingly homogeneous national states are expected to come about, at least in the industrialised Western world, and at least in its public or official domain. The other 'theory' includes, among other things, the idea of history as a continuing qualitative process of change towards increasing civilisation: from the simple to the complex, from the crude to the refined, from the primitive to the civilised, from darkness to enlightenment. Most Swedes also embraced the belief that the Western world in general, and Sweden in particular, had reached higher levels of development than most of the rest of the world, and that people with other cultural backgrounds, if and when they came to Sweden, would soon realise this and want to adopt the Swedish ways as much as possible. 'Ethnic identity' and 'religious identity' as social factors were considered historical residues which would disappear through the process of modernisation and cultural development. Economic factors would replace them as mobilising factors for political action as well as in terms of identity.

Swedes, therefore, were firm believers in a version of the melting-pot theory: a modern welfare society was thought to be almost completely dominated by its public domain, in which all differences were to be democratised away and everybody would be equal, while the private domain should in principle be confined to the privacy of one's home. So, behind the official phraseology of multiculturalism and integration there was a firm belief that a high degree of assimilation would inevitably take place.[7] This assumption did of course make it easier to be generous when it came to formulating a policy of immigration. Up to the mid-1980s, while the large majority of the refugees and immigrants came from countries belonging to the Christian-Western cultural tradition, i.e. from countries with thought and life patterns concerning basic cultural categories such as justice and law, norms and values as well as religion that were similar to those already in Sweden, these assumptions seemed also, on the whole, to be correct.

3. The 1980s: increased immigration and incipient animosity

3.1. *Policy and reality*

From the early 1980s onward, however, with the immigration of a relatively large number of people with backgrounds in countries dominated by a Muslim cultural tradition, the situation changed. The number of ethnic Muslims in Sweden illustrate this: in 1950 they were only a few hundred, increasing only marginally over the next decade. By 1970 they had increased to roughly 10,000. By 1980 this had again tripled to nearly 30,000, by 1985 to 50,000. Within five years, by 1990, this figure had doubled to 100,000 and it then took only two years for another 50,000 to be added. Today's figure may be estimated at around 200,000.[8] It came as something of a shock to many Swedes that there were an increasing number of people, mainly Muslims, who did not 'realise' the superiority of the Swedish culture and want to be like the indigenous population. An increasing number of these immigrants explicitly wanted to protect themselves (and especially their wives and daughters) from many aspects of Swedish culture. The real threat for these people was not difference and segregation, but assimilation through forced equality. That it could be possible to feel discriminated by equality, to experience equality as repression, was a totally alien concept to most Swedes.

This growing number of 'unmeltables' showed Swedish politicians to be without real strategies for handling the situation. It showed the existing policies to be nice theoretical constructs, but without any real anchoring among either politicians and bureaucrats, or the population at large. Everybody had considered the 'difference-blind' ideal as the only, obvious, ideal. The phenomenon also pointed up the wide gap between theory (multiculturalism and integration) and practice (equality implying assimilation) in Swedish immigration policies. It demonstrated that, in many ways, Swedish policies for dealing with ethnic, cultural and religious minority groups could be compared, to use a fairy-tale analogy, to the Emperor's new clothes. Despite the beautiful phraseology of established policies, the Swedes were semi-naked when it came to strategies for dealing constructively with ethnic, cultural and religious minorities that claimed their rights as minority groups.

When we turn to the goal of freedom of choice, which roughly states that members of minorities should be given the possibility to choose to what extent they would like to keep their old culture and to what extent they want to join the Swedish culture, the same biases, in combination with a strong adherence to the 'two-domain society' of a strong welfare state type, led most people to believe that society's public domain would witness a process of almost complete assimilation. In this domain everybody should be equal, have equal rights and obligations. Cultural specificity was supposed to be allowed and tolerated only in the private domain, a domain that in a strong welfare state such as Sweden is relatively small. This, I would argue, was the basic 'hidden meaning' of Swedish 'integration' and 'multiculturalism' policy: equality, assimilation and homogeneity in the public sphere, and freedom of choice, specificity and diversity in the private sphere, which, in the case of Sweden, was supposed to be more or less equivalent to the privacy of one's home.

Consequently, and despite official pronouncements to the contrary, much of the debate in Sweden centred around the conviction that giving institutional support and protection to minorities to help them keep their cultures, norms and values alive, would only serve to add fuel to discrimination and racism, to undermine the creation or maintenance of social unity and community feeling, and to be detrimental to the on-going process of nation-state building. An associated argument against supporting separate institutions for minority groups (particularly for Muslim groups) was that those institutions were considered unmodern, patriarchal, repressive, and the like, and that by counteracting them one was in fact doing these groups, and particularly their women, a favour. Behind all the pragmatic arguments, however, it was not hard to detect a spontaneous and unspoken repugnance against differentiation *per se*: the application of different rules, treatment, etc., based on belonging to different ethnic, religious, or other groups, was generally considered intrinsically bad. It is this basic attitude which, I would argue, has determined praxis.

In other words, in the implementation of Swedish immigration policy, two of its cornerstones – equality and freedom of choice – have, instead of being mutually reinforcing, been pitted against each other; equality in principle has won a knockout victory over freedom of choice.

However, it is not only in the implementation of immigration policies as they are formulated in theory, that the failure has been patent. Sweden also failed to achieve the de facto aims which had been adopted. This is true mainly for two reasons. The first is the Swedes' own inability to live up to the officially articulated goals and ideals of equality in the public domain of society. It was only too obvious that the immigrants, and particularly those from outside Europe, of which a large part were cultural Muslims, were not (or more correctly, had not been allowed to be) integrated or assimilated. They have been discriminated against and segregated in the housing market; they have much higher unemployment rates than the native Swedes; they are more affected by work-related injuries and accidents; they are over-represented in drug abuse and criminality; they have a very small symbolic presence in society; they use their voting power to a lower extent than the indigenous population; and they are facing a lack of respect in most areas of society and social life.

The second reason is that an increasing number of immigrants did not want the type of individually based freedom, limited to the private domain, which Sweden was offering them. They wanted to get recognised, for example, as Muslims first and foremost. In accordance with the official policies, they wanted Sweden and the Swedes to recognise their culture and religion as of equal value, and to have an equal right to exist, as the Swedish or any other culture. In our fieldwork and otherwise, those taking this position point out that, apart from 'equality' (the element of liberal democratic tradition which the Swedes have stressed most), multiculturalism also presupposes the kind of freedom which allows the individual with his/her identity to be coupled with a group identity that carries its own special rights and privileges. If a multicultural society is to be achieved, therefore, the collective of the Western European Christian tradition can no longer enjoy all advantages, they claim, and other cultural and religious contexts have to be promoted equally. The argument adduced in support of this contention is rendered below.

3.2. *The Muslim argument*

A fundamental liberal idea, the Muslim argument goes, seems to be that freedom should include the individual's right and opportunity to make his/her own choices when it comes to decisive questions in life such as what social, religious, sexual, and other roles he/she would like to adopt and live by. To be forced to make these choices constrained by boundaries determined by someone else's opinions of what constitutes the good or the right life, is to have one's freedom unacceptably restricted – whether these opinions are those of individuals, a state, a church, a tradition or the Pope.

In other words: people do not choose their identity – or ethnicity, religion, or many other important identifying characteristics – in a social vacuum. They choose from or within the spectrum of alternatives and options provided for them by the cultural, religious and social setting which they have been born into and are living in. An individual cannot normally choose a way of life or value system that has not been mediated through, and had its meaning determined by, (one of) the social realities of his/her everyday life and world. It is within this context that all his/her choices acquire their meaning and sense. The existence of a relatively stable, coherent and consistent culture can, in this sense, be argued both to precede any meaningful choice and to be a prerequisite, or necessary condition, for it.

This is particularly clear in the case of members of minority groups, whose separate identities are not confined only to subjective, psychological properties, or properties connected to the private life of their homes, but tied up with a particular way of public life, including culture, language, religion, dress, relations between the sexes and the age-groups, and so on. It can even be argued that some groups have their identities closely tied up with their way of subsistence – as is the case for various nomadic people such as the Lapps in Scandinavia. Their way of life is, in other words, constitutive of their identity. In these cases it is true that to recognise someone's right to her/his own identity forces us to recognise her/his right to a way of life. In these cases, acceptance of individual rights leads to acceptance of collective rights or group rights, as they are mutually dependent on each other.

In discussions of groups such as these we see the important distinction, not always easy to draw, between choice and circumstances. Differences, including material and other inequalities between individuals and groups, that are due to their own choices (in a very wide sense of the term) are not cases of injustice. But inequalities that depend on circumstances outside an individual's control and which affect her/his ability to make well-informed, rational and meaningful choices, constitute cases of injustice, and is something that a democratic, liberal state, according to its own creed, ought to counterbalance.

This is, according to Swedish Muslims, their situation in Sweden today: by being forced to be equal in, and to assimilate to, the Swedish public sphere and its culture, norms and value system, they are subjected to this kind of circumstantial handicap. They are deprived of the necessary conditions to be able to choose an Islamic identity, to choose what they consider the good or the right life: an Islamic social structure with a relatively high degree of institutional completeness. Children born to Muslim parents in Sweden, therefore, run the risk of losing their Muslim identity before they can even find it, for the simple reason that their culture, their way of life and their social structure are necessary conditions for them to be able to choose an Islamic identity.

If this is true, then it follows that the individual Muslim who experiences a threat towards his/her culture as a threat towards his/her person is not the victim of an illusion. His/her estimation of the risk is rational; the threat is real.

The Muslim argument, then, could be summarised as follows: if one seriously wants to claim that everybody should have freedom of choice when it comes to making important decisions in life like choosing one's identity, then one also has to grant them the real possibilities to create the social and other structures, the institutional completeness, necessary for them to be able to make those choices.

One presupposition for the validity of this argument is that one believes that every culture (every 'cognitive universe' and its accompanying way of life) can be considered as a historically formed and shaped attempt by the people who are the carriers of the culture in question to find and create the best and most valuable way of life. To the extent that this is true, the traditional liberal arguments for freedom of speech, freedom of religion as well as for everybody's (every cultural group's) right freely to choose how they wish to live their lives, can be used in support of the view that there is a prima facie case for every cultural group having the right to live in accordance with its own culture.

The primary goal for any cultural group is normally to survive over time, and its chances to do so are closely connected with its ability to reproduce itself, and to transmit the core items of its patterns of thought, communication, life, etc., to new group members. Normally, new members are born and socialised into the group. When the cultural group concerned dominates its territory, reproduction and socialisation do not normally pose any major problem. The biologically acquired new members of such a group have few possibilities not to be socialised into the culture in question. It is quite a different matter for small cultural groups that are embedded in a larger, dominating and often hostile majority culture, and that frequently do not have access to social institutions such as schools and mass media of their own – that is, groups with a low degree of institutional completeness. That such groups have a small chance of survival over time if they do not receive special rights and protection by the state of the dominating society, is demonstrated by many studies.[9]

If one accepts the prima facie case for every cultural group having the right to live in accordance with its own culture, and if it can be argued that an individual's identity is usually dependent upon a group identity, then a majority society can be said to have a prima facie duty to give those cultural minority groups the rights, support and protection that is necessary to secure its survival. As this presupposes that the group can transmit its patterns of life and thought to its new members, this prima facie duty includes the duty on the part of the majority society to give the minorities the possibilities to transmit their culture in an effective way.

The Muslims argue convincingly that Sweden has officially accepted these responsibilities, as illustrated by the way immigration policy is formulated. They argue equally convincingly, however, that the reality is altogether different.

The arguments which Swedish Muslims have begun to formulate and express in recent years might be translated as follows. From a reasonable interpretation of texts describing two of the cornerstones of the Swedish immigration policy – equality and freedom of choice – four general principles can be formulated. These principles seem to follow from, or be presupposed in, the classical liberal arguments[10] for freedom of speech, freedom of religion as well as freedom for individuals to choose for themselves how they want to live their lives.[11] At the same time, they are principles which most Swedes probably would endorse as guiding principles for a liberal democratic society such as their own. They might be formulated as follows:

(1) Every cultural group, with its patterns of thought, communication, and life has a positive prima facie value;
(2) Membership and participation in a cultural group should be voluntary;
(3) Competition between different cultural groups should be just and fair;
(4) Each cultural group has a prima facie right to use its own historically based traditional ways to socialise its (biologically produced) new members.

3.3. The political fallout

A result of the attempt by the Muslims to make some sort of political platform out of these principles, together with the fact that the Swedes endorse them in theory but do not abide by them in practical political action,[12] has been that various xenophobic, nationalist and extreme right-wing groups, but also many unemployed and generally politically and/or economically dissatisfied young Swedes, have reacted by turning the Muslims into a symbolic target for their complaints and dissatisfaction. In one of the most dramatic instances of this, one of three purpose-built mosques in Sweden was burnt down in early autumn 1993 by a number of nationalist right-wing youths. It must be stressed that this was not a purely anti-Islamic act. However, the fact that it was a mosque that was chosen for this 'political demonstration' shows a change in the Swedish social and political reality. Islam and Muslims have become an important pawn in the political game.

One result of the anti-Islamic lobbying is that Islam and Muslims have been brought onto the national political agenda since the early 1990s, to an extent that exaggerates their real impact on Swedish society. This in itself in return magnifies the problem as it gives rise to a general feeling that can be summarised as: 'When everybody, including people within the government and the established political parties, are discussing "them" so much, there must be something to the stereotype.' Clearly, this in its turn provides fertile soil for xenophobes and nationalists in general, and for anti-Islamic lobbying in particular.

The political impact in Sweden of what the anti-Muslim lobby often calls 'the Islamic fundamentalist project' resides mainly in the way in which the introduction of this 'project' as an item in the political debate serves to alter the parameters of acceptable political debate and action. A party that is openly hostile to Islam and Muslims may only have limited support for its own programme, and may never have any real success in an election, but it may have the effect of making what were previously seen as extreme and unacceptable actions and statements 'politically acceptable' or even mainstream.

Another result is an increased polarisation between native and immigrated Swedes, particularly those with a non-European and Muslim origin. The xenophobic nationalist complaint that 'if it was not for them everything would be all right', has been heard both more often and more loudly in the wake of Sweden's economic recession. In this development it is, again, especially the Muslim immigrants who have been victimised. On the one hand they are the first to become unemployed and otherwise marginalised; on the other, they themselves are getting the blame for the increasing unemployment. The Muslims have been increasingly subjected to this case of 'blaming the victim' in Sweden recently. Native Swedes claim that the Muslims should integrate or assimilate to the Swedish culture and society, at least when it comes to the public domain of society. At the same time these same Swedes continue to hamper such integration by systematically discriminating against the Muslims and by limiting their chances on the labour market, housing market, etc. Native Swedes then blame this failure to achieve integration, as well as many other problems in society, on the Muslims' unwillingness and inability to integrate.

If it is true, as is often claimed, that it is only a de-politicised and liberal Islam that can integrate in Sweden, and that the development of such an Islam presupposes economic and social integration of the Muslim community, then the prospects for this are bleak.

This process of 'blaming the victim' has led to the result – paradoxically, from the Swedish point of view – that the ethnic and religious consciousness of the Muslims have increased, along with a new ethnic and religious self-esteem, which in turn has had the effect that immigrant groups in Sweden have started to mobilise themselves more and more along cultural, ethnic, and religious lines. They and their organisations have also lately been increasingly successful in 'turning the tables', and in turning their disadvantage – their religiosity, their ethnicity – into a political asset and a factor for political mobilisation.

An example of this is that one of the Islamic national federations in 1993 felt strong enough to send a letter to a number of the Swedish political parties promising them 'the Muslim vote' if they in return promised to work for the realisation of a set of specific Muslim demands on Swedish society. At present it would probably be political suicide for any party to accept the offer, a fact of which the Muslims are aware.

From the Swedish point of view, this whole process of increased ethnic and religious mobilisation is, of course, looked upon as politically destabilising and dangerous to national unity. The Swedes do not want to accept people who do not 'play by the rules', into the political game.

The paradox here is that the basic cause behind this development of 'the Muslim problem' is not, as most Swedes tend to believe, primarily that the Muslims are different and behave differently from the rest of the Swedes, but rather that the majority society have not sufficiently allowed them to be, behave, and organise themselves, and to live in a different way from the rest of the society. The main

cause of 'the problem' is, in other words, that the Muslims subjectively, and probably correctly, experience a threat towards their own
identity and culture, and thereby a risk of religious, ethnic and
cultural extinction. If there is anything that can mobilise a religious,
ethnic or cultural group and weld it together, it is precisely such
a threat of extinction. For most religious, ethnic and cultural groups
in the world there is a strong metaphysical sentiment or value connected with the idea of a future existence of the group and its beliefs,
language, norms, values, and customs. This is a metaphysical sentiment which probably affects most people, even if only on the more
individual level of wishing to see what we represent to survive and to
be carried on by our children and grandchildren. It is, I believe, an
empirical fact that most individuals and collectives do resist assimilation and, particularly in times of threat, show strong preferences for
maintaining and living by their own values and according to their
own way of life.

This is, I would argue, a major reason why religious and ethnic
groups in Sweden are increasingly looking for protection and ways
to defend themselves, when they feel the basis for their existence
threatened. It is then that they will tend to ask for collective rights,
as they feel the recognition of these rights to be the only way to safeguard the reproduction of the group as a distinct entity with its own
social organisation.

4. The future

Viewed from the Swedish context, it seems clear that the process of
religious and ethnic mobilisation as a response to discrimination and
xenophobia sketched above constitutes a political challenge in the
sense that the political establishment seems to be taken by surprise
and does not know how to respond. It also, however, constitutes a scientific challenge: most social scientists also seem to have been taken
by surprise, and appear to have little to say about the phenomenon
that is enlightening or constructive. They too seem in the main to
have considered the religious factor and the ethnic factor as elements
doomed to disappear in the wake of modernisation.[13] Social conflicts
were to be explained in terms of class conflicts, economic conflicts.
Groups *qua* groups were dealt with mainly as functional aggregates –

as occupation groups, as consumer groups, as class groups and other groups united by a shared economic interest. Groups 'substantially' defined and united, united by a common ethnicity, culture or religion, have been neglected.

Recent years have shown this assumption to be wrong. If, in consequence, one abandons the belief that culturally, ethnically and religiously distinct minority groups will simply disappear over time and melt into the wider society, then there is a need to try to understand and treat these groups and their demands for recognition as groups and as group demands. Various ethnic and religious group demands for recognition, for the right to be treated as groups and be given group rights (in the context of the principles of equality, freedom of choice, etc.) are very likely to prove one of the larger questions the people and decision-makers of Sweden, as elsewhere, will have to address. The question is a difficult one because, among other things, an 'ethnic or religious group-based society' and a traditional Swedish 'individual-based society' represent two different types of social organisation and two different conceptions of society and of the rights, freedom, value etc., of the individual. It forces us to rethink, among other things, the relations between the individual and the group as well as the relation between the ethnic group (and other groups) and the national state. This rethinking is made especially problematic because most people in Sweden consider mobilisation and organisation around religious and ethnic lines as anti-modern and reactionary, something belonging to a period of history left behind by the modern, developed West. Within the modernistic and evolutionistic assumption which many still more or less consciously embrace, the way to define and solve conflicts that have been dominating the last 100 years – 'class struggle' – is in a vague manner considered as something of an improvement over the old way, largely based on 'ethnic group struggle'. It is not only Marxists who view this change as having 'brought history forward'. By the same token, it seems clear that people in general consider a 'return' to ethnic and religious mobilisation and struggle as a step back, particularly as it negates the idea of modernisation and development and also, to some extent, our idea of the nation state.

Yet I believe that any solution to 'the problem' requires that the majority population in Sweden realise that Sweden is, and will continue to be (probably increasingly), a multiethnic, multicultural and multireligious society, that repression only makes the problem worse, and that we must learn to live with true plurality, even at the price that the Sweden we have known during the last decades will change or disappear. There is not, I would submit, any way back, at least not without much reactionary violence and ethnic cleansing. The Swedes have to realise that Sweden is going to contain an increasing number of 'unmeltable' individuals and groups, of which Muslims and Islamic groups are prime examples, and that every attempt to melt them down by force for casting in the traditional Swedish mould is going to be counterproductive in the sense that it will make them unite more strongly around their religion and ethnicity, thereby only – from the point of view of the workers in the Swedish smelting works – making the problem worse.

There are likely to be increasing instances of religious and ethnic conflict in the future. The challenge will be to learn to handle and solve them in a democratic and constructive way, i.e. a way that all involved experience as a fair balance between equity and freedom. Some of the key questions we have to address and find workable answers to in order to meet this challenge are: (1) what is a democratic multicultural, multiethnic and multireligious society? (2) How are the different actors in such a society going to be allowed to compete with each other on reasonably equal terms about status, power, work, education, money, and so on? (3) How does one solve conflicts in such a society? To answer those and similar questions will be a key challenge for social science in the future.[14]

Notes

1   R. Stavenhagen, *The Ethnic Question, Conflicts, Development and Human Rights* (Tokyo, 1990), p. 157.

2   A century ago Sweden was among the poorest nations in Europe. Up to the First World War Sweden was, largely owing to that and other factors indicated above, a country of emigration. More than 1.3 million Swedes – a fifth of the population – left the country between 1850 and 1930. Sweden was also among the last countries in Europe to industrialise; at the turn of the century 90 per cent of its people lived in the countryside, where they clung to social traditions handed down to them from the Middle Ages.

3   J. Nielsen, *Muslims in Western Europe* (Edinburgh: Edinburgh University Press, 1992), p. 80.

4   In this official policy, the part about freedom of choice runs as follows: 'The goal of *freedom of choice* implies that public initiatives are to be taken to assure members of linguistic minorities domiciled in Sweden of a genuine choice between retaining and developing their original cultural identity and assuming a Swedish cultural identity.' (SOU, *Invandrarutredingen 3, Invandrarna och minotiteterna*, Stockholm, 1974), p. 25. *Regeringsformen* (the Swedish Constitution), Chapter 1, 5.2 says: 'The ability of ethnic, linguistic and religious minorities to retain and develop their own cultural and community life should be reinforced.' In a later document (Proposition 1989/90:86, *Om åtgardner mot etnisk diskriminering m. m.*, Stockholm, 1990), the minister of immigration explained that this goal was to be understood as 'an assertion that different cultures and groups, including the Swedes, have the same value and the right to exist simultaneously and in parallel.'

5   A more detailed discussion of these terms and the various ways they can be broken down into sub-categories can be found in Å. Sander, *Får Man Slå Sin Fry Om Man Är Invandrere? Några reflektioner rörande valfrihetens gränser för minoritetsgrupper i Sverige*, KIM-Rapport No. 13 (Göteborg, 1991).

6   My interlocutors in the course of my fieldwork more than once pointed out that this picture of the isolated, individualistic, atomistic man as the basis of all rights is not shared by all cultures, and that it has its limits if and when we emphasise everybody's right to her/his own identity.

7   This means of course that 'multiculturalism' has become a meaningless catchword, standing for more or less everything that has to do with immigration policy and ethnic relations. The more watered-down the concept has become, and the less the term has to do with reality, the more it has been used. That the term was traditionally used to denote a strategy for overcoming nation-state traditions in the context of continuing migration, and to denote the togetherness of ethnic communities with independent conceptions of the world and organizations, values and behaviours, seems, on the whole, to be unknown in Sweden today. That 'multiculturalism' implies that the majority society should accept

independent social entities and sub-societies, that it implies a strategy for recognition of 'foreign' corporate individuality, in its nation-state context, is totally forgotten.

8   A detailed discussion of these figures can be found in Å. Sander, *I vilken utsträckning är den Svenske muslimen religiös? Någre överväganden kring problematiken med att ta reda på hur många muslimer som deltar i verksamheten vid de muslimska 'församlingarna' i Sverige*, KIM-Rapport No. 14 (Göteborg, 1993); and Sander, 'The Muslim Community in Sweden', *New Balkan Journal*, 1994.

9   See for example L. Driedger, 'Ethnic self-identity: A comparison of ingroup evaluations', *Sociometry*, Vol. 39, No. 2 (1976); and L. Driedger and G. Church, 'Residential segregation and institutional completeness. A comparison of ethnic minorities', *Canadian Review of Sociology and Anthropology*, Vol. 11 (1974). A minority group's chances of survival over time with a relatively stable cultural identity seems from these and other studies to be more or less directly correlated with its degree of institutional completeness, which, to use the terminology of P. Berger and T. Luckmann, *The Social Construction of Reality: A Treatise in the Sociology of Knowledge* (Garden City, New York, 1966), can be said to be the legitimation and plausibility structures for the world view and life-world of the group.

10   As they can be deduced from the writings of, for example, John Locke, above all in *Two Treatises of Government*, second thesis, John Stuart Mill, above all in *On Liberty*; and, in France, François Voltaire, for example, *Traité sur la tolérance*.

11   All this, of course, as long as there do not arise any real conflicts between different people's choice of lifestyle, i.e. as long as the implementation of one individual's choice of lifestyle does not prevent another from implementing his choice of lifestyle (the distinction between real and spurious conflicts in such cases is discussed in Sander, 'Får Man Sla Sin Fru Om Man Är Invandrare?').

12   As the Muslims also point out, Swedish officialdom even criticises other countries, not the least Muslim ones, which do not endorse them and/or do not follow them in practice.

13   See, for example, Stavenhagen, *op. cit.*, pp. 6 ff.

14   A somewhat more detailed discussion of some of the issues touched upon under the last heading can be found in Sander, 'Får Man Sla Sin Fru Om Man Är Invandrare?'; Sander, 'Det inter-kulturelle samhället' in E. Abiri (ed.), *Miljoner på flykt*, World House Papers No. 1 (Göteborg, 1992); Sander, 'Världen i Sverige – Sverige i Världen. Ett försök till belysning ur ett globalt och internationellt perspektiv, inkluderande någre spekulationer kring vad man på basis dårav kan säga om framtiden' in *Den religiösa närvaron i ett mångkulturellt Sverige, Symposium på Aspenås Herrgård*, Lerum, 21–22 October 1992 (Norrköping, 1992), pp. 45–59; and Sander, 'Do national cutlures vary in their capacity to integrate minorities?' (to be published by the Swedish Ministry of Culture, Stockholm).

14

Muslims in Denmark

Jan Hjarnø

1. Introduction

In a popular handbook on world religions published in Denmark in 1974 there is a photo of an Ahmadiyya Mosque, built in Denmark in 1969. The text states that this is the first and only mosque in Denmark.[1] Two decades later, there are 75 to 100 places in Denmark that could be classified as mosques.[2]

The presence of Muslim communities in Denmark is a new phenomenon. Denmark converted to Christianity over a thousand years ago, originally as Roman Catholics. The Reformation came in 1536, since when the Lutheran Church has been the State church. Religious freedom was introduced in 1849; since then there have been a few religious minorities, such as Jews and Catholics, and now also Muslims. The exact number of residents in Denmark with a Muslim background is not known. According to Danish law it is illegal to register people by race, religion or ethnic background, but it is estimated that 1–1.5 per cent (50,000–75,000) of all residents of the country have a Muslim background.[3]

Apart from a few Danish converts, most of the Muslim presence in Denmark traces its origin to the import of labour from Yugoslavia, Turkey, Morocco and Pakistan, which started in the late 1960s, or to political refugees. The import of foreign labour was stopped as of 1 January 1971, except for a short break in 1973, since when Denmark has officially not been a country of immigration. However, the number of foreigners has constantly increased due to permitted family reunions, and to the granting of political asylum.[4] In reality, therefore, Denmark remains a country of immigration.

Most Muslims in Denmark identify themselves by national origin, only then adding that they are Muslims. This applies to most immigrants from Turkey, Pakistan and Morocco. A few identify themselves as Muslims and state that Islam is a unity which cannot be divided into national units. This small group mention their national or ethnic origin only when asked. Finally, there is a group who maintain that they are of Turkish, Kurdish, Pakistani or Moroccan origin, adding that the question of Islam is of no importance to their relation to society. The majority of Muslims are Sunni, but various Shiite groups are also represented, as well as a small group of Ahmadiyya.[5]

Some Muslims have become Danish citizens: this applies to more than 80 per cent of the people from Pakistan and to a small percentage of those from Turkey.[6] Applications for naturalisation are considered by the Ministry of the Interior and are granted by law, passed in Parliament. The usual criteria in such cases is that the applicant must be 18 years old; have been residing in the country for more than seven years; have good knowledge of the Danish language; have incurred no legal sanctions (other than small fines); have paid taxes without delay; and not have been in receipt of certain forms of public assistance.

Regarding legal status, foreigners have almost the same rights as Danish nationals. However, they cannot become Government officials; they receive no assistance from Danish representatives while abroad; they cannot become owners of a dwelling unless they have resided in Denmark for five years (nationals of the EU countries are exempt from this rule; they may purchase a house for their families); and they cannot vote in elections to the Danish Parliament nor be elected to it. Since the 1978 election, nationals of the other Nordic countries have been given the right to vote and to be elected to Municipal Councils. This right was extended to all foreign nationals in 1981.

As regards schooling, children who do not have Danish citizenship and who have a different cultural background, are offered the same education as Danish children, free of charge. However, the Danish language is the medium, and knowledge of Danish is the precondition for benefiting from the Danish educational system. Children with a non-Danish mother tongue are offered courses in their own language and in social studies of their home country. Such courses are usually given after normal class hours. Immigrants who do not wish to have their children educated in the Danish medium are free to establish private schools, and provided these schools meet certain requirements on the standard of education, they may receive public support. A few groups of Muslims have founded their own private Islamic Schools where the education is paid for by the Danish State.[7]

At the end of the 1960s, when the first labour migrants arrived, they were welcomed and looked upon as a necessity in order to provide continued economic growth. There were, of course, linguistic, ethnic and cultural problems connected with the integration of foreign labourers, but these were not regarded as a burden compared to the economic advantages of admitting them. The immigrants took on the lowest paid and least pleasant but necessary jobs, and were therefore regarded as a cheap but vital labour force. They arrived at a time of full employment and were not regarded as competitors to the native Danish labour force. It was generally accepted that these workers should pay tax in the same way as Danish citizens and have the right to receive the social benefits of the welfare state and remain residents. If they wanted, they could eventually become Danish citizens. The fact that most of the foreign labourers were Muslims was hardly ever mentioned. It was the general opinion that the influx of foreign labour was a temporary phenomenon. They had come to work for a few years in order to save up so they could return to their countries of origin after a few years. They were never referred to as immigrants but as 'foreign workers' or 'guest workers'.[8]

2. Unemployment and increasing anxiety: The 1970s and after

2.1. Immigration and unemployment

In the early 1970s the economic situation changed. The boom came to an end. Full employment was replaced by a situation with some unemployment, which has become permanent and is slowly increasing.[9] The foreign workers did not return to their countries of origin as most Danes had expected; on the contrary, they started to bring their wives and children to Denmark, and by the end of the 1970s it was generally realised that the 'foreign workers' had turned into 'immigrants'. At the same time the number of political refugees rose. Problems in Vietnam, the war between Iran and Iraq, the civil war in Lebanon, the Sri Lanka situation, etc., brought refugees to Denmark who applied for political or humanitarian asylum. The number of people who were granted asylum rose, and many brought their wives and children with them.

Gradually Danish attitudes towards foreign workers who turned out to be immigrants, and towards the increasing number of refugees, changed. The ethnic, religious and cultural 'otherness' of the immigrants and refugees became an important issue in the public debate. Culture came to be regarded as a problem for integration – and when Danes and Danish politicians talk of culture as a problem for integration they tend to talk of the Muslim immigrants and refugees rather than of the refugees from Vietnam and Sri Lanka.[10]

The main targets of criticism are Islam and Muslims. 'Only a fool does not fear Islam' read a 1994 headline of a daily column in one of the largest Danish newspapers.[11] In the same year, the Liberal Party's spokesman on naturalisation in the Danish Parliament wrote an article in a well-known Danish newspaper, under the headline: 'Muslims are a problem'.[12] The following excerpts illustrate the view of a spokesman from the Liberal Party, one which is not generally considered extremist:

The number increases constantly due to family reunions and a high birth rate. In addition, new refugees are coming from the Balkans, Turkey, the Middle East, Afghanistan and Africa . . . They are people with a cultural pattern quite different from that of European people.

It is not a question of the text of the Koran or other Muslim writings. It is also possible to find texts in the Bible and the Jewish scriptures which can be misused by fundamentalists. But in a modern democratic society there are other much stronger forces which keep these people in check. It is not so in the Muslim countries or in Muslim communities in Europe.

Researchers in religion have drawn attention to the fact that Islam is 600 years younger than Christianity. They point to the horrors which took place in Christian Europe 600 hundred years ago in form of wars, genocide, etc. In other words, we have only got to wait 600 years and Muslims will be as rational as we normally are (except of course for Hitler, Stalin, Zhirinovsky and other similar charmers).

It is a long time to wait, when the Muslim refugees and immigrants are pouring into the country. Some Danes cling to the fact that it is Shia Muslims related to the regime in Iran who passed the fatwa death sentences on Rushdie and on the super model Claudia Schiffer. Shia Muslims only make up 10% of the Muslims of the world. Unfortunately not only Shia Muslims run wild. The fundamentalists in Egypt, the Sudan, Algiers, Tunis and a number of other countries are Sunnis.

It is Sunnis who kill foreigners in Algeria and Egypt. It is Sunnis who are killing or driving out millions of Christians in Sudan and hundreds of thousands in Chad, or who drive Christian Palestinians from the West Bank. And it is a mixture of Shia and Sunni Muslims who have driven a quarter of a million Christians out of the Lebanon and who have removed nearly all the Jews and Christians from the Arab countries. The Revival of Islam, the new Fundamentalism, affects the whole of the Muslim world, including the immigrants in Denmark.

It is a huge problem that there are Muslims in Denmark who support the sale of brides and forced marriages (also of minors); circumcision of women; polygamy, and other types of oppression of women; assault on children; medieval socialisation of children; punishment for crimes, and many other things which are against Danish Law or, at least, against current morality in Denmark. Muslims try to practise their medieval ideas in Denmark.

I believe we must take these facts into account when we decide granting asylum in Denmark and whom we shall expel under the Aliens legislation, because they represent a danger to the security of Denmark or commit serious crimes. Even more so when we decide who shall be granted Danish citizenship. We must not forget to show consideration to the Danes.

Statements like these are not at all uncommon. Why, then, has opinion among Danes and Danish politicians changed so that they now regard immigrants or refugees as a problem? Why do the words 'Islam' and 'Muslim' trigger associations of cruelty, fanaticism, oppression of women etc., which most people do not approve of? Why do Danes mainly view immigrants and refugees of Muslim origin as a problem, but not refugees from Vietnam and Sri Lanka?

The change in attitudes towards immigrants and refugees in general would appear to be related to the change in the economic situation. In the early 1970s the boom came to an end. Full employment was replaced by a degree of unemployment which became an especially heavy burden on immigrants and refugees. Social welfare arrangements suddenly and quite unexpectedly came under heavy pressure. Huge sums had to be paid out in unemployment benefit and other types of social assistance. To finance these benefits, taxes increased and strong competition between private consumption and public spending emerged.

Many taxpayers felt taxation to be a heavy burden, and began to support the populist agitation against taxes.[13] At the same time the majority were against demolishing the existing social welfare system. This has led to a contradictory position. Many people were against high taxes but did not wish to give up the right to social welfare – regardless of the impossibility of achieving both goals simultaneously.

In this situation, which persists today, more and more Danish taxpayers are listening to populist agitation which claims that the high rate of unemployment among immigrants, and the continued growth in numbers due to family reunification and the addition of political refugees, represent an economic burden on, and a threat to, the existing social welfare system. This has increased xenophobia and nationalism, such that one now finds politicians on the extreme Left as well as the extreme Right demanding repatriation of all foreigners.[14] This agitation from the extreme Left and Right has an impact on the other parties. In order to avoid losing voters, they, too, have started to talk about the problems of integration by criticising immigrants and refugees for not wanting to learn Danish, and for practising old-fashioned customs such as arranged marriages. An increasing number of Danes want the borders closed as long as the present high rate of unemployment continues, and nothing indicates that this situation will change in the near future. Because of the high rate of unemployment, immigrants are looked on as competitors to Danes in the labour market.

This is acute mainly among unskilled and semi-skilled Danes who are competing for the same types of job as the immigrants.[15] But also in a wider section of the population, immigrants and refugees are regarded as an economic burden and a threat to the social welfare arrangements. Immigrants are no longer regarded as a cheap and necessary source of labour and as a precondition for continued economic growth.[16] In a way, therefore, the social welfare arrangements have become an important hindrance to immigration.

At the same time, the pressure of immigration to Denmark is increasing. Through the modern media, people in the poorer parts of the world learn about the affluence of Western Europe and wish to share in it. Many do indeed try to get into Denmark posing as political refugees. Even though a large proportion of these are turned back, many Danes believe that the majority of those who are granted asylum are not real refugees. They come to Denmark, it is believed, not because their life is in danger but because they want to exploit the Danish public welfare system, which in the eyes of many Danes is the best in the world.

2.2. *The European Union factor*

The development of the European Union (EU) also caused increasingly hostile attitudes towards foreigners. The political and geographical precondition of the European Union (or its predecessors) was the division of Europe into East and West and the confrontation between the two sides. These preconditions have disappeared. The response of the EU to the new situation has been to speed up the process of integration on the basis of the original concept in order to keep up the momentum of the process of integration and the development of the new Germany. Many European politicians argued that, following German unification, the country's integration into European institutions became all the more important for long-term security. In the opinion of many Danes, attempts to accelerate the process of integration proceeded too fast. They voted 'No' to the Union in 1992, and later, in 1993, only a reluctant 'Yes'.[17] Nobody in Denmark feels sure what will happen except that a giant market with free movement of capital, commodities and labour will be created. Danish voters also know that Denmark must accept migration between countries. Many feel uneasy about this, believing that foreigners will flood Denmark looking for work. They expect that these job hunters will mainly be non-EU immigrants and refugees who will be leaving other EU countries. They suffer more than any other group from unemployment and are more mobile than the natives of these countries, because they are not tied by the same historical ties to certain geographical localities. These immigrants and refugees, it is feared, will then compete for jobs with unemployed Danes, and if they become unemployed it will be Danish taxpayers who have to pay as they become a burden on the Danish social security arrangements.

Denmark, many Danes feel, has the most attractive social security system in the EU; they believe this will draw foreigners to the country, thus eventually undermining the system. Danes have become very conscious about taxation and social rights. This applies especially to the social groups which are most threatened and who most eagerly wish to preserve the existing social security arrangements.

The European Union contains an important contradiction: it is only a market; there is no real social dimension. This would not have been a problem if the social security systems had been similar in all member states. This, clearly, is not the case. In most member states people tend to prefer their own system, and it is difficult to harmonise them. Each system is the result of a specific historical development.[18] The values, norms and beliefs attached to these systems cannot quickly be replaced by new ones. This contradiction will remain for a long time to come, and will no doubt cause considerable tension in the Union and within each member state.

Although the creation of the European Union was potentially an important step towards internationalisation, all evidence points to its creating more nationalism, more xenophobia and less solidarity with the poor and disadvantaged. All over the Union one can expect people to defend their system of social security. People defending job opportunities and their right to social benefits may turn their anger and fears against the immigrants, especially those with other than a European-Christian cultural background. The victims, then, will be these immigrants – not the inadequate EU structures.

3.   A bleak future for Christian–Muslim relations in Denmark?

Since the onset of the economic crisis, ethnic problems have increasingly been used by Danish social and political actors in connection with costs, taxes and social welfare. The appeal to the workers and the poor is strong – although such hostile activities may in fact lead to a termination of the social welfare systems they believe they are defending. In Denmark, as in all countries in Western Europe, one observes an increasing popular aversion to paying for foreigners who are unable to get jobs. Perhaps in part as a reflection of this attitude, the level of aversion to funding the public authorities by taxes has also increased. Fewer and fewer people have faith anymore that the public authorities are administering their system efficiently. An often-heard question, for instance, is, in one of its variants: 'Why should I go on paying for people who cannot be bothered to make an effort for themselves?' There is also a widespread feeling that, while Denmark has become a target of immigration, Danish politicians have no real control over the situation: the number of foreigners, after all, continues to rise in spite of the officia immigration stop from 1 January 1971.

Why is it that Islam and Muslims are subject to attack, and not refugees from Vietnam, with their Buddhist religion, or the Tamil refugees and their Hinduism? This is no doubt related to history. Danes in general hardly know anything about Buddhism or Hinduism, whereas Islam and Muslims have been part of European and thus Danish history for centuries. In an historical analysis, Peter Christiansen[19] has shown that it is possible in most of Europe to trace a hostile image of Islam back to the Middle Ages. Though this image has undergone change through time, it has some constant basic elements which even today have an impact on the way many Danes interpret what takes place in the Middle East. One such element is *Jihad*, usually translated as 'holy war', one meaning of which implies the demand on Muslims to propagate Islam.[20] The Middle East is identified in the popular perception with violence and fanaticism. Events which would otherwise be explained by reference to political, social or ethnic differences are, in cases involving the Middle East and Muslim communities, usually explained by references to Islam.

Another constant basic element in the European perception of Muslims, is that the latter have always been 'the others' in contrast to whom one has identified oneself. Islam has always appeared as the negative image of Christian Europe, and as its absolute opposite. In the Middle Ages, when Christianity was by definition the truth, Islam was identified as false and Muhammad as the work or the agent of the devil. Later the image changed to Islam being characterised by fanaticism, violence and irrationality, while Christian Europeans were thought of as humanistic, tolerant and rational. The hostile image of Islam has been revived and continues to have an effect on the perception of Muslim immigrants and refugees in Denmark.

The hostile image of Islam and Muslims has gradually become dominant in the public debate since the 1980s. At the end of the 1960s and in the early 1970s, the hostile image of a foreigner was that of a southern European: a treacherous, lazy, hot-headed, spaghetti-eating person.[21] Only after the economic crisis of the 1970s, and when the extreme Left and Right began to focus their agitation on the fact that most immigrants and refugees were Muslims, did the image change. There is now a tendency among many politicians and the media to make Islam the explanation for all problems related to immigrants and refugees.[22] Even political parties which claim to work for ethnic and religious equality regard the culture of the immigrants and refugees as a problem.

No research has yet been undertaken on the response among Muslims to the massive criticism of their cultural and religious background. Analysis has shown how immigrants and refugees are socially marginalised in housing, employment and education. Nevertheless, they themselves are accused of being the cause of the marginalisation, because they stick to their own culture and will not adapt (read 'assimilate') to Danish norms and values. The high rate of unemployment among Muslims in Denmark has the unfortunate effect that Danish workers no longer meet Muslims on the factory floor: this creates an information gap which prevents people from determining whether the detrimental reports they read about Muslim migrants in the media are true or not. Muslims continue to be forced in relatively large numbers into the role of welfare clients.

What does it mean to belong to a religious minority which is constantly identified as a problem? What does it mean constantly to be subject to discrimination? Do they become defeatist or will they fight back? The ideal picture of Denmark of the late 1960s as a tolerant society unmarred by discrimination against ethnic minorities no longer holds true. The 'ideologised' development of Danish attitudes towards the new Muslim minority in Denmark would appear to hold out bleak prospects. However, in November 1993 the Danish Parliament passed a law setting up a committee for ethnic equality, which may provide Muslims and other ethnic and religious minorities in Denmark with a platform from which they may raise a voice against discrimination. At the time of writing it was not yet known if sufficient funds would be made available for the committee, for it to wage a forceful campaign against discrimination.

Notes

1   J. Aagaard, *Håndbog i Verdens religioner* (Copenhagen, 1974).
2   J. Simonsen, *Islam I Danmark* (Aarhus, 1990); and J. Hjarnø, *Research on Muslim Communities in Denmark, 1980 to 1991* (Sydjysk Universitetscenter, 1992).
3   Simonsen, *op. cit.*
4   *Statistik om Invandrere om Flygtninge 1993. Dokumentation om invandrere,* No. 1/1993 (København, 1993). These are statistics on foreign nationals in Denmark, and on foreign nationals who have become Danish citizens.
5   Simonsen, *op. cit.*
6   J. Hjarnø and I. Abdulrahman, *Statistics on Immigrants and Refugees in Denmark* (Esbjerg, 1994).
7   J. Hjarnø, *Islamic Private Schools in Denmark* (Esbjerg, 1994); K. Just Jeppesen, *Unge indvandrere. En undersøgelse af andengenerationen fra Jugoslavien, Tyrkiet og Pakistan* (Scoalforskningsinstituttet, Rapport 89:6, Copenhagen, 1989).
8   J. Würtz-Sørensen, *Der kom fremmede*, Arbejdspapir nr. 1 (Aarhus: Center for kulturforskning, 1988); Würtz-Sørensen, *Velkommen Mustafa? Debatten om gæstearbejderne i det danske samfund i starten af 1970'erne*, Arbejdspapir nr. 17 (Aarhus: Center for kulturforskning, 1988); J. Hjarnø, *Kurdiske indvandrere* (Esbjerg: Sydjysk Universitetsforlag, 1991).
9   Hjarnø, *op. cit.*
10   C. Schierup, *På Kulturens Slagmark* (Esbjerg, 1993).
11   *BT*, March 1994.
12   I. Dahl-Sørensen, 'Muslimer er et problem', *Politiken*, 28 February 1994, Section 2, p. 2.
13   Schierup, *På Kulturens Slagmark*; Hjarnø, 'Causes of the increase in xenophobia in Denmark'; *Migration – A European Journal of International Migration and Ethnic Relations*, Berlin, Vol. 18, No. 2 (1993), pp. 41–63.
14   Schierup, *op. cit.*; Hjarnø, 'Indvandrernes boligforhold', *Byplan*, No. 5, 1993, pp. 227–32.
15   J. Hjarnø, *Synet på indvandrere og flygtninge*, Ungdomsbilleder i Esbjerg, Rapport nr. 4 (Esbjerg: Sydjysk Universitetscenter, 1989); and Hjarnø, 'Migrants and refugees on the Danish labour market', *New Community*, Vol. 18, pp. 75–87, pp. 80–2.
16   P. Gundelach, 'Danskernes intolerance', *Dansk Sociologi*, 2, 1992; Hansen, *Tal dansk din hund!* (Herning, 1992); M. Heide Ottosen, 'Os og dem – gensidig tilpasning?' *De fremmede i Danmark*, 2 (Copenhagen: Social-forskningsinstituttet, pjece 37, 1993).
17   K. Siune, P. Svensson and O. Tonsgaard, *Det blev et nej* (Aarhus, 1992).
18   J. Petersen, *Dansk pensionspolitik i fortid, nutid og fremtid* (CHS Arbejdsnotat 1991) (Odense Universitet, 1991).
19   P. Christiansen, 'Opfattelser af Islam i Vesten' in K. Kristiansen and J. Rasmussen (eds.), *Fjendebilleder og fremmedhad* (Copenhagen, 1988).
20   In fact, the term strictly speaking means 'effort' or 'struggle'. This encompasses in the first instance a personal spiritual effort at self-improvement.

The propagation of the faith is the other main meaning. Armed struggle and 'holy war' are therefore only a secondary meaning of the term – contrary to Western interpretations.

21 S. Dindler and A. Olesen (eds.), *Islam og muslimer i de danske medier* (Aarhus, 1988); J. Würtz-Sørensen, *Der kom fremmede, op. cit.* and *Kulturmøde/kulturkonfrontation. Tendenser i 80'ernes debat om danskerne og de fremmede.* Arbejdspapir No. 60 (Aarhus: Center for kulturforskning, 1990); *id.,* Enestående fremmedhad. 25 år med fordomme og fjendebilleder. In Exil, No. 1, 1992; Hansen, *Tal dansk din hund!*; M. Hussein, 'Billeder af muslimer i pressen. Et mediesociologisk perspektiv' in Dindler and Olesen, *Islam og muslimer i de danske medier.*

22 Schierup, På Kulturens Slagmark; J. Hjarnø, 'Indvandrernes bolig-forhold', *Byplan*, No. 5, 1993, pp. 227–32; C. Horst, 'Marginalisering og etnicisme' in *Dansk Sociologi*, 1991, No. 4.

15

THE MUSLIM COMMUNITY IN SPAIN

Nuria del Olmo Vicén

1. Introduction

This chapter outlines the emergence, development and the present position of the Muslim community in Spain. The context of a specific set of historical circumstances that have made it highly problematic for its people to coexist with different cultures. For centuries concerted efforts were made to keep the existing heterogeneous cultures united within the Spanish state. Ever since the expulsion of Muslims and Jews began in the late 15th century (the last Muslims were expelled in 1609), the coexistence with different communities has proved very difficult.

More recently, under General Franco's dictatorship Spain was very much a Catholic country, politically isolated from other religious communities. However, in the final years of his reign, diplomatic links between Spain and the Arab world increased. In the 1970s the first significant numbers of immigrants from the Middle East began to arrive to Spain. Some came for political reasons, others as students or looking for business. All were aware both of the friendly relations between Spain and their countries of origin, and of the part of Spain which had been most influenced by Islamic civilisation. By the same token, some in Spain in the late 1970s were looking for ideas for societal renewal and identity, by contemplating new ways of life based on nostalgia for the eight centuries of Hispano-Arabic co-existence. All of this led to the formation of several Muslim associations, especially in the southern territories of the old Muslim Spain, in Andalucia.

Article 16 of the new constitution of 1978, which accompanied the arrival of democracy, foresees the possibility of reaching agreements between the Spanish Government and the religious communities with old and deep roots in Spain. As a result, Islam was recognised in 1989 by the Advisory Commission on Religious Freedom. Historical reconciliation, therefore, became possible: in 1992 the Spanish government, together with the Islamic Commission of Spain, signed an agreement of cooperation that enhanced the Constitutional Law of Freedom of Religion passed by the Parliament in 1980.

Today, the Muslim community in Spain is growing, mainly as a result of the arrival of immigrants from countries with a Muslim majority population. One can usefully classify the members of the Muslim community in Spain into two main groups: convert Islam and immigrant Islam. Within the latter group two sub-groups may in turn be identified, namely immigrants from the Mashriq (the 'Middle East' proper), and those from the Maghreb. Each has its own characteristics, about which more later. The number of non-immigrant Spanish Muslims today stands at about 13,000, distributed among converted (1,000), nationalised (5,000) and about 7,000 who were born Muslims in Ceuta and Melilla (Spanish territories in North Africa).[1]

A description of both the immigrant and non-immigrant groups is offered below, with special attention to their formation and their associational networks: that is, for their members and their geographical origins, their source of financial aid, their activities, their relationships with other Muslim associations, and their expansion – but non-assimilation – into Spanish society.

2. Spanish convert Islam

As part of our research on the role of Islam in the formation of ethnic groups among economic immigrants (March 1992), a questionnaire was sent to 30 Spanish Muslim associations registered at the office of the Ministry of Justice.[2] The response showed that more than half of the Muslim associations had been founded by converted Spaniards. Nevertheless, the number of such converts is low, standing at about 1,000, including the converts' families.

Most converted Muslims are Sunni with a tendency towards 'fundamentalism'. As indicated earlier, the increase in conversions during the 1970s is a peculiar phenomenon, when viewed against the absence of a multiconfessional tradition. Several authors have put forward explanations. Greater religious freedom during the last years of the dictatorship, together with the social disappointment of new generations, led to a search for different ways of life inside the established social structure. In the end, the attempt to 'legitimise' their position led to a search for historical roots. For some of the converts, more than eight centuries of Hispanic–Muslim coexistence were enough to justify embracing Islam. From this time onward, much has been written about the desire to establish 'the *umma* in al-Andalus' (the former being the Arabic word for the community of all Muslims, the latter the name for Arabo-Islamic Spain).[3] Among non-immigrant Spanish Muslims, however, the converts are only the second-largest component: the largest consists of those born in Ceuta and Melilla.[4]

The associational network for all these Spanish Muslims developed mainly in Andalucia (especially in Cordoba, Granada and Seville), Madrid, Ceuta and Melilla.[5] The first Muslim association was established in Melilla in 1968; during the following twenty years another fifteen were founded.[6] These associations, founded by converted Spaniards, naturalised, or original Spanish Muslims, were established with similar structural, organisational and social networks, activities and aims. Some of them have now disappeared, but those that remained, together with those founded by early Muslim migrants (especially upper-middle-class people from Middle Eastern countries active in the liberal professions, business, or as students, or from the diplomatic corps), united on 23 September 1989, under the umbrella of the Spanish Federation of Islamic Religious Entities (FEERI). Between 1989 and 1990, other religious associations were founded, eight among which came from the old Muslim Association in Spain. In 1990 these were unified in the Islamic Community's Union in Spain (UCIE). Finally, in April 1992 the Federation and the Union were brought together as the Islamic Community of Spain.[7]

Their activities, generally, have had not much influence on Spanish society. Most of these associations describe themselves as religious associations, and their main activities are religious and cultural, functioning in Spanish and sometimes Arabic. However, the infrastructure to develop these activities is limited: only some of them have their own place as a library or meeting place, or have their own publications. The main source of finance is the members themselves, although in some cases they receive financial support from the Ministry of Social Affairs or the Municipal Government, and from a number of Arab Embassies. Generally, the number of members is few; usually they are Spanish, and they do not have much contact with other religious or cultural associations.

3. Immigrant Islam

At present, it is difficult to know the exact number of Muslim immigrants in Spain. There are several reasons for this. One is the unknown extent of clandestine migration; another, that even among legal immigrants from mainly Muslim countries, it is not easy to determine exactly the numbers of those who practise Islam, especially because in some of these countries other religions are practised in addition to Islam. The numbers may be estimated, however, at between 111,000 and 175,000.[8] In any case, the important point is that in recent years the Spanish Muslim community has grown, due to immigration from countries with a majority Muslim population. These immigrant Muslims, moreover, also constitute the main source of the future increase in the Muslim community. It is worth dwelling at some length, then, on this aspect of the Muslim presence in Spain.

3.1. *Early immigrants*

The immigrant Muslim community falls into two categories, according to their time of arrival and the type of immigration. In the context of the friendly relations between the Spanish dictatorship and Arab–Islamic countries, Muslims mainly from these countries began arriving. Most of these were students, liberal professionals and businessmen, that is, upper-middle-class people who ended up staying in Spain and adopting Spanish nationality. The majority came from Syria, Lebanon,[9] Jordan and Iraq. Later this group was added to by political refugees, such as the Palestinians,[10] who started to arrive around 1977. In the beginning these were mainly students, but after 1982 whole Arab families began escaping to Spain from difficulties in countries such as Lebanon, Jordan and Kuwait. A further group of Muslim immigrants to Spain are the Iranians, who began arriving as a result of the 1979 revolution and the Iran–Iraq war. Some of them arrived in Spain with the intention of emigrating later to Great Britain or the United States. Finally, there are also small numbers of Muslim immigrants from other Arab, Central African and Asian countries.

The associational network of these Muslim immigrants is basically similar to that of convert Islam: they are largely religious and cultural associations, except that some of them have greater economic possibilities, due to the financial aid received from their countries of origin or from other friendly states or organisations. As among the converts, the majority of immigrant Muslims are also Sunni, at times with radical Islamist tendencies.

3.2. Economic immigrants of the 1980s

While the kind of immigrants discussed above are, by and large, the first chronologically, they are not so in size. The largest Muslim sub-group in Spain – even if smaller in number than in other European countries – is made up of later economic immigrants from North African countries and, less prominently, Sub-Saharan Africa, who began arriving during the 1980s. There are deep differences among these migrants and the earlier ones. They differ in the number, type of migration, socio-economic status and cultural level; there is also a distinction in where they tend to settle, in how their group has developed and is developing, and in their associational network.

The main difference between the two sub-groups is perhaps that, while the first often *choose* to stay apart from the rest of Spanish society, the later, economic, migrants are excluded from it (and often find themselves rejected by the Muslim communities as well). This is basically a case of economic and racist discrimination, spurred on by the very widespread survival in Spanish folklore and collective memory of the idea of 'the Moor' (*El Moro*).[11] This group does not identify with the Spanish Muslim community. They tend to identify themselves instead according to their nationality and the circumstances of their immigration.

The group is mainly composed of Moroccans,[12] who started to arrive on the Peninsula during the 1960s, as a consequence of the colonial period.[13] The total has increased since 1973, when the Western European countries closed their borders. But the massive economic migration flow only began in the 1980s; this is where the origins lie of Spain's largest Muslim community today. Given the reason for their migration, it comes as no surprise that this group is characterised by low levels of education and low socio-economic status. The majority is settled in Catalonia, Madrid, Andalucia, Valencia, and the Canary Islands. Their precarious living conditions, together with their cultural differences, make their integration into Spanish society very difficult.

In spite of these conditions, the group has developed only a low degree of solidarity.[14] This is reflected, on the one hand, in their low participation in the Muslim religious associations founded by other Muslims, and, on the other, in the low development of their own associational network. As an illustration and a consequence of this phenomenon, Spain's 'official' Islam – the Islamic Commission – is not concerned with this group of immigrants.[15]

Their associational network distinguishes them from other Muslim associations mainly in its syndicalist character, whereby the national, immigrant and worker identities have priority over the religious identity. This, indeed, would seem to be another explanation for their low level of membership in the Islamic Associations.[16]

The main associations founded by immigrants of this subgroup[17] have focused on three issues. The first is legal advice on the protection of immigrants. Secondly, they have developed a 'social relation' function, facilitating the immigrant's integration into the immigrant community itself (and even into the receiving society). Thirdly, they have worked towards cultural development, which is intended both to ease social integration into Spanish society and to engender new manifestations of their own culture.

In summary, then, while Islam is of course one of the defining features of this sub-group,[18] this has not led to the development of a network of Islamic associations. At present, the largest Muslim group in Spain, that of the 'economic immigrants', has primordial and subsistence needs. For this reason, and because they are the seeds of the future Muslim community in Spain, through family reunion and new births, this group must be the prime concern for Spanish social and political actors.

4. The socio-economic and cultural impact of the presence of Muslim communities on Spanish society

As the formation of a Muslim community in Spain is so recent, coming

after centuries of cultural and religious isolation, it is worth elaborating, first, on the impact of its presence on Spanish society, before
briefly addressing the questions of the political position of the
Muslim community in Spain, its economic conditions, and its role in
international relations.

As illustrated above, the Muslim community in Spain is characterised by its heterogeneity (both in its formation and in its subsequent development), its recent origins, its small size, and its rapid
growth. As a consequence, the impact on Spanish society remains
basically an 'immigrant', marginal matter; it is only with future
generations of Muslims in Spain, that Islam will perhaps begin to
constitute a homogeneous and well-structured community with a
strong cultural impact on the community from the dominant culture.

The impact of the different Muslim groups on Spanish society
varies considerably, both because of the origin of the groups, and
because of the specific socio-political and economic context in which
they have developed. Thus, the impact of the converted Muslims is
limited to marginal groups of society. There has been only sporadic
cultural contact even with immigrants from Middle East countries.

The first settled groups of Muslim immigrants from Middle
Eastern countries have gradually integrated into Spanish society.
Islamic activities have been restricted to the private sphere, with Islam
being experienced as a religion rather than as a whole way of life.

However, the so-called economic immigrants present a different
case. As mentioned above, they have arrived more recently, in worse
conditions, and were more numerous. Thus, their impact on the
Spanish society is felt at several levels: in the political arena, on
the external relations, in the educational and cultural areas, and
especially on the matter of peaceable social coexistence.

That the largest impact of this group should regard the issue of
coexistence, has increased Spanish society's awareness of the new
elements in the composition of its once ethnically stable population:
the first waves of xenophobia are now arriving. The so-called
'Moors', who have been rejected for centuries, are now at times the
object of violent attacks, due, firstly, to the fact that they are immigrants, and secondly, to their geographical-cultural origins.

In recent years, the increase of the unemployment rate, together
with the falling-off in quality of life, have provoked some reactions
against these immigrant workers, from the most affected sectors of
Spanish society. Generally, perhaps due to the influence of some

nationalist hectoring, this feeling against immigrants is spreading through the working class, where the immigrant is seen as a competitor. Also, the difficult economic situation in Spain does not allow the provision of the levels of aid to this group of immigrants which might otherwise be contemplated. As a result, both the development and the implementation of any integration programme is proceeding only very slowly. The most important activity in this regard relies on non-profit organisations, especially those linked to the Catholic Church. However, a lack of clear division of labour and responsibility regarding immigration, between the central, regional and municipal administrations, adds to the difficulty of properly carrying out any such programmes.

Their geographical origins engender a mixture of curiosity and distrust toward this sub-group of more recent, mainly economic, immigrants. Muslim immigrants from Maghreb countries are the most affected by this. The difference in this respect from the perception of converts or even those coming from the eastern Arab world, can be explained by historical events and the difficult relationship between Spain and the North African countries. For centuries, this has put these people in a bad light.

Even though, on the whole, the Islamic identity of these migrants has appeared to be a secondary factor only, it is still true that their impact in society has become significant. This has at times been beneficial for the rest of the established Muslim community, as in the case of the Agreement of Cooperation signed in 1992, between the Islamic Commission of Spain and the Spanish Government. Thus they have benefited, for example, from labour exemption for the compulsory prayers, and they have the right to finish their job one hour early during Ramadhan.[19] However, generally the impact does not relate to their status as Muslims so much as to their immigrant status. The relatively sudden arrival of significant numbers of immigrants from countries with a Muslim majority in a country such as Spain brings in new elements of ethnic, linguistic, religious and cultural differentiation. As a consequence it leads to legal and educational modifications in the receiving country and may, possibly, also help lead to instances of social destabilisation.

As was already highlighted, the Muslim community of Spain is heterogeneous with a low degree of solidarity, and, consequently, without a strong associational network through which the common interests of the whole Muslim community in the country could be pursued. As a consequence, it is not possible to identify a particular political status for 'the Muslim community' as a whole. Neither has their presence a particularly important meaning for, or impact on, international relations. It may be noted, though, that recent years saw an improvement in Hispano-Moroccan relations, although this has been mainly related to the regulation of the migratory flow from Morocco, and to economic agreements.

However, the presence of Islam in Spanish society has started to arouse certain popular reactions to Islam in general,[20] with the Spanish considering Islam as a symbol of violence, fanaticism and backwardness.

Regarding the economic position of Muslim communities in Spain, some data have been gathered by category of labour activity.[21] However, such data not surprisingly differ very much between Muslims integrated into Spanish society, on the one hand, and the recent immigrants on the other. Again, we have to differentiate particularly between the economic immigrants and the rest of the Muslim community of Spain.

The immigrants coming from the Mashriq (the Middle East 'proper'), who initially arrived as students, over the years have integrated into a middle class with a high percentage of professionals and executives. However, the recent, mainly economic, immigrants, make up the most marginal social class, living for the most part at subsistence level.

In all, it is still accurate today to state that, because the incipient expansion of the Muslim community in Spain is of such recent origin, the presence of this community has no more than a small impact on Spanish state and society, whether in cultural, economic or political terms.

5.   Conclusions: what about the future?

In spite of the heterogeneity and the small size of the Muslim community in Spain, it has begun to constitute a concern for Spanish political and social actors. As happened in other European countries, this concern is increasing as a consequence of the comparatively sudden arrival of relatively large numbers of immigrants from countries with a Muslim majority. Indeed, while today's rate of immigration is low, compared with other states of the European Union, an increase is imminent. This will be the result particularly of the decision by current immigrants to remain in Spain and to try to regroup their families, thus giving rise to a second generation.

To sum up: first, Islam in Spain is composed mainly of an immigrant community. By far the largest part of this group are recent and mainly economic migrants. This sub-group is the only one that may develop a strong social pressure. Secondly, today this immigrant sub-group – coming from countries with a Muslim majority – finds itself in the first stage of its migratory project. Thus, the real needs and claims from them at present regard subsistence. In this context, Muslim immigrants in Spain have not so far proved prone to using Islam as a prime feature of identity, nor, therefore, as a tool for social dialogue or political struggle.

However, with regard to the future, there is no reason to expect that, given a major growth of this immigrant community, Spain's experience would be much different from that of the other European host states. Spanish political and social representatives have tried to develop a number of policies on immigration, but Spanish society is still a long way from considering seriously the presence of Islam in its daily life.

Precisely such consideration is nevertheless needed. An awareness should develop that, as a result of the migratory process, the individual migrants generally find themselves in a disrupted social context. Thus disoriented, people (here as elsewhere) may take refuge in particular aspects of their life and identity, such as religion, emphasising these and seeking confidence and context through them. This (again, here as elsewhere) may be a source of social conflict. The conclusion must be that Spain as a receiving society needs to make it easier for this community to reproduce some of the original religious and cultural aspects of their lives and contexts, thus reducing alienation and disorientation – and with it the risk of disruption, radicalism and social conflict.

These new cultural elements should then enter the Spanish environment, bringing to a close, at last, the centuries of isolation. Spanish society cannot wait for the future of the Muslim community; it must facilitate its development from the start.

Notes

1   See E. Alonso, *De las Taifas a la Federación. La larga marcha hacia la unidad de las Asociaciones Islámicas Españolas* (Madrid: Comisión Episcopal de Relaciones Interconfesionales, 1990).

2   The survey was composed of a blank form of three pages with the following sections: (1) Association's structure: number of members according to original nationality and present nationality; (2) Relationships between the association and other associations (Spanish and foreign); (3) Typology of activities; (4) Sources of finance. The form was sent together with an explanatory letter regarding our research and a stamped envelope. This research constitutes the empirical part of my doctoral thesis on *The Formation of New Identities among Muslim Immigrants*, being undertaken at the European University Institute, Florence, under the supervision of Professor Klaus Eder.

3   Indeed, most of these Muslim Associations are located in Andalucia, Spain's southernmost province, where the Muslim civilisation remained from 711 until 1609 (that is, even after the fall of Granada in 1492).

4   Generally, due to the fact that in Spain nationality is acquired on the basis of the *ius sanguinis*, this population had kept their Moroccan nationality until the first regularisation process (1985/6); afterwards they could adopt Spanish nationality.

5   As of 4 February 1993, according to the General Direction of Religious Affairs of the Ministry of Justice, the Muslim organisations are settled in the following places: Andalucia (19), Madrid (9), Ceuta y Melilla (6), Catalonia (3), Canary Islands (2) and in the regions of Valencia, Zaragoza, Galicia and Asturias (1). These associations were founded by both converted and naturalised Muslims. See B. López García and N. del Olmo Vicén, 'Islam e Inmigración: El Islam en la formación de grupos étnicos en España' in M. Abumalham (ed.), *Actas del Simposio Internacional: Comunidades Islamicas En España Y En La Comunidad Europea* (Madrid: Ediciones Trotta, Universidad Complutense de Madrid, 1993).

6   Most of the Muslim associations have been founded by Muslim converts, naturalised Spanish Muslims and born Muslims from Ceuta and Melilla, in addition to non-naturalised Muslims from Middle Eastern (not North African) countries. The immigrants coming from the Maghreb have not developed religious associations but other kinds of associations, as will be seen below.

7   A full listing of the various associations and their details can be found in the paper by B. López García, 'Estatuto del Islam e immigración musulmana en España', for the conference *Islam y Occidente: Las condiciones para un diálogo* (Granada: February 1993).

8   See López García and del Olmo Vicén, *op. cit.*

9   It should be emphasised that not all the Lebanese citizens settled in Spain are Muslims: a considerable number of them are Christians.

10   In 1977 the PLO opened an office in Madrid, where it has been helping

the Palestinian community, as well as giving classes about Palestinian geography and history, and various other activities.

11   On the origins of the pejorative use of the word 'Moor' (*Moro*), see B. López Garcia, 'La Historia y las Raíces de la Xenofobia Antiárabe en España' in I. Arias *et al.*, *Racismo y Xenofobia. Búsqueda de las Raíces* (Madrid: Fundación Rich, 1993), pp. 203–20.

12   More recently and in smaller numbers, but no less important in social repercussions, is the group coming from Sub-Saharan countries with a Muslim majority (particularly from Senegal).

13   Morocco and the 'Spanish Sahara' were a Spanish protectorate for half a century (1906–56).

14   Several authors have written about the strong links of solidarity that groups usually develop under difficult and marginal situations: see the 'circumstantialist' approach.

15   It must, at the same time, be remembered that embassies are usually affiliated to the Islamic Association; immigrants therefore suspect possible manipulation.

16   Due to the short track record of immigration in Spain, it is difficult to make a confident comparison with other European countries with longer experience of inward migration, such as France. Perhaps, in a first step of the migratory process when the individuals have primary needs, the associations are founded as para-syndical ones. But, according to Kepel, Islam is used later as a tool of social phenomena, being an important element in the identity of these immigrant groups (G. Kepel, 'Islam en Francia: ¿inserción o integración?' in B. López García *et al.*, *Inmigración Magrebí en España: el retorno de los moriscos* (Madrid: Mapfre, 1993), pp. 161–80.

17   These associations have a strong trade-union nature and are defined mainly according to nationality. For example, there are the Association of Moroccan Emigrants in Spain (AEME) and the second, more important one, the Association of Moroccan Immigrant Workers in Spain (ATIME).

18   Our empirical work indicates that there are substantial differences in this group regarding religious matters. However, among the Moroccan students who arrived after the Moroccan disturbances of 1984, Islam is a part of their culture.

19   These types of social benefits can be a double-edged sword, however: in the present time of high unemployment, the demand for certain exemptions may be to the detriment of the Muslim worker community, reducing the employment possibilities of Muslims.

20   According to the surveys undertaken by several sociological research centers (for instance the CIS), and to the work of D. Nyumba and E. Galindo, *Encuentro Islamo-Cristiano*, No. 236.

21   See López García, 'La Historia y las Raíces de la Xenofobia Antiárabe en España' *op. cit.*

16

THE MUSLIM COMMUNITY IN ITALY

Stefano Allievi

1. The return of Islam

From a broad historical perspective, today's presence of Islam in Italy is not new: to speak of a 'return' is more accurate. Italy, indeed, witnessed an occasional Arab presence in Sicily since the 7th century – the very beginning of the history of Islam – and a real Islamic domination of the island from the 9th to the 11th century. But the Islamic heritage is visible also elsewhere, from the South up to the North, all along the coast of the country. Moreover, there was some Muslim presence also subsequently, up to the 19th century.

In more recent times the importance of Islam in Italy was much reduced, particularly if compared to the cases of France, Britain or Germany. This is largely so because Italy does not have as important a colonial past, and never developed a real policy towards Islam. The only exception was arguably in the fascist period, when Mussolini tried to adopt the role of 'protector' of Islam: he liked to be pictured with the 'sword of Islam' in his hand (and in 1928 even on occasions defined Italy not only as a 'friend of the Islamic world', but as a 'great Muslim Power') but these political posturings never developed into reality. In 20th-century Italian culture, Islam remains an unknown quantity. If there is any perception of it, it is mainly as an old enemy. In Italy's case, this may be due less to the Crusades (which, even with the Pope established on the Italian peninsula, were in many respects more of a French affair), than to the frequent incursions on the Italian coasts of the 'Saracen' pirates, whose traces remain clearly visible in several popular traditions.

Considering the present resurgence of Islam in the world, the presence of Islam in contemporary Italy could therefore be characterised as a 'double return', with roots both in the past and in the topical issues of today, from history and from geography.[1]

From the sociological point of view, however, the Islamic presence is a new phenomenon, paralleling the arrival of inward migration. For more than a century, until the early 1970s, Italy still had its own migrants going to different receiving countries, having been the largest European reservoir of labour for the Western economies. The symbolic turning point was 1973 – the year in which the number of immigrants for the first time exceeded that of those leaving. The real boom in immigration is even more recent, dating back only to the 1980s. It started with the arrival of different groups of immigrants, mainly from the Philippines and other Catholic countries, such as El Salvador, particularly as domestic workers, and continued in several waves. The most recent groups of workers, both legal and illegal, came from the Maghreb, some Sub-Saharan countries, as well as Albania, Peru, etc.[2] Among these immigrants there were also Muslims: it is here that the return of Islam to Italy finds its origin.

Islam's return to Italy, then, is very recent. It arrived, for all practical purposes, twenty years ago, with the first mosques organised in several university towns by the Union of Muslim Students in Italy (USMI) in the early 1970s. This, however, was a small presence, and rather untypical for Europe. Before the establishment of the USMI mosques, there was only a single mosque in Italy, located, not surprisingly, in Rome. What is peculiar in the Italian situation is that the first mosques were created not by and for communities of foreign workers, but by and for an elite of students, mainly coming from the Middle East (Syria and Jordan among others, many of them Palestinians). Only later did the number of workers exceed that of the students; the mosques have, consequently, changed their role and frequently their legal statutes, even if their leadership has, so far, often remained the same.

Clearly, though, Islam in Italy is establishing itself very rapidly. The whole typology that characterises the Islamic institutionalised presence elsewhere is already visible: mosques, associations, Sufi orders (turuq), political movements, intellectual production, transnational powers (particularly in Rome), intervention of states of origin, converts, freelancers, etc.[3] While all of this is in evidence, however, it is still at a very fragile stage of organisation. For one thing, the leadership of emerging communities, as well as on the national level, remains ill-defined: this process (and this competition) is still on-going.

2. Towards a morphology of Islam in Italy[4]

2.1. *Some statistical data*

The Muslim presence in Italy today is difficult to evaluate; even the overall number of migrants can only be estimated. While Italy has one of the smallest migrant communities in Europe, the percentage of non-EU foreigners in this community is one of the highest, and its number of illegal immigrants is probably also the highest, both in relative and in absolute terms.

Just over 900,000 foreigners were legally resident in Italy at the end of 1992. Among these, some 760,000 were non-EC citizens, and around 280,000 (31 per cent) were from Muslim countries, or from countries with a major Muslim presence. If one adds a conservative estimate of illegal immigrants in addition to converts and those who have obtained Italian citizenship, the number of persons of Muslim origin in Italy (excluding those who only stay for a short time), can be estimated at about 500,000. This number does not, of course, tell us anything about the level of their effective and practical 'Islamicity'. Higher figures do circulate occasionally in the press and elsewhere, but these lack serious credibility.

Approximately one-third of these Muslims come from Morocco, but the origin of the rest (contrasting with the absolute pre-eminence of the Turks in Germany, the Algerians in France or the Indians and Pakistanis in Great Britain, for instance) is divided across a range of countries, including Tunisia, the former Yugoslavia, Senegal, Albania, Egypt, Iran, Somalia and Pakistan. Among the illegal immigrant Muslims, most are from the Maghreb (mainly Morocco and Tunisia), but especially the number of Bosnians and Albanians is increasing.

Italy's Muslim community is peculiar in European terms, therefore, because of its diversity, the almost complete absence of Turks, the small presence of Asian Muslims, and no more than a symbolic presence of migrants from former colonies.

2.2. *The mosques*

As regards religious organisation, Italian Islam is following the path of Islam elsewhere in Western Europe, except more quickly. Until

1970, there was only one mosque in Italy. In the 1970s six new mosques were created. The period between 1981 and 1990 witnessed a first expansion of mosques in various regions of the country; seven out of the 23 established in this period were in fact opened only in 1990. But the real 'boom' is even more recent: at the time of writing, Italy counted more than 60 mosques, and up to 120 prayer-halls.

In so far as it is at all possible to distinguish it, the national community behind the establishment of such mosques is often Moroccan, although there are also Tunisian, Algerian, Iranian, Egyptian, Pakistani, Libyan, Turkish and Italian mosques. More frequently, however, the origin of the mosques is not ethnic/national but associative and, for the earlier mosques, connected to the USMI network.

All of them are what may be called 'first-generation mosques'. In contrast to the sequence observed in most EU countries, the Muslims of Italy began building their mosques soon after arriving in Italy, and did not wait for a second generation that had to be Islamically educated.

2.3. Sufi orders and religious movements

The organisation of the *turuq*, the Sufi orders, is not easy to study. Even when they are not secret societies, they are always at the very least publicity-shy; those who belong to a *tariqa* (singular of *turuq*) often do not willingly declare their membership, and indeed sometimes deny it. This is the case also for some other religious and political Islamic movements.

Probably, though, *turuq* membership is higher, proportionately, among converts than among those who are Muslims by birth. There are, however, exceptions. The most evident of these is the Senegalese *tariqa* of the *Mourides*, to which the majority of the Senegalese living in Italy refer to, even if they are not explicitly members, or if they were not members while still in Senegal. This is because the *tariqa* plays not only a religious role, but also a social one of protection and insertion, and even an economic one.

There is evidence of others Sufi orders as well. Two branches of the *Tijaniyya* are active: one is Senegalese (in Senegal it is probably still numerically the most important *tariqa*), and the other is mainly composed of converts. The *Burhaniyya*, an Egyptian *tariqa* that is very active also in Europe and has its European centre in Germany, is also present among certain groups of converts. Groups which refer to the *Naqshbandiyya*, the *Darqawiyya*, the *Alawiyya* and others, all with some dozens of members at most, are made up mostly of converts. The *Ahmadiyya* is also present, as are the Baha'is.

Also of some importance are the political and religious movements that are beginning to make their existence felt in the Italian Muslim community. Some of these are more established than others: for instance the *Jama'at at-Tabligh*, which, having started with two mosques, is now rapidly increasing; and the Muslim Brotherhood, which is in fact more important as an ideological point of reference than as an organised structure. The ideas of the Brotherhood are popular among the leaderships of the USMI and some Islamic centres. Perhaps a parallel could be drawn between the widespread acquaintance with the writings of Sayyid Qutb and Mawdudi on the one hand, and those of Marxism on the other: the latter, too, it was long virtually indispensable to be conversant with, but one did not have to belong to a Communist organisation to read them. This distinction must be kept in mind with regard to the Muslim Brotherhood in Italy.

Finally, note must be taken of what might be termed the wider non-Sunni 'religious families', not beholden to any of the above groups. The most important of these is that of the Shi'ites, but Ismailis and others also have a presence. These also have their own organisational structures.

Contrary to the situation in most other Western European countries, in Italy the organisations based on country of origin (what the French call the *amicales*) play only a very modest role. This is related to the lesser degree of concentration of migrants in any particular nationality. Recently, however, some change may have begun to appear in this picture.

2.4. *Social actors*

At the time of writing, the 'competition' for representing Islam in Italy remained unclear and far from concluded. No single figure or organisation can at present lay claim to the leadership of Italian Islam. The most important actors are reviewed below:

The Islamic Cultural Centre of Italy (*Centro Islamico culturale d'Italia*). This is the group which is at the origin of the great mosque of Rome. It might perhaps be defined as 'diplomatic' or 'state' Islam: the board of the Centre is officially composed of the ambassadors of the different Islamic countries, even if the leading role is played by Saudi Arabia through the *Rabita*, the Muslim World League.

The Union of Islamic Communities and Organisations in Italy (UCOII) was founded in 1990 in order to be the representative of the 'real' Islam, in opposition to the 'official' Islam of the centre of Rome, this has in its committee of promoters the Islamic Centre of Milan, historically one of the most powerful and best organised in Italy, and the Union of Muslim Students (USMI). The UCOII is quite active both in internal organisation and in external public relations with the media and Italian society. It publishes a new Muslim bi-lingual (Italian and Arabic) monthly, *Il musulmano*, and its main purpose is to obtain an *Intesa* (agreement) with the Italian state in order to recognise Islam as one of the religions of the country (to join the other denominations that have already obtained a similar recognition, such as a number of Protestant churches, the Jews, etc.).

Other Islamic social actors are also playing a role. In some areas of the country regional networks, with at their centre the oldest or the best organised mosque, are quite active and relatively independ-ent from the bodies referred to above. Some transnational organ-isations, such as the Saudi-sponsored *Rabita* and the Libyan *Da'wa*, also exert some influence. In addition, some states (particularly Morocco, Tunisia, Egypt and Iran), have attempted to establish a degree of control over their citizens, with varying degrees of success. The converts (including Shi'ites) recently also started to build their own networks, both at the national and at the European level. A final group of social actors might be called the 'freelancers', a type not uncommon in Europe, even if unimportant in the Islamic countries of origin. They are also referred to as 'sociological' Muslims, quite often intellectuals, who perform (or try to perform) a linkage or bridging role between the Muslim world and non-Muslim society, but who are often more recognised as Muslim representatives by the non-Muslim majority than by the Muslims themselves.

2.5. *The intellectual output*

The intellectual output of Italian Islam is surprising, given the latter's recent establishment. There have already been a dozen attempts to create Islamic magazines in Italian, and some of these have survived. To this must be added various publishers who count Islam among their main interests (not scholarly literature on Islam, but more or less militant publications). The role played in this field by converts is easily ascertained. They are the ones who have the best grasp of the Italian language, have the best know-how, and are able to find the necessary financial resources. The result is that it is the converts, with their peculiar way of practising and thinking about Islam, who have become the interlocutor with the media and, more generally, with society as a whole. This is probably a temporary phase, but one that may have nefarious effects: the image of Islam thus given Italian society is often both more mystical and more radical and militant than the reality lived by the Muslim immigrants.

3. Islam and society

Although it is necessary always to keep in mind the novelty of the phenomenon of Italian Islam, it is nevertheless possible to outline some of the features of the on-going process of contact and interaction between Islam and the State or, more precisely, some analytical comments on the growing question of the visibility of Islam in the public sphere.

Italy presents the spectrum of a relatively acceptable level of social integration of the Muslim communities. Moreover – and perhaps this is one of the causes of this acceptance – these communities are not even perceived, for the moment, as *Muslim* communities, but much more as *migrant* communities. Indeed, they are not commonly identified even by their ethnic communities, but, more in general, as *non*-members of the community, as *extracomunitari* (i.e. not from the EU); this is how they are usually defined in statistics, in the press, in the socio-political jargon, but also, very often, in research).

A number of phenomena can currently be observed with regard to the socio-economic integration of foreign workers, that have implications also for the spread of Islam.

The first one is a visible marginality of a certain segment of the migrant population, and particularly of the illegal one. This group can be described by the popular label of the so-called *vu' cumprà*[5] (foreign street sellers), *vu' lavà*[6] (traffic light windscreen washers), small smugglers (particularly of cigarettes), etc. While this part of the migrant population is not the largest, it is by far the most visible and, inevitably, the most quoted, discussed, and reported. At the other end of the social spectrum, there is an elite composed of entrepreneurs, businessmen, professionals, intellectuals and diplomats, among others. This elite, much less visible and in any case not focused on by public opinion, journalists, or researchers, in fact plays an important role for the social integration of the other members of the foreign community, and particularly of the Muslims. This is not only through the financing of Rome's Islamic cultural centre by the embassies of Muslim countries, but also, far more importantly, because this elite is at the origin of most of the more important Islamic centres and associations, and even of the umbrella organisations. A particular role has been played by a group of university-educated professionals (mainly doctors, but also architects etc.), most of whom hail from the Middle East (Palestinians, as well as Syrians, Jordanians and others). These not only founded the USMI, but also became the actual leaders of several local or regional networks of mosques, as well as the UCOII.

In between these two ends of the spectrum, there is the majority of the Muslims in Italy: common believers, followers rather than organisers of various groups and participants in the activities of various mosques. There is at present little emphasis on, or attention for, their presence and role, or concern for their position. One Muslim leader in fact stated in an official speech, that from the religious point of view many Muslims have more freedom in Italy than in most of the so-called Islamic countries.[7]

4. Institutional relations

While relations between the Muslim community and the population and society are, then, relatively good so far, it is fair to describe relations with the government and the public institutions similarly. It should be noted that these latter relations exist more at the local (municipal and to some extent regional) level, than at the national one.

At the local level the evidence is clear: many of the mosques and prayer-halls (both usually modest halls) are located in centres for migrants, in hostels, or in other places offered by the municipalities, often for free or for a symbolic rent. In one striking example, in Palermo, a former church was restored by the regional government of Sicily and given to the Tunisian community (the most important Muslim community of the region) practically for free. In this particular case a linkage between domestic and international politics is in evidence, particularly via the linkages between the Socialist Party in Italy (whose former leader Bettino Craxi, is a personal friend of prominent members of the Tunisian leadership and owns properties in the holiday resort of Hammamet) and the Tunisian government. This type of international linkage is also visible in the case of Rome – more of which below.

Quite apart from the matter of the mosques, relatively good relations are in evidence also in the discussions in several towns on the problems of schools (particularly the question of *halal* food for Muslim students), Arabic and Quranic courses, Islamic cemeteries, etc. – even if these have not always been followed by decisions.

Similarly positive relations exist between the Muslim community and religious and church organisations, particularly concerning the problems of migrants, and with public opinion. There have thus far been very few acts motivated or justified in anti-Islamic terms: it seems clear that curiosity and 'the exotic' still play a larger role than rejection and racism, exceptions notwithstanding.

At the national level the situation is quite different. The Islamic community, particularly through the action of the UCOII, is trying to establish an *Intesa* (agreement) with the Italian government, in order to obtain a status compared with that of other religious minorities.[8] But the actual process – or, indeed, the discussions – have not yet officially started. This can be ascribed to several factors.

The first of these is the problem of determining which Islamic body should be taken as the official representative of the Muslim communities. The first text of a possible *Intesa* was proposed by the UCOII; while this is the most representative umbrella organisation among the Muslim communities, it is only a de facto association, not recognised by the State. The latter, indeed, has recognised the Islamic Cultural Centre of Rome as a 'moral body', but not a 'church' and even less a 'religion', but something more than a private association. The Centre, which obviously does not want to be excluded from this process and in fact claims exclusive representation of the Muslims in Italy, can count on the important support of the Islamic countries.

The second obstructive factor resides with the State itself. Italy's political scene in 1993–4 was occupied with more urgent matters. More specifically, the country has been undergoing a dramatic process of change in the structure of the State and its institutions. If pursued along the lines advocated by the main political party in northern Italy,[9] this could well lead to a less centralised system and possibly a (at least administrative) division of the country. Also on the part of the State, in other words, there are serious questions of representativeness and leadership.

5. Muslim communities and international relations

It is difficult to distinguish which is the more relevant impact: that of the Muslim presence on the international relations or that of international affairs and relations on the Muslim presence. One example, which is not an isolated case, illustrates this well.

The decision to permit the building of the mosque of Rome[10] and the present of 30,000 square metres in a valuable area just outside the city of Rome (near the residential quarter of Parioli) was taken in 1974, after a visit of King Faisal of Saudi Arabia to Rome in 1973 – the year of the first oil shock. The Islamic Cultural Centre of Rome was created officially in 1966, but it is only in 1974 that, a mere three months after the King's request, in an unusually fast procedure, it was recognised as a 'moral body'. This clearly fits an international pattern. Islam was recognised in Belgium as one of the religions of the State in 1974. And several Islamic institutions received a discreet impulse in the same period. There is little doubt that the Italian and other European governments were intent on showing goodwill towards Islam, in their determination to safeguard economic relations with the oil-rich Middle East.

This, of course, is neither a surprise nor a scandal. The whole history of the relations between religion and the State is replete with instances of such bargains, as attested by the history of Christianity in Europe. It is argued here, that, in line with this tradition, Western governments were using Islam as an *instrumentum regni*, under the assumption that supporting the establishment of a few mosques would have few appreciable consequences for Europe itself, beyond the economic advantage to be gained. Little or no thought, therefore, went into the matter beyond these calculations (as, indeed, was the case for the importing of foreign labour). Inevitably, the increased presence and visibility of Islam in Italy – as elsewhere in Western Europe – *did* have consequences: both for these countries, and for Muslims and Islamic institutions. Admittedly, it seems probable that the Islamic countries, and particularly the Saudi *Rabita* – the financial partner of many Islamic centres in Europe – did not themselves know or consider in depth the implications of these developments, as would become evident when events at times eluded their control and, indeed, went against their interests.

Another process of sociological and political interest is the Muslim communities' own internationalisation. They are not interested in, and do not recognise in the same way, national and European borders. What has been happening in this respect, is that 'their' Europe, as represented in their international organisations and networks, extends from the Atlantic to the Urals, and is not restricted to the territory of the European Union. This is quite apparent in the case of the Italian Muslims, perhaps because, with Islam in Italy having been introduced more recently than in other European countries, they have been assisted and influenced by those longer-established communities.

A footnote must be made, in this connection, to the role of the converts. They *are* Europeans, and in some countries, certainly in Italy, they play an important role in Islamic associations and media. They also have their European networks. It comes as no surprise, that they should be in search of a European Islam. This search in turn can, as in Italy, have a certain feed-back effect on the wider Muslim communities.

6. Conclusions

A country that long believed itself to be monolithically Catholic is, in the mid-1990s, beginning vaguely to become aware that this image is no more than an ideal construct: Islam is the second religion in the country. Even if this religion has not yet reached a high level of organisation, and has not yet become very visible, Italy has, in this respect, clearly reached an historical turning-point. After centuries of being identified with 'the enemy', Islam has now begun to form a part of the social and cultural landscape of the country, and mosques and minarets have begun to figure in the skyline of the city: Islam, in other words, has become an 'internal' element, no longer a purely international one.

For Italy, this is a dramatic change, more so than for many other West European countries – indeed, potentially representing a revolution in its self-perception. At the same time, the process might also in fact prove easier here than in the rest of Europe, because of the role of the Catholic Church.

Reference was made earlier to the role of the Church structures in assistance to migrants in general, and to the attention paid to Muslim migrants in particular. It must, in addition, be remembered that the Church based in Rome is not only Italian, but very much universal: the centre of the most widely-connected religious institution in the world. This has a number of implications.

A universal body has universal needs. For Muslims, this means among other things, being constantly reminded of the need for reciprocity, for respect for the rights of minorities (*in casu* the Christian minorities in Muslim countries who are in some instances living through a critical period), for a minimum of equality, justice and freedom of religion in the treatment of these minorities. For the Catholic Church, it means the equivalent need to give the example: demonstrating that in countries with Christian majorities, Muslims can freely live their religious life. On both sides, there is clear evidence of a desire for mutual understanding, as illustrated for instance by the meetings of religious leaders in Assisi and elsewhere, and of a recognition for the needs of diplomatic contact between religions. This explains the largely positive attitude of the Catholic hierarchy towards Muslims, even if there may be some resistance on the part of some members. It explains also why the attitude of the Vatican (and particularly of the Pontifical Council for Interreligious Dialogue) appears more open than the attitude prevailing in several dioceses.

In the absence of a State strategy, this Church policy represents the only nation-wide long-term thinking and policy towards Muslims. Rome, the seat of the Vatican, therefore has a crucial role with regard to Italy's Muslims. But the city's centrality also derives from a different, Islamic factor. This factor is contained in a *hadith* (tradition of an alleged sayings or practices of the Prophet), according to which Muhammad, in answer to the question of a disciple whether the Constantinople or Rome would be the first to be 'opened' or conquered, said: 'The city of Heracles will be opened the first, that is Constantinople.'[11] In the discourse of Muslims living in Italy this text simply means that Rome too will become a Muslim city. It is therefore not surprising that this argument is taking on increasing importance in the ideological (and not only in the eschatological) discourse of Italy's Muslims. It also adds to the centrality of Rome in the internal politicking of the Muslim community in Italy – quite apart from the obvious centrality of Rome for the whole *umma*, as argued above.

The whole process of interaction within the Muslim community, as well as between the community and Italian society, the state and the Church, is at its very beginning in Italy. It will be of enormous interest to follow the next stages, both in and outside Rome.

Notes

1   Hence the choice of the title for the book by F. Dassetto and the present writer: *Il ritorno dell islam. I musulmani in Italia* (Rome: Edizioni Lavoro, 1993).

2   For an historical analysis and a panorama of the actual situation of migrations in Italy, see S. Allievi, *La sfida dell'immigrazione* (Bologna: EMI, 1991).

3   In Allievi and Dassetto, *op. cit.*, we have tried to develop the first morphology of Italian Islam in its various forms. This is both a theoretical approach and based on lengthy and wide-ranging fieldwork throughout Italy. Because of the lack of sources of information (there were practically no studies, very little local research, and not even sufficient empirical evidence of the Islamic presence, our study took the character of an exploration, a voyage of discovery – indeed covering thousands of miles in the process (for some of the reasons, see S. Allievi, 'Muslim minorities in Italy and their image in the Italian media' in S. Vertovec and C. Peach (eds.), *Islam in Europe: The Politics of Religion and Community* (London: University College London Press, 1994). After one and a half years of travel, observation, interviews and other research, the results are a map of the mosques, the meeting places of the organisation of the Muslim communities living in Italy, a quantitative evaluation of their weight (in every region of the country), an analysis of their activities, a first interpretation of the social and religious role they are playing, and of the reactions of the dominant non-Muslim society.

4   An earlier, shorter version of this section was published in S. Allievi, 'Muslim minorities in Italy', *op. cit.*

5   Broken Italian phrase, meaning 'Won't you buy?', with which foreign street sellers, very often Moroccans and Senegalese, offer items from lighters to socks, from sunglasses to alarm clocks (and, on rainy days, umbrellas), and by which Italians commonly refer to them.

6   'Do you want washing [of your windscreen]?'

7   At the launch of the book *Il ritorno dell Islam*, in Milan, September 1993.

8   In Italy the State has a central agreement with the Catholic Church (the *Concordato*); the origins lie in the 1929 Pact of Lateran, signed by the Italian State, represented by Mussolini, and the Vatican, and the text of which was revised in 1984. The other religions, once 'tolerated' and then 'admitted cults', are now simply referred to, in the republican constitution, as the religious confessions 'different from the Catholic', and can apply for an *Intesa* with the State. This has already been obtained by some Protestant denominations and by the Jews, and has been applied for by several other religious denominations. The proposal for an *Intesa* for Islam was formulated by the UCOII; the text is a virtual copy of the one of the Union of the Jewish Communities. On these problems see G. Long, *Le confessioni religiose 'diverse dalla cattolica'* (Bologna: Il Mulino, 1991).

9   See S. Allievi, *Le parole della Lega. Il movimento politico che vuole un'altra Italia* (Milano: Garzanti, 1992).

10   For further details, see S. Allievi, 'La moschea di Roma', *Africa*, No.1, 1994.

11   For the complete text and some considerations on the meaning of this *hadith*, see Allievi and Dassetto, *Il ritorno dell'islam, op. cit.*, pp. 289–91.

NOTES ON EDITORS

Dr Gerd Nonneman is Lecturer in International Relations at Lancaster University, with a particular interest in the politics of Islam and the Middle East. He previously worked in Iraq and taught at the Universities of Manchester, Exeter and the International University of Japan. His most recent books include *The Middle East and Europe: the Search for Stability and Integration,* and *Political and Economic Liberalisation: Dynamics and Linkages in International Perspective.*

Professor Tim Niblcock is Director of the Centre for Middle Eastern and Islamic Studies, University of Durham, and has written widely on questions of Middle East politics, Islam and ethnicity, and questions of democratisation and citizenship. His latest book (with E. Murphy) is *Political and Economic Liberalisation in the Middle East.*

Dr Bogdan Szajkowshi is Senior Lecturer in Politics at the University of Exeter, and a specialist in post-Soviet and East-European politics. His latest book is *Encyclopaedia of Conflicts, Disputes and Flashpoints in Eastern Europe, Russia and the Successor States.*

NOTES ON THE OTHER
CONTRIBUTORS

Dr Stefano Allievi teaches urban sociology at the University of Milan, and has written several books on immigration, minorities and Islam.

Dr Elira Cela is attached to the School of Slavonic and East European Studies, University of London; previously, she was Lecturer in the Sociology of Religion at Tirana University (Albania).

Yorgos Christidis is currently completing doctoral research into the politics of the Balkans and Turkey's relations with the region, at the Department of Politics, University of Exeter (UK).

Professor Felice Dassetto teaches sociology and the sociology of Islam at the Université Catholique de Louvain, Louvain-la-Neuve (Belgium).

Nuria del Olmo Vicén is Researcher at the European University Institute, Florence (Italy). An Arabist by training, she is also completing a doctoral dissertation on Muslim immigration in Spain.

Dr Natasha Gaber is Researcher at the Center for Ethnic Relations of the Institute for Sociological, Juridical and Political Research, Sts. Kiril & Metodij University, Skopje, (Republic of Macedonia) and a specialist in comparative law and politics.

Jan Hjarnø is Associate Professor at the Danish Centre for Migration and Ethnic Studies, South Jutland University Centre, Esbjerg.

James House is currently engaged in doctoral research on ethnic relations and politics, at the Université Paris XII (France) and Leeds University (UK).

Dr Ivan Ilchev is Associate Professor of History at Sofia University (Bulgaria).

Yasemin Karakaşoğlu is Researcher at the Zentrum für Türkeistudien, Essen, and teaches at the University of Essen.

Dr Alexander Lopasic, formerly of the Department of Sociology at Reading University (UK), specialises in Islam and Eastern Europe.

Robert W. Mickey, currently at Harvard University, was until 1995, Project Manager, Managing Ethnic Conflict, at the Institute for EastWest Studies (Prague, Czech Republic).

Dr Mirjana Najecevska is Director of the Center for Ethnic Relations of the Institute for Sociological, Juridical and Political Research, Skopje (Republic of Macedonia).

Duncan Perry is Executive Director of the Open Media Research Institute in Prague (the successor institution to the RFE/RL Research Institute) (Czech Republic).

Dr Åke Sander is Associate Professor of religious studies at Göteborg University (Sweden), and Director of the Centre for the Study of Cultural Contact and International Migration (KIM) at that university.

Dr Emilija Simoska has been Minister of Education of the Republic of Macedonia since 1994. She was previously the Director of the Center for Ethnic Relations of the Institute for Sociological, Juridical and Political Research, Skopje.

Dr Steven Vertovec, previously at Oxford University and the Humboldt-Stiftung (Berlin), is Principal Research Fellow at the Centre for Research in Ethnic Relations, University of Warwick (UK).

INDEX